BENJAMIN FRANKLIN

BENJAMIN FRANKLIN

The Religious Life of a Founding Father

* * *
* *

THOMAS S. KIDD

Yale

UNIVERSITY PRESS

New Haven and London

Published with assistance from the Annie Burr Lewis Fund.
Published with assistance from the foundation established in memory
of Amasa Stone Mather of the Class of 1907, Yale College.

Yale University Press books may be purchased in quantity
for educational, business, or promotional use. For information,
please e-mail sales.press@yale.edu (U.S. office) or sales@yaleup.co.uk
(U.K. office).

Set in Janson type by IDS Infotech Ltd., Chandigarh India.
Printed in the United States of America.

ISBN 978-0-300-21749-0 (hardcover : alk. paper)

Library of Congress Control Number: 2016956723

A catalogue record for this book is available from the British Library.

This paper meets the requirements of ANSI/NISO Z39.48–1992
(Permanence of Paper).

10 9 8 7 6 5 4 3 2 1

Contents

Introduction

1787. THE CONSTITUTIONAL CONVENTION, Philadelphia. Time dragged as delegates bickered about representation in Congress. Virginia's James Madison insisted that states with more people (including slaves) should possess more power. The small states knew that under the Articles of Confederation—America's existing national government—all states had equal authority, regardless of population. Why should the small states give that power up under a new Constitution? The convention might have failed at this point. If it had, the country would have continued to struggle under the inefficient (some said feckless) Articles government. Or the new American nation might have disintegrated.

At this critical moment, the octogenarian Benjamin Franklin took the floor. Calling for unity, he asked delegates to open sessions with prayer. As they were "groping as it were in the dark to find political truth," he queried, "how has it happened that we have not hitherto once thought of humbly applying to the Father of lights to illuminate our understandings?" If they continued to ignore God, they would remain "divided by our little, partial, local interests, our projects will be confounded, and we ourselves shall become a reproach and a by-word down to future ages." This man, who called himself a deist, now insisted that delegates should ask God for wisdom. This was strange: classic deists did not believe that God intervened in human affairs.[1]

Even more strange, he was one of the few delegates who thought opening with prayer was a good idea. His motion was tabled. What kind of deist was this elderly man, dressed in his signature Quaker garb, calling on America's greatest political minds to humble themselves before God?

"Franklin, of Philadelphia." In our mind's eye, the man seems ingenious, mischievous, and enigmatic. His journalistic, scientific, and political achievements are clear. But what of Ben Franklin's faith? Was Franklin defined by his youthful embrace of deism? His longtime friendship with George Whitefield, the most influential evangelist of the eighteenth century? His work with Thomas Jefferson on the Declaration of Independence, and its invocations of the Creator and of "nature and Nature's God"? Or his solitary insistence on prayer at the convention? When you add Franklin's propensity for joking about serious matters, he becomes even more difficult to pin down. Regarding Franklin's chameleon-like religion, John Adams remarked that "the Catholics thought him almost a Catholic. The Church of England claimed him as one of them. The Presbyterians thought him half a Presbyterian, and the Friends believed him a wet Quaker."[2] This biography illuminates Ben Franklin's faith, even as it tells the story of his remarkable career in printing, science, and politics.

The key to understanding Franklin's ambivalent religion is the contrast between the skepticism of his adult life and the indelible imprint of his childhood Calvinism. The intense faith of his parents acted as a tether, restraining Franklin's skepticism. As a teenager, he abandoned his parents' Puritan piety. But that same traditional faith kept him from getting too far away. He would stretch his moral and doctrinal tether to the breaking point by the end of his youthful sojourn in London. When he returned to Philadelphia in 1726, he resolved to conform more closely to his parents' ethical code. He steered away from extreme deism. Could he craft a Christianity centered on virtue, rather than on traditional doctrine, and avoid alienating his parents at the same time? More importantly, could he convince the evangelical figures in his life—his sister Jane Mecom and the revivalist George Whitefield—that all was well with his soul? (He would have more success convincing his sister than Whitefield.) When he ran away from Boston as a teenager, he also ran away from the city's Calvinism. But many factors—his Puritan tether, the pressure of relationships with Christian friends and family, disappointments with his own integrity, repeated illnesses, and the growing weight of political responsibility—all kept him from going too deep into the dark woods of radical skepticism.

Franklin explored a number of religious opinions. Even at the end of his life he remained noncommittal about all but a few points of belief. This elusiveness has made Franklin susceptible to many religious interpretations. Some devout Christians, beginning with the celebrated nineteenth-century biographer Parson Mason Weems, have found ways to mold Franklin into a faithful believer. Weems opined that "Franklin's extraordinary benevolence and useful life were imbibed, even *unconsciously*, from the Gospel." There is something to this notion of Christianity's "unconscious" effect on Franklin. But Weems had to employ indirection because of Franklin's repeated insistence that he doubted key points of Christian doctrine. Other Christian writers could not overlook those skeptical statements. The English Baptist minister John Foster wrote in 1818 that "love of the useful" was the cornerstone of Franklin's thought, and that Franklin "substantially rejected Christianity."[3]

One of the most influential interpretations of Franklin's religion appeared in Max Weber's classic study *The Protestant Ethic and the Spirit of Capitalism* (1905). For Weber, Franklin was a near-perfect example of how Protestantism, drained of its doctrinal particularity, fostered modern capitalism. Franklin's "The Way to Wealth" (1758), which distilled his best thoughts on frugality and industry, illustrated the spirit of capitalism "in near classical purity, and simultaneously offers the advantage of being detached from all direct connection to religious belief," Weber wrote. Franklin's maxims conveyed an "ethically-oriented" system for organizing one's business. For Weber, Franklin's virtues were no longer a matter of just obeying God. Virtue was also useful and profitable. Franklin, admonished by his "strict Calvinist father" about diligence in one's calling, presented money-making and success as products of "competence and proficiency" in a vocation. Weber's Franklin grew up in an intense Calvinist setting but redirected that zeal toward virtuous labor in a profession (namely, printing). There is much to recommend in Weber's portrait. As an adult, Franklin touted ethical responsibility, industriousness, and benevolence, even as he jettisoned Christian orthodoxy.[4]

Many recent scholars have taken Franklin at his word by describing him as a "deist." Others have called him everything from a "stone-cold atheist" to a man who believed in the "active God of the Israelites, the prophets, and the apostles." Deism stands at the center of this interpretive continuum between atheism and Christian devotion. But other than indicating skepticism about traditional Christian doctrine, deism could mean many things in eighteenth-century Europe and America. The beliefs of different "deists" did not always sync up. Some said they believed in the Bible as originally written. Others doubted the Bible's reliability. Some believed that God remained involved with life on earth. Others saw God as a cosmic watchmaker, winding up the world and then letting it run on its own. Deism meant different things to Franklin over the course of his long career, too. He did not always explain those variant meanings. I am not opposed to calling Franklin a deist—indeed, I do so in this book—but "deist" does not quite capture the texture or trajectory of Franklin's beliefs.[5]

So what did Franklin believe, precisely? As with so many issues about Franklin, the answer has been elusive. Political philosopher Ralph Lerner put it well when he wrote that "this man of many masks and voices, our native master of satire and hoax, of parable and bagatelle, preserves to himself a core that defies simple explanation." Earlier studies of Franklin's faith have offered a range of perspectives. Alfred Owen Aldridge's *Benjamin Franklin and Nature's God* (1967) holds that Franklin "completely disbelieved Christianity; yet he was attracted by it as a system of worship." Aldridge was right—to an extent. But Aldridge should have emphasized Franklin's ambivalence about Christianity even more. Especially after his teenage rebellion, he wavered in his views of Christianity, Jesus, and Providence, never making any orthodox profession but rarely denying orthodoxy outright. Franklin's certitudes about religion included the obligations of benevolent service and toleration of religious differences. These were the only "unchanging dogmas in his creed," Aldridge noted.[6]

In *Benjamin Franklin and His Gods* (1999), Kerry S. Walters emphasizes the fluidity of Franklin's religious views more than Aldridge did. But Walters believes that as a young man Franklin discovered a religious model—"theistic perspectivism"—which framed many of his thoughts on religion. Franklin, according to Walters, never questioned God's existence. But he believed that a thorough knowledge of God was inaccessible. Thus, Franklin held that people "symbolically represent God to themselves in such a way as to establish some sort of contact with the divine." But Walters gives too much weight to just one of Franklin's writings, his 1728 "Articles of Belief." There Franklin puzzlingly speculated about the Creator God also creating "many Beings or Gods" who help people worship the one true God. This was an intriguing thought, but not one to which Franklin gave sustained attention after 1728.[7]

I gratefully draw from aspects of Weber, Aldridge, Walters, and many other commentators on Franklin's religion. But adding to the themes of Franklin's skepticism and ambivalence, my book shows how much Franklin's personal experiences shaped his religious beliefs. Like Abraham Lincoln, Franklin's early exposure to skeptical writings undermined his confidence in Christianity. But books alone could not erase Franklin's childhood immersion in Puritan piety. His ongoing relationships with evangelical Christians made it difficult for him to jettison the vocabulary and precepts of traditional faith altogether. Although his view of Providence vacillated, the weight of the American Revolution fostered a renewed belief that history had divine purpose. Franklin and Lincoln—both self-educated sons of Calvinist parents, both of whom had much of the Bible committed to memory—gravitated toward a revitalized sense of God's role over history, as war and constitutional crises racked America in the 1770s and 1860s. Neither man's beliefs could escape the influence of their daily relationships and stressful experiences.[8]

It is difficult to overstate just how deep an imprint the Bible itself made on Franklin's (or Lincoln's) mind, or on his ways of speaking and writing. Even many devout Christians today are unfamiliar with large sections of the Bible (especially in the Old Testament) and do not know much about current theological debates. Franklin knew the Bible backward and forward. It framed the way he spoke and thought. Biblical phrases are ubiquitous in Franklin's vast body of writings. Even as he embraced religious doubts, the King James Bible colored his ideas about morality, human nature, and the purpose of life. It served as his most common source of similes and anecdotes. He even enjoyed preying on friends' ignorance of scripture in order to play jokes on them.

Franklin once explained the Bible-saturated environment in which he grew up in a letter to Reverend Samuel Cooper of Boston. He was arranging for the publication of one of Cooper's sermons in Europe. But Franklin needed to annotate it with biblical references. "It was not necessary in New England where everybody reads the Bible, and is acquainted with Scripture phrases, that you should note the texts from which you took them," he told Cooper. "But I have observed in England as well as in France, that verses and expressions taken from the sacred writings, and not known to be such, appear very strange and awkward to some readers; and I shall therefore in my edition take the liberty of marking the quoted texts in the margin." Franklin did not need Cooper to insert the Bible references. He knew them by heart. As a child of the Puritans, Franklin instantly recognized Bible phrases when he read them, even from obscure sections of the text. The shadow of scripture loomed over his long life.[9]

Franklin, then, was a pioneer of a distinctly American kind of religion. I'm tempted to call it an early form of "Sheilaism," the individualist religion described in Robert Bellah's *Habits of the Heart* (1985). In Bellah's Sheilaism, the individual conscience is the standard for religious truth, not any external authority. But Franklin's protégé Thomas Paine might be a better choice as a founder of Sheilaism, with his declaration in *The Age of Reason* (1794) that "my own mind is my own church." No, Franklin was too tethered to external Christian ethics and institutions to be a forerunner of Sheilaism.[10]

Instead, Franklin was the pioneer of a related kind of faith: *doctrineless, moralized Christianity*. Franklin was an experimenter at heart, and he tinkered with a novel form of Christianity, one where virtually all beliefs became nonessential. The Puritans of his childhood focused too much on doctrine, he thought. He wearied of Philadelphia Presbyterians' zeal for expelling the heterodox, and their lack of interest (as he perceived it) in the mandates of love and charity. For Franklin, Christianity remained a preeminent resource for virtue. But he had no exclusive attachment to Christianity as a religious system or as a source of salvation. In Franklin's estimation, we cannot know for certain whether doctrines such as God's Trinitarian nature are true. But we *do* know that Christians—and the devout of all faiths—are called to benevolence and selfless service. God calls us all to "do good." Doctrinal strife is not only futile but undermines the mandate of virtue.

Doctrineless Christianity, and doctrineless religion, is utterly pervasive today in America. We see it most commonly in major media figures of self-help, spirituality, and success, such as Oprah Winfrey, Houston megachurch pastor Joel Osteen, and the late Stephen Covey, author of *Seven Habits of Highly Effective People* (1999). Teresa Jordan's 2014 book *Year of Living Virtuously (Weekends Off)* used Franklin's ethical program as a framework, and commended the way that Franklin never forced his beliefs on others, focusing "on practical rather than spiritual values." Although they might differ on specifics, the common message of these authors (and their countless followers) is that a life of love, service, and significance is the best life of all.[11]

God will help you live that kind of life, but your faith should be empowering and tolerant, rather than fractious and nit-picking. Sociologist Christian Smith says that these characteristically American beliefs amount to "moralistic therapeutic deism." Many of its most prominent exponents, such as Osteen, live out their faith in particular congregations and traditions. Even Winfrey has testified that "I am a Christian. That is my faith." However, she says, "I'm not asking you to be a Christian. If you want to be one I can show you how. But it is not required." Doctrineless Christians agree that people *may* need to believe in doctrines. Our personal understanding of God can help us. We may need particular beliefs to enable our "best life now," in Osteen's phrase. But ultimately, the focus of doctrineless Christianity is a life of good works, resiliency, and generosity—*now*. Faith helps us to embody disciplined, benevolent success in this life. That's what God wants for us.[12]

It is easy to dismiss this kind of pop faith as peddled by wealthy media superstars. But it is America's most common code of spirituality. Throughout American history, Franklin's sort of religion has fueled a multitude of related trends, such as anticlericalism (suspicion of ministers), opposition to creeds, and religious individualism. For Franklin, doctrineless, moralized Christianity was serious intellectual business, born out of contemporary religious debates and dissatisfaction with his family's Puritanism. Like many skeptics in the eighteenth century, Franklin was weary of three hundred years of fighting over the implications of the Protestant Reformation. Much of that fighting concerned church authority and particular doctrines. Franklin grew up in a world of intractable conflict between Catholics and Protestants, but also between and within Protestant denominations themselves. What good was Christianity if it precipitated pettiness, persecution, and violence? Unlike some self-help celebrities today, Franklin and his cohort of European and American deists reckoned that in promoting a doctrineless, ethics-focused Christianity, they were redeeming Christianity itself. How successful that redemptive effort was, readers will have to decide for themselves.

Could you really have a nonexclusive, doctrinally minimal, morality-centered Christianity? Or did the effort fatally compromise Christianity? Franklin, Thomas Jefferson, and many of their friends in America, Britain, and France wanted to give it a try. Thirteen years after Franklin's death, Jefferson wrote that he considered himself "a Christian, in the only sense [Jesus] wished any one to be." He admired Jesus's "moral doctrines" as "more pure and perfect" than any other philosopher's. But to Jefferson, Jesus's excellence was only human. Jesus never claimed to be anything else. His followers imposed the claims of divinity on Jesus after he had gone to his grave and *not* risen again.[13]

Franklin did not go as far as Jefferson. He preferred not to dogmatize, one way or the other, on matters such as Jesus's divinity. Late in life Franklin told Yale president and Congregationalist minister Ezra Stiles that he had doubts about whether Christ was God. He figured that he would find out soon enough, anyway.

In a classic tension that still marks American religion, Franklin's devout parents, his sister Jane, and the revivalist George Whitefield all found doctrineless Christianity dangerous. Yes, they agreed that morality was essential. And yes, it was better not to fight over pointless issues. But true belief in Jesus was necessary for salvation. To the Puritans and evangelicals, Jesus was fully God and fully man. Doubting that truth put your soul in jeopardy. Jesus had made the way for sinners to be saved, through his atoning death and miraculous resurrection. It was not enough to emulate Jesus's life, as important as that was. More than a moral teacher, Jesus was Lord and Savior. Honoring Christ required belief in doctrinal truth. Franklin was not so sure. Perhaps the Puritans and Presbyterians of his youth had gotten it all wrong. Perhaps he was the one who was getting back to Jesus's core teaching. But he was sure that doing good was the grand point.

Benjamin Franklin: The Religious Life of a Founding Father focuses closely on the period of Franklin's life between the beginning of his publishing and writing career in the early 1720s and his departure for London in 1757. The final two chapters of the book cover his diplomatic career in London and Paris, and his last few years in Philadelphia. But the majority of the vast bulk of Franklin's reflections on faith came in the decades prior to his diplomatic missions. Franklin likely published more on religion than any other layperson of the eighteenth century. His religious musings did continue during his final three decades of life, as did the tensions among his traditionalist background, his adult skepticism, and his quest for doctrineless Christianity. But matters related to the American Revolutionary crisis and war also dominated much of his time and thinking in those decades.[14]

For readability, I have silently modernized much of the spelling and capitalization in Franklin's writings and correspondence. For exact transcriptions, readers should consult the Yale University Press volumes of Franklin's papers.

CHAPTER ONE

Child of the Puritans

AT YALE'S COMMENCEMENT IN 1722, college rector
Timothy Cutler blew up conservative New England's
religious world. At first glance, what he did might
seem innocuous. He just concluded a prayer with "let all
the people say amen." But this was telltale language from the
Anglican Book of Common Prayer. Cutler was repudiating his
Congregationalist (Puritan) convictions, the founding faith of Yale,
Harvard, Connecticut, and Massachusetts. Cutler was becoming an
Anglican, or Episcopal, minister. The "Yale apostasy" shook the
traditional Puritan culture of New England to its core. It also set
the stage for young Ben Franklin to register some of his earliest
surviving writings and first known opinions about religion.

That this sixteen-year-old's first publications focused on religion
signals the pervasive Christian controversies in Ben's world. Writing
under the pseudonym "Silence Dogood," Franklin touted themes
that would become representative concerns: people's overemphasis
on doctrine and their neglect of Christian morality. Quoting the
Bible, the middle-aged widow Dogood worried that those wanting
radical religious change "neither fear God, nor honor the King."
"Blind zealots" insisted that they had a monopoly on truth, but they
failed to reform their proselytes' morals.[1]

Franklin's background prepared him well to comment on religious topics. He grew up in early eighteenth-century Boston as a child of Puritans. His parents were tradespeople who came to New England seeking freedom to practice their faith. They even imagined that Ben might become a minister, as he showed early aptitude for theology. Franklin was familiar with the Puritans' zealous promotion of Calvinist doctrine, such as the predestination of God's chosen elect to salvation, and with Congregational church polity. But he also knew that they sometimes failed to love God and neighbor. Franklin's voracious reading habits, and the unfolding of Christian pluralism (as illustrated by Cutler's switch to Anglicanism) in New England, inaugurated his lifelong musings on true Christian devotion. Whatever his changing convictions about God over the decades, Franklin always believed that faith without works is dead.

Much of Franklin's Reformed Christian inheritance came from his father, Josiah, and Uncle Benjamin (Benjamin "the elder," as he came to be known). They tutored Ben in biblical truth and in dissent from the Anglican Church, or Church of England. Uncle Benjamin wrote a poem for his nephew in 1710. This was one of the earliest surviving writings related to Franklin, who was then four years old. For Uncle Benjamin, moral duty was rooted in devotion to God. He emphasized his nephew's obligation to be an "obedient son" who attended to his daily duties, never giving "sloth or lust or pride" a foothold. The threats of "Satan, sin, and self" always loomed. "Virtue, learning, and wisdom" would keep them at bay. These themes would mark Benjamin's moral code too. But he would downplay Uncle Benjamin's priority of giving God one's heart and adoring "none but the Three in One forevermore."[2]

Franklin's family had deep religious roots in England. As Franklin recalled in his autobiography, his ancestors were early joiners in the Reformation. The Protestant Reformation had sparked in 1517 with the German leader Martin Luther's "protest" against the abuses of the Roman Catholic Church. Luther excoriated the church's sale of indulgences as means to secure reduced penances for the living, or for the dead who had already passed on to Purgatory. Luther, reading scripture with fresh eyes, came to the conviction that salvation was entirely a work of God's mercy.

Protestants across Europe began preaching salvation by grace alone and attacking the corruptions of Rome.[3]

The Reformation came to England in a halting, politicized manner. England broke with Rome when King Henry VIII sought but failed to receive the pope's permission to annul his marriage to Catherine of Aragon. Henry declared himself head of the church in England, resulting in Henry's excommunication by the pope. But when Mary I (known to Protestants as "Bloody Mary") became queen in 1553, she reestablished Roman Catholicism as England's official religion. She unleashed a wave of anti-Protestant persecution that threatened to engulf the Franklin family of Ecton in Northamptonshire.

Protestants desired access to the Bible in the vernacular, instead of just Latin. Ben's great-great-grandfather Thomas Francklyne procured an English Bible. Possessing such a Bible during Queen Mary's reign was dangerous. So Thomas built a contraption to hide it at a moment's notice. "It was fastened open with tapes under and within the frame of a joint stool," Ben wrote. When Thomas "read in it to his family, he turned up the joint stool upon his knees, turning over the leaves then under the tapes." One of the children stood at the door to raise the alarm should Mary's minions approach. If an unfriendly visitor arrived, "the stool was turned down again upon its feet, when the Bible remained concealed under it as before." Proud Uncle Benjamin told Ben that story to illustrate the Franklin family's "zeal against Popery."[4]

England returned to the Protestant side, seemingly for good, when Queen Elizabeth I began her reign in 1559. But Puritans wanted further reform, or "purification," of the Anglican Church. To Puritans, the church still had too many "Romish" features that were out of line with the Bible. The Franklin family adhered to the Church of England through the trials of the English Civil War in the 1640s and 1650s. Although they did not affiliate with the most radical Puritans, Ben's grandfather, Thomas, Jr., certainly raised father Josiah in a Bible-centered setting. On the wall of their parlor, the family inscribed the words of John 3:16: "For God so loved the world, that he gave his only begotten Son, that whosoever believeth in him should not perish, but have everlasting life."[5]

To many English Protestants, the fate of Reformed Christianity seemed at risk with the Restoration. This 1660 event put Charles II, son of the executed King Charles I, back on the English throne. Charles II despised Puritans, who had helped to engineer the beheading of his father in 1649. The king set out a legal program, the Clarendon Code, designed to require strict conformity to the Church of England and root out Puritans. Parliamentarians had banned the Anglicans' Book of Common Prayer in the 1640s. But Charles II demanded that all Church of England ministers comply with the manual's rituals. Many Reformed-minded clergy resented this edict, believing that the prayer book enforced practices (such as kneeling during services) that were not biblical. Charles's church expelled some two thousand ministers for refusing to adhere to the prayer book. The episode became known as the "Great Ejection."[6]

Although most of the Franklin family remained Anglicans, father Josiah and Uncle Benjamin began attending "nonconformists'" private meetings in Northamptonshire. In the late 1670s, a wave of persecution came against nonconformists across England. The nonconformists, critics feared, might once again threaten the stability of the nation, as they had during the Civil War. University of Oxford officials burned non-Anglican writings by English luminaries such as John Milton. Even pacifist Quakers, who would soon found Pennsylvania, were jailed under brutal conditions and died by the hundreds during the 1680s. The Franklins' Northamptonshire was a hotbed of nonconformity. In one episode there in the mid-1680s, more than fifty members of the landowning gentry were arrested for seditious religious activity.[7]

This intense hostility led Josiah Franklin to leave England in 1683 and move to America with his wife, Anne, and their children. As Ben told the story, the nonconformists' meetings were "forbidden by law, and frequently disturbed." Some of the gentry convinced Josiah to go to Massachusetts, "where they expected to enjoy their mode of religion with freedom." The autobiography is keen to highlight his father's experience with religious intolerance, helping to frame Franklin's own passion for liberty.[8]

As with most of the Puritan migrants, Josiah Franklin did not see America only as a spiritual sanctuary. Massachusetts offered financial opportunity in addition to religious freedom. Josiah had worked as a clothes dyer in England, but, "things not succeeding there according to his mind," the Franklins sailed across the Atlantic in 1683. They went on a tightly packed ship with a hundred other passengers. For the journey, they paid fifteen pounds, or about six months' wages. There must have been considerable spiritual and financial pull drawing them to the New World.[9]

Boston in 1683 was impressive—by American standards. It was the largest town in English North America at about five or six thousand people, but only slightly bigger than Banbury, Northamptonshire, from which the Franklins had departed. Of course England's metropolis of London, about a hundred times larger than Boston, dwarfed the Franklins' new home. The Quaker William Penn had only just founded Philadelphia the year before the family arrived.

The first wave of English Puritans had settled Massachusetts in 1630, hoping that New England would become, in Governor John Winthrop's words, a "city on a hill." The initial settlers, who endured harassment by English authorities in the 1620s, hoped that they could establish a godly refuge in the New World. It would be a bastion of biblical religion, though not of religious "freedom." The Puritans, like most seventeenth-century Christians, believed that the Bible was clear about biblical faith and practice. They saw no reason to allow non-Puritan Christians to provoke God with unbiblical behavior. Puritan religion was individualistic yet communal. A person's sins impacted the lives of neighbors. For example, if any person violated the Sabbath (thus breaking one of the Ten Commandments) without consequence from the authorities, then people could expect the judgment of God to fall on them all. Some critics, including Franklin, would later react against the Puritans' confidence about knowing God's will. But in these early years, the Puritans enforced their brand of religious conformity.

By the 1670s, many New England Puritans believed that their society was in decline. Massachusetts was falling away from God and the commitment of the New England founders. Signs of God's displeasure abounded. Instead of bringing most Native Americans to the Christian faith, New Englanders engaged in brutal wars with them. Occurring in the mid-1670s, King Philip's War was, by percentage of population killed, the deadliest conflict in American history. The English committed grotesque violence against Native Americans. In one attack on a Narragansett fort in Rhode Island, Puritan fighters slaughtered hundreds of Indians, many of them women and children, by setting fire to the building and shooting victims as they fled. Few whites wondered whether such tactics met Christian standards for a just war. Pastors interpreted King Philip's War as God's judgment on the colonists for their lack of faithfulness to the original Puritan mission. Pastor Increase Mather (whose son Cotton would be an important early influence on Ben) lamented that the "heavenly Father should be provoked to set vile Indians upon the backs of his children to scourge them so severely."[10]

King Charles II's disdain for the Puritans also put Massachusetts at risk. The year after Josiah Franklin's family came to Boston, the crown nullified Massachusetts's charter and placed New England under royal administration. To independent-minded New Englanders, this was a disaster. Colonists consequently ousted this new Dominion of New England government at their first opportunity, during the Glorious Revolution of 1688–1689. Protestants called it "glorious" because the revolution removed the openly Catholic King James II, who had replaced Charles II in 1685. Parliamentarians and Protestants installed King William and Queen Mary in James II's place. To many in England and the colonies, the Glorious Revolution seemed to secure England once again for biblical faith. Massachusetts would receive a new charter (negotiated in part by Increase Mather) in 1692, but it did not afford as much independence as the original one had. Still, the colonists were eager to accept the authority of the Protestant monarchs William and Mary. Americans needed Britain's power to help them in wars with France and Spain that would span the next two generations.

The changes of the 1680s meant that Boston was becoming less of a Puritan town. But nonconformists like Josiah Franklin still sought religious refuge there. Church life structured Boston society. The Franklins moved into a home across from the Old South Church, where Reverend Samuel Willard began serving in 1678. Willard's magnum opus was the thousand-page *Compleat Body of Divinity*, a series of 250 lectures on doctrine. This compilation was arguably the most comprehensive theological treatise ever produced in New England, drawing from the Westminster Shorter Catechism (1647), the most frequently used guide to English and Scottish Reformed theology. (This catechism was reprinted eight times in New England prior to 1714.) When Willard's book was posthumously published, Josiah was one of 450 subscribers who underwrote it. He ordered two copies.[11]

Willard performed Josiah's marriage to Abiah Folger in 1689, after the death of Franklin's first wife, Anne. Abiah would become the mother of Ben Franklin. The Folger family had come to Massachusetts in 1635, among the charter generation of Puritan settlers. Josiah and Abiah both joined the Old South Church, and Ben would later memorialize them on their tombstone as a "pious and prudent man" and a "discreet and virtuous woman." In settings reminiscent of the old conventicles in Northamptonshire, Josiah participated in home group prayer meetings with the judge and celebrated Boston diarist Samuel Sewall. Josiah was also elected as a "tithingman," an officer tasked with confronting and informing the authorities about "disorderly persons." A tithingman might report any practices "tending to debauchery, irreligion, profaneness, and atheism amongst us." Although such mandates sound ominous to modern ears, Ben contended that in his duties Josiah won "a good deal of respect for his judgment and advice." In the Massachusetts of Ben's youth, New Englanders widely agreed that virtue and morality were public concerns.[12]

As Max Weber explained more than a century ago, Puritans like Josiah Franklin embraced a "Protestant work ethic," or the worldly calling to labor and contribute to society. In Boston, Josiah found his calling as a tallow chandler, a maker of candles and soap. He had worked as a dyer of fabrics in Northamptonshire, but he found demand for silks and other fancy clothes somewhat limited in Boston where there were laws against common people wearing such fabrics. These statutes remind us of the profoundly hierarchical nature of English society, including that society's manifestation in the New World. Massachusetts law frowned on the non-genteel adopting the "garb of gentlemen by wearing gold or silk lace, or buttons, or points at their knees, or to walke in great boots, or women of the same ranke, to wear silk or tyffany hoods, or scarfs, which though allowable to persons of greater estates, or more liberal education, yet wee cannot but judg it intollerable in persons of such like condition." This statute passed originally in 1651 and was reaffirmed in 1672.[13]

The market for candle- and soap-making was relatively open, so Josiah began rendering animal fat (tallow) for a living. This was tedious, smelly work, and many colonists were happy to pay someone else to do it. Few common people needed to purchase candles, and soap remained a luxury. But Josiah did find that growing numbers of pastors, officials, and merchants required candlelight to read in the evenings, especially in the dark wintertime. As a boy, Ben probably delivered candles to Reverend Cotton Mather, who lived four blocks from the Franklins. The scholars at Harvard College (founded in 1636) were regular customers for Josiah. Harvard president John Leverett once purchased nearly a hundred candles from Josiah in a single order.[14]

As a boy Ben helped his father make soap and candles. "I was employed in cutting wick for the candles, filling the dipping mold, and the molds for cast candles, attending the shop, going of errands, &c.," Franklin recalled. But he "disliked the trade." His thoughts turned to rambling. Perhaps he would try working as a sailor. Lessons from making those greasy candles stayed with him through old age, however. When Franklin proposed in the 1780s that the French government adopt a plan for daylight savings time, his argument hinged on the tallow candles it would save. He guessed that over the course of six months, Parisians would preserve 64 million pounds of wax and tallow. If people were encouraged to begin their workday when the sun rose, it would be much more efficient. "It is impossible," Franklin concluded, "that so sensible a people, under such circumstances, should have lived so long by the smoky unwholesome and enormously-expensive light of candles, if they had really known that they might have had as much pure light of the sun for nothing."[15]

Ben Franklin was a bookish boy. "All the little money that came into my hands was ever laid out in books," he said. Because of his autobiography, we know quite a lot about what Franklin read as a young man. He said less about what he read as an adult. Once his diplomatic career commenced, he seems to have read fewer books than in prior decades. In any case, the foundational texts from his youth were mostly Reformed Christian and classical. Like count-less English-speaking children of his age, one of the most forma-tive books he read was *Pilgrim's Progress* (1678) by John Bunyan. Bunyan was, like Josiah Franklin, a nonconformist. He ran afoul of Charles II's persecution, spending twelve years in jail for preaching in conventicles. While confined he began writing *Pilgrim's Progress*, which became one of the English language's bestselling works ever. The allegory tells the story of "Christian" and the trials on his journey from the "City of Destruction" to the "Celestial City." Franklin supposed that *Pilgrim's Progress* "has been more generally read than any other book except perhaps the Bible." It was a wor-thy text, Franklin explained, as "honest John was the first [author] that I know of who mixed narration and dialogue, a method of writing very engaging to the reader, who in the most interesting parts finds himself as it were brought into the company, and pres-ent at the discourse." A collection of Bunyan's books was Franklin's first multivolume set. It included Bunyan's *Grace Abounding to the Chief of Sinners*, as well as titles such as *Sighs from Hell; or, The Groans of a Damned Soul.*[16]

Franklin sold Bunyan's works to purchase a collection of forty or fifty popular titles called "Burton's Books" (compiled by an author us-ing the pen name Robert Burton), which featured tales from English history and the natural world. It included *Admirable Curiosities, Rarities, and Wonders in England* and *The Kingdom of Darkness; or, The History of Daemons, Specters, Witches, Apparitions, Possessions, Disturbances, and Other Supernatural Delusions, and Malicious Impostures of the Devil.* The latter was written to combat the "Atheists and Sadducees of this age" who denied "the being of spirits." It promised to give examples of "Satan's possessing the bodies of men."[17]

Franklin read books from his father's library, too. First up was the Bible. He had read the scriptures all the way through by the age of five. He found many of his family's other books deficient, at least in retrospect. Many were "books in polemic divinity," he re-called, "most of which I read, and have since often regretted, that at a time when I had such a thirst for knowledge, more proper books had not fallen in my way." This was the adult Franklin speaking, of course. By then he had come to believe that the phrase "polemic divinity" was oxymoronic.[18]

Still, some of the books he found at home profited him. One text was Plutarch's *Lives*, in which he "read abundantly, and I still think that time spent to great advantage." The *Lives* was widely available in English or Latin, for those who could not read the original Greek. The figures it profiled—such as Cicero and Demosthenes—showed up frequently as historical references and pseudonyms in the revolutionary era. Plutarch also highlighted the classical virtues, such as selfless benevolence, which the Founders celebrated. One of Franklin's friends claimed that no reading ever made a "stronger impression" on Franklin than the "wise and generous" philosophy of Plutarch.[19]

Daniel Defoe likewise captured the boy's attention, with his *Essay upon Projects*. Like John Bunyan and Josiah Franklin, Defoe was an English nonconformist. Defoe participated in the ill-fated 1685 rebellion by James Scott, Duke of Monmouth, which sought to overthrow the openly Catholic King James II. (Three years later, the Glorious Revolution would succeed where Monmouth failed.) Franklin loved Defoe's style, and his ideas for profitable and charitable projects. In his early writings as Silence Dogood, Franklin quoted Defoe at length on two of these projects—his plans for educating women and for relief of widows. Like Bunyan, Defoe would go on to become a giant of English literature, especially with his grand tale of Robinson Crusoe's shipwreck, devotion to God, and friendship with his "man Friday."[20]

Franklin also relished Cotton Mather's oft-reprinted *Bonifacius: An Essay upon the Good.* (Franklin, and titles of later editions, called Mather's book "Essays to Do Good.") Mather might seem like a peddler of the kind of "polemic divinity" that Franklin disliked. In Franklin's youth, Mather was one of Boston's leading ministers. He was also, to critics, one of the chief culprits behind the Salem witchcraft controversy that ravaged Massachusetts in 1692. But Mather's defenders have argued that he was really "peripheral" to the proceedings at Salem. He was certainly an avid scientific reader and researcher, an early proponent of smallpox inoculations, and an advocate of creative charity. Franklin's pseudonym Silence Dogood seems to have been a mocking play on Mather's book. But in Mather's work, Franklin found confirmation of the principle that true religion meant doing good. Mather would have cautioned

Franklin that a person needed faith, and regeneration in Christ, in order to do God-glorifying good. Still, Mather insisted that no man should "pretend unto the name of a *Christian*, who does not approve of the proposal of *A Perpetual Endeavour to Do Good in the World*." For Mather, these good works would make "God and His CHRIST" known more widely. Even as a teenager, Franklin believed that serving God first required doing good for others. Franklin, Defoe, and Mather all agreed that people did the greatest good when they employed the most strategic means possible. As Defoe put it, theirs was a "Projecting Age" of invention and social experiment in which benevolent new measures might solve perennial social problems of poverty, ignorance, and irreligion.[21]

Late in life, Franklin corresponded with Cotton Mather's son about the profound influence that *Essays to Do Good* had on him:

> When I was a boy, I met with a book entitled *Essays to do Good*, which I think was written by your father. It had been so little regarded by a former possessor, that several leaves of it were torn out: But the remainder gave me such a turn of thinking as to have no [little] influence on my conduct thro' life; for I have always set a greater value on the character of a *Doer of Good*, than on any other kind of reputation; and if I have been, as you seem to think, a useful citizen, the public owes the advantage of it to that book.

Franklin preferred to be remembered as a "Doer of Good" more than the proponent of a creed.[22]

Mather's courageous defense of medical inoculation in 1721 must have boosted Franklin's "turn of thinking" about Mather. Ben's brother James, a printer, and his *New-England Courant* newspaper reviled Mather for his support of the treatment. Physicians administering it would intentionally introduce smallpox into patients, hoping to produce a mild, survivable case of the disease and thus convey immunity in the future. Mather learned of the technique from his slave Onesimus, who told him that inoculations were common in Africa. When Boston suffered a major outbreak of smallpox in 1721, killing nearly a tenth of the town's population, Mather urged doctors to begin an inoculation campaign. Assisted

Cotton Mather, *mezzotint, [London?], 1797 (detail). Courtesy New York
Public Library.*

by James Franklin, most physicians in the area resisted Mather's
pleas, scoffing at the reverend's "negroish" medicine.[23]

One antagonist was so incensed by Mather's support of inoculation that he bombed Mather's home. Fortunately for Mather, the
fuse burned out before igniting the explosive. The shaken pastor
found a note attached saying, "I'll inoculate you with this, with a
pox to you." Young Ben did not take a public stance on inoculation,
but he may have already believed that Mather was on the side of
progress and public good. When Franklin's four-year-old son died
of smallpox in 1736, Ben began advocating for inoculation. In his
autobiography, Franklin spoke of his regret for having not supported the technique sooner. "This I mention for the sake of parents, who omit that operation on the supposition that they should
never forgive themselves if a child died under it," he wrote. He believed that his experience of losing his son showed that "the regret
may be the same either way, and that therefore the safer should be

chosen." He may have wished that he had listened to Mather in the 1720s.[24]

Franklin's "Silence Dogood" essays appeared in 1722, after the smallpox epidemic and Mather's brush with the bomb. But if Franklin's memory served him correctly, he had a positive encounter with Cotton Mather a year later. The meeting confirmed his hunch that Mather was not so bad. The seventeen-year-old Ben ran an errand to Mather's home. "I had been some time with him in his study, where he condescended to entertain me, a very youth, with some pleasant and instructive conversation," Franklin recalled in a 1773 letter.

> As I was taking my leave he accompanied me through a narrow passage at which I did not enter, and which had a beam across it lower than my head. He continued talking which occasioned me to keep my face partly towards him as I retired, when he suddenly cried out, Stoop! Stoop! Not immediately understanding what he meant, I hit my head hard against the beam. He then added, *Let this be a caution to you not always to hold your head so high; Stoop, young man, stoop—as you go through the world—and you'll miss many hard thumps.* This was a way of hammering instruction into one's head: And it was so far effectual, that I have ever since remembered it, though I have not always been able to practice it.

There was much to glean from Cotton Mather's advice and example. Mather's Calvinism, however, Ben would leave behind.[25]

Bookish boys in Puritan Boston often became pastors. Josiah certainly noted the boy's love for reading. He wanted to offer up at least one of his sons as a "tithe" to the church. So Josiah arranged for Ben to attend South Grammar School (which became Boston Latin), in preparation for Harvard. Cotton Mather had also gone to this school. Uncle Benjamin gave Ben a stock of sermon outlines that he might use when he got his own pastorate. Ben excelled at his studies and moved to the top of his class.

Josiah abruptly removed Ben from the school, however, and set him back to working in the candle business. Ben recalled overhearing

Josiah telling friends that Harvard was too expensive. And it was true that many graduates did not make enough money to justify the costs. But this explanation seems dubious, as Harvard scholarships were not that difficult to obtain. The college routinely admitted students from a range of economic backgrounds—and Josiah and Abiah were not desperately poor, in any case. Other factors may have played a role in Ben's removal from school. Perhaps Franklin's skepticism about Christianity was already becoming known. Josiah may have also realized that many Harvard graduates were entering careers other than the ministry. And the college had developed a reputation for anti-Calvinist "rational" theology. Ben would continue to sample the classics and theology, but only in his autodidactic reading, not in college.[26]

Franklin's horizons widened when he was apprenticed to his brother James, a printer in Boston who himself had probably apprenticed in Boston. James seems to have gone to London to buy printing equipment and returned to Boston with it by mid-1718. For boys not on a college track—most boys, that is—an apprenticeship was the standard method of acquiring skills in a manual trade. Although printing might seem like a more glamorous career than candle-making, it still remained a manual job. It required physical strength to run the press. Ben was a strapping twelve-year-old, on his way to reaching nearly six feet tall. So his brother signed him on for nine years, a lengthy term for an apprentice.[27]

Working for James expanded Ben's menu of readings. He sometimes borrowed books from other apprentices, promising to return them quickly in pristine condition. "Often I sat up in my room reading the greatest part of the night, when the book was borrowed in the evening and to be returned early in the morning lest it should be missed or wanted," he recalled. Franklin began reading poetry, and writing some of his own. His brother even printed a couple of his early poems, including one about Blackbeard the Pirate. The verses sold well, but later in life Franklin regarded them as "wretched stuff." Josiah did not like the poetry, either, telling his brother that he would never make a living as a writer. Thus Ben "escaped being a poet, most probably a very bad one."[28]

In these months Franklin discovered a volume of Joseph Addison's essays in *The Spectator*. The English writer Addison was the son of an Anglican minister and an entrepreneurial, brilliant essayist. Franklin was smitten. In *The Spectator* he found a resource for understanding the latest in English philosophical writing. Addison promoted rationalism and denounced religious bigotry, placing virtue at the center of true piety. As Addison wrote, "I love to see a man zealous in a good matter, and especially when his zeal shows itself for advancing morality, and promoting the happiness of mankind: But when I find the instruments he works with are racks and gibbets, galleys and dungeons; when he imprisons men's persons, confiscates their estates, ruins their families, and burns the body to save the soul, I cannot stick to pronounce of such a one, that (whatever he may think of his faith and religion) his faith is vain, and his religion unprofitable." Franklin read *The Spectator* over and over, trying to memorize the essays. These labors, and the improvements they produced in his own writing, encouraged him to think he "might possibly in time come to be a tolerable English writer, of which I was extremely ambitious."[29]

To Josiah's chagrin, Ben started hiding out at the printing house on Sundays when he was supposed to be at worship. Even though Ben still regarded church attendance as virtuous, he was now "evading" that duty as often as he could. He could not "afford the time" for going to church meeting when he had so little time for reading. As Addison wrote, "The mind that lies fallow but a single day, sprouts up in follies that are only to be killed by a constant and assiduous culture." Franklin regarded Addison as the author "whose writings have contributed more to the improvement of the minds of the British nation, and polishing their manners, than those of any other English pen." He had discovered his most significant literary influence and had begun to slip away from Josiah's faith.[30]

Franklin read widely and voraciously. At sixteen he consumed Thomas Tryon's popular manual *The Way to Health*, which convinced Franklin to stop eating meat. For Tryon, an English nonconformist, vegetarianism was a matter of Christian discipline and health. Tryon did not approve of people gorging "themselves with the flesh of their fellow-animals." For Franklin, Tryon's philosophy represented practical self-improvement. He could save money by not buying meat and by eating potatoes and rice. The money saved represented "an additional fund for buying books," he said. Staying behind while his companions went out to procure their meals, he kept reading books on arithmetic, geometry, and navigation.[31]

Franklin's vegetarian phase did not last, however. When he left Boston at age seventeen, his ship was delayed at Block Island, south of Rhode Island. Up until that point he had maintained his conviction that "the taking every fish [was] a kind of unprovoked murder, since none of them had or ever could do us any injury that might justify the slaughter." But then his shipmates began catching fish and frying them. "It smelt admirably well," he recalled. "I balanced some time between principle and inclination: till I recollected, that when the fish were opened, I saw smaller fish taken out of their stomachs: Then thought I, if you eat one another, I don't see why we mayn't eat you. So I dined upon cod very heartily and continued to eat with other people, returning only now and then occasionally to a vegetable diet."[32]

This episode illustrated reason's weakness as a moral guide. "So convenient a thing it is to be a *reasonable Creature*, since it enables one to find or make a reason for everything one has a mind to do," he mused. The theme of temperance stayed with Franklin, however. In his 1742 almanac, Franklin claimed that a "sober diet" would preserve the memory, mitigate the "heat of lust," and make "the body a fit tabernacle for the Lord to dwell in." That would make us happy in this world, and the world to come, "through Jesus Christ our Lord and Savior."[33]

Franklin still occasionally made orthodox-sounding statements about Jesus as Lord and Savior, and comments about the limited powers of the unaided mind. But he was starting to value reason over revelation. One of his key texts on the topic was the great English philosopher John Locke's *Essay Concerning Human Understanding*, which he read during his apprenticeship. Locke conceded that, for some kinds of knowledge, we need revelation. But reason was a stronger basis than revelation for what we *know* to be true. Whatever God has revealed to humankind must be correct, but only reason can judge whether claims of revelation are plausible. This undercut the traditional assumption that the Bible, and the church's understanding of it, was rooted in divine revelation. "Reason must be our last judge and guide in everything," Locke declared.[34]

Locke also argued against religious "enthusiasm." This was a derogatory term that both Locke and Franklin associated with intense Protestants, such as those who attended Josiah Franklin's conventicles. Authentic revelation and reason were two primary means of understanding truth. Enthusiasts claimed to possess a third way: hearing directly from the Holy Spirit. More often than not, such communications were "the conceits of a warmed or overweening brain," Locke wrote. Although his ideas had skeptical implications, Locke did not question the existence of divine truth itself. He brilliantly employed traditional Christian categories to undermine church authority. Every Christian knew that the devil was a great deceiver, so Locke asked how anyone could "distinguish between the delusions of Satan, and the inspirations of the Holy Ghost"? Those deceived by Satan often considered themselves "enlightened by the Spirit of God." Reason was the God-given tool with which people could distinguish between the godly and the infernal.[35]

Locke's packaging of rationalism and traditional Christian concepts made him irresistible to Franklin, who was seeking an intellectual map with which to escape his Reformed Christian background. Already by his teen years, Franklin was pursuing a Christianity based on virtue and reason, not doctrine. Poor Richard, the voice of Franklin's almanacs, would commemorate Locke as the "[Isaac] Newton of the microcosm" of the human mind. Even though he would later befriend Calvinist Christians such as the evangelist George Whitefield (whom critics accused of enthusiasm), Franklin found in Locke and similar sources a vocabulary for combining rationalism and Christianity. Of course, evangelicals such as Whitefield did not repudiate reason. But they saw an unregenerate person's reason as less reliable than did Locke or Franklin. Franklin, conversely, would dismiss the necessity of evangelical conversion.[36]

Franklin also devoured the works of Anthony Ashley Cooper, Third Earl of Shaftesbury, and Anthony Collins, both of whom were connected socially to Locke. From Shaftesbury, Franklin adopted the conviction that whatever one believed about God should be held with lighthearted flexibility. Anger and dogmatism were the worst threats to authentic religion. "Good humor," however, "is not only the best security against enthusiasm, but the best foundation of piety and true religion," Shaftesbury wrote. Shaftesbury also contended that the "end of religion" was to make us more virtuous. Collins, the author of the notorious *Discourse of Free-Thinking*, was more radically skeptical than Shaftesbury or Locke. Franklin owned a copy of Collins's *Philosophical Inquiry Concerning Human Liberty* (1717), in which Collins argued that people's actions were determined by psychological inclinations over which they have no control. As a freethinker, Collins insisted that people must ask hard questions about received dogma. If they did not, they would simply default to the "opinions they have imbibed from their grandmothers, mothers, or priests." (Franklin might have added "fathers" to that list.) Collins argued that reason must triumph over faith, "unless it is to be supposed that men are such absurd animals, that the most unreasonable opinion is as likely to be admitted for true as the most reasonable, when it is judged of by the reason and understanding of men." Collins suggested that the Bible was mistranslated by priests with worldly agendas. Thus, even the scriptures were unreliable.[37]

Reading Shaftesbury and Collins led Franklin to become "a real doubter in many points of our religious doctrine." Calling it "our" doctrine suggests Franklin's sense of communal and familial identification with Reformed Christianity. This was not just a solitary individual picking what system of thought made the most sense to him, nor was Franklin's trajectory a path to solitary, individualistic "Sheilaism." As much as Franklin framed himself as a new modern man, he knew that his upbringing exerted a powerful influence. His parents' effect was preeminent, but it could not constrain his skeptical tendencies: "My parents had early given me religious impressions, and brought me through my childhood piously in the dissenting way. But I was scarce 15 when, after doubting by turns of several points as I found them disputed in the different books I read, I began to doubt of Revelation itself." His faith in the Bible and Reformed theology was crumbling.[38]

Perhaps at Josiah's insistence, Franklin also read some anti-deist books. But they had an unintended influence. "Some books against deism fell into my hands. . . . They wrought an effect on me quite contrary to what was intended by them: For the arguments of the deists which were quoted to be refuted, appeared to me

much stronger than the refutations. In short I soon became a thorough deist." Josiah and Abiah knew that their child's eternal fate
was ultimately in God's hands, but they worried as they saw Ben
slipping away into skepticism. Franklin drafted a letter to them in
1738 in which he noted that his parents were "concerned for my
orthodoxy."[39]

What did Franklin mean when he said that he became a "thorough deist"? The answer is elusive. Pastor and future Yale president Ezra Stiles wrote in 1769 that as a young man, Franklin "read
himself almost into deism." "Almost" into deism? But not quite
into it, perhaps? Deism in eighteenth-century Europe and Anglo-
America could mean many things, from modest anti-Calvinism to
near-atheism. Deists could be anti-Christian, to be sure, but they
often thought of themselves as recovering true Christianity. They
would strip down Christendom's abuses and myths that had grown
up since the time of Christ, uncovering the original faith. In this
sense, the deists were not that different from the leaders of the
Reformation. That the term "deism" was often used by opponents
as a pejorative makes the concept even more difficult to define.[40]

Nevertheless, Franklin's deism included at least four major tenets, or inclinations: (1) doubts about Calvinism, (2) qualms about
the Bible's reliability, (3) resistance to churches' claims of religious
authority, and (4) a focus on ethics. For Ben, these did not require
a rejection of Christianity, or of God's providential work in the
world. He just wanted to distill the pure faith. In doing so, he fancied that he might bring New England theology out of its intellectual ghetto.

Although Ben would surpass his brother in publishing greatness,
James Franklin's *New-England Courant* revolutionized America's
newspaper culture. Earlier newspapers tended to be staid, reprinting
many stories received from London papers. None had ever sought
out controversy the way the *New-England Courant* did, regularly
criticizing colonial authorities. The publication generated an angry
response from New England's political and religious leaders. One of
them (possibly Cotton Mather) denounced the Franklins' newspaper as "full freighted with nonsense, unmannerliness, railery, profaneness, immorality, arrogancy, calumnies, lies, contradictions, and

what not, all tending to ... debauch and corrupt the minds and manners of New-England." James Franklin wanted to create sensational arguments because he knew that controversy drives the media business. The first major brouhaha that James Franklin stirred up was with Mather and the advocates of smallpox inoculation.[41]

James initially tasked Ben, his apprentice, with delivering papers around Boston. But Ben wanted to write. All of Franklin's reading to that point had prepared him to take on the role of Silence Dogood. Silence Dogood employed the taut, humorous style of *The Spectator.* Fourteen Dogood essays, including the one regarding Timothy Cutler's "apostasy," appeared in the *Courant* in 1722. As unlikely as it seems, Ben says that he kept his identity as the author hidden from James. Ben suspected that James would not take the essays seriously if he knew who had written them. So Ben disguised his hand and put the first composition "in at night under the door of the printing house. It was found in the morning and communicated to his writing friends. . . . They read it, commented on it in my hearing, and I had the exquisite pleasure, of finding it met with their approbation." James's friends guessed at the author's identity but only came up with names of established writers.[42]

Silence Dogood was the first-ever American-authored series of essays. It is striking that as a first-time author, Franklin chose to take on a woman's persona. The choice was not typical, and it suggests Franklin's emerging conviction about women deserving a more public role in society. The pseudonym, as we have seen, was an unsubtle reference to Cotton Mather. "Dogood" was derived from Mather's *Essays to Do Good,* even though several of the *Courant*'s writers had commented favorably on that book. "Silence" was drawn from Mather's recent sermon *Silentarius* (1721), but it also alluded sarcastically to Mather's prolific writings. Mather was many things but "silent" was not one of them. The widow Dogood was a complex figure both in name and character. She was not simply reviling Reverend Mather, in spite of the *Courant*'s history of conflict with him.[43]

One of Franklin's chief targets in the Silence Dogood essays was Harvard College, where he once thought he might matriculate. Now he saw the college as a mind-numbing holding tank for children of the wealthy. In Silence Dogood's fourth essay, she relates a dream about the "Temple of Learning" where every peasant father plans to send at least one of his children. They consider only "their own purses instead of their children's capacities" when deciding whether to place a student there, so most of the temple's students "were little better than dunces and blockheads." In the temple Dogood encounters the figure of "LEARNING," who, in spite of her "awful state," is busy writing an issue of the *New-England Courant*. Figures called "Ignorance" and "Idleness" command much of the curriculum, which is dominated by the "Antique Figures" of Latin, Greek, and Hebrew, at the expense of English.[44]

Further along, Dogood sees the Temple of Theology, centered around the "fraudulent contrivances of Plagius, who ... was diligently transcribing some eloquent paragraphs out of Tillotson's *Works*" to enhance his own compositions. This was a swipe at Harvard's love for John Tillotson, the broadminded former Archbishop of Canterbury. Among other doctrinal innovations, Tillotson had proposed that the souls of unrepentant sinners might be annihilated at their death, rather than suffering eternal torment in hell. Tillotson was a favorite at Harvard, and popular throughout the Anglo-American world. Indeed, the *Courant*'s own library held Tillotson's works. Franklin admired Tillotson, but Harvard's slavish devotion to the archbishop illustrated their lack of originality. (Traditionalists were suspicious of Tillotson. Revivalist George Whitefield contended that Tillotson "knew no more of true Christianity than Mahomet.") Dogood finishes her account by wondering at parents sending their children to such a school, "from whence they return, after abundance of trouble and charge, as great blockheads as ever, only more proud and self-conceited." Ordinarily Franklin's writing leaned more on irony and satire, but here we see his unvarnished teenage anger against privilege.[45]

In another composition, Silence Dogood addresses the dangers of religious establishments (state-supported churches) and the temptations they presented for hypocrisy. Franklin posited that "hypocritical pretenders to religion" were more damaging to a commonwealth than the "openly profane." The scandalous person damaged himself and those close to him, but a hypocrite could gain power by simply knowing how to sound pious. The public witness of Christianity was damaged when people lionized charlatans as saints. Franklin warned of the deceiver who "leaves the gospel for the sake of the law." Law and grace were classically at odds in scripture. Christ directed his strongest indictments against the Pharisees, who heaped extralegal requirements on the Jews. But Franklin was also hinting at the unsavory connection between New England's court system and religious leaders. He may have been satirizing Massachusetts chief justice Samuel Sewall, who, like Franklin, had once considered going into the ministry. As we have seen, the pious Sewall also prayed occasionally with Josiah Franklin.[46]

In the last Silence Dogood essay, Franklin critiqued the overwrought zeal of the Yale apostates to Anglicanism. Overall, the short series reviled the religiously powerful, from the Mathers and Samuel Sewall to John Tillotson and Timothy Cutler. The essays mocked the mixing of religious, political, and educational authority (the last seen in the case of Harvard). They shamed those whose faith was more show than practice. In the voice of a marginalized widow, Franklin was criticizing much of New England's Congregationalist establishment.[47]

Conflict between James and Ben Franklin was inevitable. They were both big, strong-minded personalities. Ben ran the newspaper for a month while his brother was jailed for slandering government officials. But James was less than delighted when he found out that Ben had written the Silence Dogood essays. The discovery confirmed to James that Ben no longer wished to be treated as an apprentice, but as an equal and a brother. James insisted that he was the "master" and Ben was the servant. Ben admitted that he "expected more indulgence" than this, and that he was probably "too saucy and provoking" toward James. Sometimes when they would argue, James would physically beat him.[48]

Ben was in a desperate situation. But as a literate white man, he could entertain hope of getting out, unlike most of the servants and slaves in the colonies. A door of opportunity opened when Massachusetts authorities banned James Franklin from publishing the *Courant*. In a letter to the editor, probably written by Ben, the *Courant* noted that if a newspaper abused the clergy, "you may be sure that they will improve their influence to the uttermost, to suppress your paper." The ban forced James to publish the paper under

Ben's name. He also sought to make Ben serve the remaining time of his apprenticeship. To Ben, this arrangement was utterly unacceptable. Ben had few places to turn to in Boston, especially after word got out that he was Silence Dogood. "My indiscrete disputations about religion," Ben recalled, "began to make me pointed at with horror by good people, as an infidel or atheist."[49]

It was time for Ben Franklin's Exodus journey out of captivity. In the fall of 1723, a friend convinced a sloop captain bound for New York that Ben had gotten a girl pregnant and that her relatives were demanding that he marry her. He needed to steal away secretly. To pay for the passage, he sold some books. So he went to New York, and then to Philadelphia. He was "a boy of but 17, without the least recommendation to or knowledge of any person in the place, and with very little money in my pocket." His passage to independence had begun.[50]

CHAPTER TWO

Exodus to Philadelphia, Sojourn
in London

ALMOST THE FIRST THING Benjamin Franklin did when he arrived in Philadelphia was to attend a Quaker meeting. Quakers designated no one to give sermons in their assemblies. They waited in silence until the Holy Spirit prompted someone to speak. The teenage Franklin sat there in the quiet room. He had not gotten a good night's rest. Soon he fell asleep. A kindly Quaker woke him up at the end of the meeting. "This was therefore the first house I was in or slept in, in Philadelphia," Franklin wrote.[1]

The City of Brotherly Love was a Quaker town of about six thousand people. Its founders had laid it out in a neat grid pattern like a "Chess-Board" between the Delaware and Schuylkill Rivers. It was a city on the rise. In the mid-1720s, it was still a new place in a new colony. Unlike Boston, which would struggle economically throughout the eighteenth century, Philadelphia was the ideal American town for an artisan on the make. It was the perfect place for Franklin to emerge "from the poverty and obscurity in which I was born and bred, to a state of affluence and some degree of reputation in the world," as he recalled in his autobiography.[2]

The city was not all opportunity and ease, though. Burgeoning numbers of African slaves and European (Scots-Irish and German) indentured servants labored in the city's wharves. Fluctuations in the Atlantic markets, especially in grain prices, routinely sent Philadelphia into economic turmoil, which happened shortly before Franklin arrived. In 1722, Pennsylvania's governor lamented that many artisans were out of work, interest rates were crushing, "and the usurer grinds the face of the poor so that lawsuits multiply, our jails are full, and we are justly apprehensive of falling into debt." But rebounding demand and tinkering with the currency supply righted the city's economic fortunes.[3]

All in all, Pennsylvania was "the best poor man's country" in America. Philadelphia offered more opportunity compared to other American seaports. Artisans like Franklin, those who had resources, education, and connections, could find customers and the "way to wealth." Franklin was not alone as a Philadelphia artisan who entered the middle or upper class in the mid-1700s. Friends of his who worked as blacksmiths, brickmakers, pipemakers, and shoemakers enjoyed similar successes. Not all artisans prospered, but those who did enjoyed a wealth of material goods that suffused the American colonial towns. A thriving artisan's family could eat from pewter plates instead of wooden trenchers, recline on mahogany furniture, and buy ornate houses. At home and in public, they could enjoy global imports of coffee and chocolate. And, of course, they could drink tea. Franklin's papers contain receipts for purchases of green and bohea teas, as well as regular invitations from friends to join them for evenings of tea-drinking.[4]

Franklin's journey from abused apprentice to prosperous printer was a story that most of the major Founders did not share. The best-known ones, except for Franklin and Alexander Hamilton, came from relatively privileged backgrounds. They were a hard-working group when it came to politics, but few had to work as hard as Franklin to make their way in the world. While many contemporary artisans who became wealthy did everything in their power to obscure their humble origins, Franklin reveled in his life story. His celebration of his working-class background helps to explain why his autobiography has become the genre's most popular book in world history. It has made him a hero for many "leather-apron" types in America, Europe, and around the globe.⁵

We should not forget, though, that the prosperity of free whites like Franklin depended on the enslavement and servitude of others. Franklin had been one of those "others" when he ran away, but this did not keep him from building his own fortune partly through the labor of servants, slaves, and the transatlantic markets that needed them. Philadelphia and its hinterlands employed thousands of servants and slaves in shipbuilding, iron forges, farming, and more. One of the most important exports for the Middle Colonies was grain, much of which fed the enslaved workers of the South and Caribbean. Franklin would go on to own slaves himself. That fact is generally forgotten today, as Americans have (rightly) lamented the slave-owning of the major southern Founders. Franklin also printed slave and servant ads in his *Pennsylvania Gazette*. Franklin's growing wealth depended on such ads—more than 20 percent of the paper's notices concerned servants or slaves. Often these ads described runaways in attempts to apprehend them and force them back into slavery. Ironically, a return to his oppressive apprenticeship was what young Ben also feared most as he arrived in Philadelphia.⁶

Making the journey from Boston to New York and Philadelphia introduced Ben to a wider world. One segment of the trip saw him walk across New Jersey, from northeast to southwest, often trudging through torrential rains. The runaway stayed a night at the inn of Dr. John Browne, who would become a longtime friend. Seeing past the seventeen-year-old's soaking clothes, Browne talked with Franklin and was surprised to find him so well read. They became "sociable and friendly." The admiring boy listened to the doctor's stories of travel in Europe, where he had seemingly visited every town and country. Browne, who was in his mid-fifties, had also embraced an even fiercer skepticism about Christianity than Ben had. He was "much of an unbeliever," Franklin recalled, "and wickedly undertook some years after to travesty the Bible in doggerel verse. ... By this means he set many of the facts in a very ridiculous light, and might have hurt weak minds if his work had been published." Browne could not get a publisher to print his mock Bible, however. Printers may have feared legal repercussions. If Browne ever asked

Ben to publish it, Franklin declined. Directly assaulting faith was never really Franklin's style. It was not in good humor.[7]

In Philadelphia, Franklin approached the town's two printers, Samuel Keimer and Andrew Bradford, both of whom offered him some work. He was not overly impressed with either of them. Franklin sized up the colony's top printer, Bradford, as ill-suited to the job and "illiterate." Franklin regarded Keimer as "something of a scholar," but he suffered from a former association with an ecstatic sect of radical French Protestant émigrés in London known as the "French Prophets." He still "could act their enthusiastic agitations," Franklin noted, but at that moment Keimer "did not profess any particular religion." Following his mother and sister (who served as a lay preacher) into the ranks of the so-called Prophets, Keimer had also established a print shop in London, serving clients including Daniel Defoe. Keimer soon fell out with other members of the sect, partly due to his financial difficulties. Some of his former religionists denounced him and had him sent to Ludgate Prison for failing to pay debts. Sometime in 1722 or 1723, Keimer followed his preaching sister to Pennsylvania, where he sought to pass himself off as a Quaker. He wore a long beard and spoke in the typical thees and thous of Quaker manners.[8]

Doing occasional work for Bradford and Keimer was no sure way to wealth. Franklin needed a patron. Skills for making a desirable product were helpful, but eighteenth-century America was no pure meritocracy. To enter the ranks of elites, a young man needed an older merchant or politician to open doors. Franklin caught a break when his brother-in-law, a shipmaster with business in Philadelphia, wrote to Ben asking him to come back to Boston. Franklin replied with one of his characteristically articulate missives. The brother-in-law received the letter during a visit with Pennsylvania governor William Keith. He showed the composition to Keith, and it was not long before the "finely dressed" governor himself was dropping by Keimer's print shop. Keimer assumed that the governor was there to see him. "But the governor enquired for me," wrote Franklin, and "made me many compliments." Wouldn't Franklin like to come to the tavern to taste "some excellent Madeira," the governor asked? Franklin was shocked, and Keimer was appalled. The elder printer watched them walk out of his shop, staring "like a pig poisoned." Keith offered to set Franklin up as an independent printer and to contract him to publish materials for the Pennsylvania government. For a lucky young man with the right timing and connections, catapulting into elite circles could happen just as quickly as that.[9]

Keith instructed Ben to approach his father, Josiah, about supporting the new printing business. So Ben made his way back to Boston in 1724. It was a triumphant return for the runaway, and his family was surprised to see him. All were delighted, except for his brother and former master, James. Ben visited James at his printing house, pompously wearing "a genteel new suit from head to foot" and a nice watch. His pockets jingled with cash. James watched him walk in, looked him up and down, and turned sullenly back to his work. Ben chatted with James's assistants and gave them a piece of eight to buy drinks. The visit offended James "extreamly."[10]

Father Josiah was pleased to see Ben doing well. But he did not want to invest in his son's business, fearing that he was still "too young to be trusted." Still, Josiah consented for Ben to run his own shop in the Quaker city. He advised Ben to "behave respectfully to the people there . . . and avoid lampooning and libeling to which he thought I had too much inclination," Franklin wrote. Josiah hoped the Puritan habits of "steady industry and a prudent parsimony" would undergird the business. After a few years of work, perhaps Ben could save most of what he needed to open the print shop. Then Josiah might help him out with the rest of the money. Ben left for Philadelphia again, this time as a man of opportunity, carrying his parents' "approbation and their blessing," if not their finances.[11]

Franklin was finding his way in the world, but he was still naive. Temptations enticed him as he traveled through America's port towns. His ship put in at Newport, Rhode Island. It became the stage for a tale of temptation and danger worthy of Bunyan's *Pilgrim's Progress*. Two young women boarded the ship, bound for New York, as did a "grave, sensible matron-like Quaker woman with her attendants." When the matron noticed the two ladies showing an interest in Ben, she pulled him aside. "Young man, I am concerned for thee," she said, "for thou has no friend with thee, and seems not to know much of the world, or of the snares youth is exposed to." She warned him that "those are very bad women . . . if thee art not upon thy guard, they will draw thee into some danger." Franklin thanked the lady and resolved to be careful. When they disembarked at New York, however, tension rose as the mysterious young women told him their address and invited him to visit. Franklin declined. He was glad that he did, for the captain soon discovered that a silver spoon and other valuables were missing from the ship. Realizing that the women were "a couple of strumpets," the captain got a warrant to search their home, and found the stolen items. "Though we had escaped a sunken rock which we scraped upon in the passage," Franklin mused, "I thought this escape of rather more importance." The delights and dangers of the flesh would remain consistent themes in Franklin's life story.[12]

His escape from the thieving temptresses was followed immediately by another moral lesson. In New York, he met up with childhood friend John Collins, whom Franklin regarded as well-read and ingenious. In Boston, Collins had attracted prospective patrons, but in New York he displayed an emerging problem with drinking. "He had acquired a habit of sotting with brandy," Franklin lamented. Collins had also begun gambling, so he lost all his money, and Franklin had to pay for his friend's lodging and transportation.[13]

Franklin and Collins reaped the respective fruits of sobriety and drunkenness. Franklin's unusual knack for attracting the attention of elites continued when New York governor William Burnet, having heard there was a teenage boy in town carrying "a great many books," summoned Ben to a meeting. Franklin would have taken Collins with him, but "he was not sober." (Collins and Franklin would fight about Collins's dissolute habits, and before long Collins had departed for Barbados and fallen out of Franklin's life.) Franklin went to meet the governor alone, and Burnet treated him "with great civility, showed me his library, which was a very large one, and we had a good deal of conversation about books." The governor was the son of Bishop Gilbert Burnet, who served as King William's chaplain and was one of the fiercest defenders of England's Glorious Revolution of 1688–1689. It was exciting to

chat with a politician who was so well connected in English literary, political, and religious circles. "This was the second governor
who had done me the honour to take notice of me, which to a poor
boy like me was very pleasing," Franklin recalled.[14]

Back in Philadelphia, Franklin kept working for the eccentric
prophet-printer Keimer. They got along fairly well, though they
argued a lot. Both seemed to appreciate a good sparring partner,
especially on matters of faith. Franklin said that Keimer "retained a
great deal of his old enthusiasms," about which he quizzed Keimer.
Franklin was at his best when he raised questions about religion,
rather than when he expressed definite opinions about faith.[15]

Skepticism marked Franklin's intellectual awakening.
Skepticism was likewise the hallmark of what historians call the
"Enlightenment." Many have regarded Franklin as the paradig-
matic figure of America's Enlightenment. There was no single
"Enlightenment" in the eighteenth century: there were many national differences and ideological contradictions among its proponents. The concept of the Enlightenment also presupposes a
"dark" age of faith that preceded it, which raises immense historical difficulties. Many Enlightenment figures, such as the great Isaac
Newton, were people of deep Christian commitment. Skeptics
such as Franklin were indelibly marked by foundational theistic assumptions, even as they moved away from basic Christian doctrine.
Still, increasing numbers of philosophers and scientists in the eighteenth century doubted all kinds of traditional knowledge.

Franklin manifested his doubts by challenging logical inconsistencies. He loved to probe Keimer's assumptions for weak spots,
asking questions until he caught the printer in a contradiction.
Realizing Franklin's strategy, Keimer "grew ridiculously cautious."
The simplest question would put Keimer on the defensive. He
would demand to know what Franklin was getting at before he
would answer. Working with Franklin must have been exhausting
at times, especially for lesser mortals such as Keimer.[16]

Although the hectoring was frustrating, Keimer appreciated
the teenager's intellectual skills. Keimer thought he might put
those skills to good use in his one-man sect. In a new religious
scheme, Keimer would "preach the doctrines," while Ben was to

"confound all opponents." Franklin apparently agreed to this plan
for some time, perhaps hoping it would secure him more work.
Maybe this was also another opportunity for fun at Keimer's expense. (Or perhaps Franklin was more under Keimer's spell than
his autobiography conceded.) Franklin accepted parts of Keimer's
spin on Christian devotion, but he wanted to introduce some precepts of his own. Showing a penchant for Old Testament law,
Keimer wore a long, bushy beard, in accord with a prohibition in
Leviticus against beard trimming. Moreover, he observed a
Saturday Sabbath, as did Jews and certain sectarian Protestants.

The long beard and Saturday Sabbath were "essentials" to
Keimer, Franklin recalled. He, however, thought both regulations
were silly. But Franklin agreed to adhere to the rules, if in exchange Keimer would commit to vegetarianism. Even though
Franklin had already rationalized his switch back to occasional
meat-eating, Franklin still appreciated the way that vegetarianism
helped him save money. As Franklin suspected he would, Keimer
"suffered grievously" through his vegetarian experiment. It lasted
for three months, until the longing for the "flesh pots of Egypt"
(Exodus 16:3) overtook Keimer's resolve. Thus he ordered a roast
pig, and invited two women and Franklin to dine upon it. But
Keimer ate it all up before the guests arrived. "Deist" though
Franklin may have been, he showed a lifelong attraction for experiments in religious devotion, like Keimer's, and enjoyed the friendship of a number of figures whom he regarded as "enthusiasts,"
most notably the revivalist George Whitefield. At the time of
Franklin's short-lived spiritual alliance with Keimer, Whitefield
was a precocious ten-year-old in Gloucester, England.[17]

Franklin's "chief acquaintances" in Philadelphia besides Keimer
were clerks named Joseph Watson and James Ralph. They were
"lovers of reading" on their own religious pilgrimages. Watson, a
Quaker, was serious about his faith and (most importantly to
Franklin) a person of good sense and "great integrity." Ralph was a
skeptic like Franklin. Ralph succumbed to Franklin's usual method
of criticism: asking questions until the interrogated person was
flabbergasted. The bright young men would stroll in the woods
near the Schuylkill River, reading and criticizing one another's efforts at poetry. Once they agreed to each compose a paraphrase of

the eighteenth psalm, and to compare one another's work. Even as Franklin embraced skepticism, the King James Bible remained one of his key literary resources.[18]

Governor Keith had promised that he would help Franklin set up his printing shop, and encouraged him to travel to London to procure the required equipment. With more than half a million souls, London was the center of British politics and culture. Any young man wanting to make a mark in the empire needed to visit the city. As Samuel Johnson said, "You find no man, at all intellectual, who is willing to leave London. No, Sir, when a man is tired of London, he is tired of life." Keith's promises of support convinced the teenage Franklin that now was his time, so he boarded a ship bound for the great metropolis. Arriving on Christmas Eve, 1724, Franklin and his companion James Ralph must have found the city overwhelming. If Franklin picked up a newspaper, he would have discovered familiar material. The London papers were tracking news of colonial religious and military conflict. The Christmas Day edition of the *Daily Post*, for instance, included a speech by Massachusetts's lieutenant governor addressing the war with Abenaki Indians in northern New England. A French Jesuit missionary named Sebastien Rale had convinced the Abenakis to stand against English land incursions. Massachusetts forces would execute and scalp Rale for his role in the conflict, which many called "Father Rale's War."[19]

The city of London was disorienting even to regular visitors. Its streets were loud and smelly, teeming with people and refuse. Daniel Defoe hailed the Fleet Ditch, a city stream that doubled as a sewer, as a "nauseous and abominable sink of public nastiness." Unaccustomed to the city's odoriferous dazzle, Franklin became more distressed when he realized that Governor Keith had failed to deliver on his promises. The governor had not even sent introductory letters or credit with which to buy printing equipment. "What shall we think of a governor's playing such pitiful tricks, and imposing so grossly on a poor ignorant boy!" Franklin wondered. The distraught teenager turned to Thomas Denham, a Quaker merchant whom he had met on ship. He confided in Denham about the debacle. Denham commiserated with Franklin, telling him that there was no way that the governor had written any such letters for him. "No one who knew him had the smallest dependence" on Keith, Denham warned. The merchant "laughed at the notion of the governor's giving me a letter of credit." The governor had no "credit to give." Denham helped Franklin gather himself. He advised the teenager to seek employment with a London printer.[20]

The resilient Franklin took Denham's advice and found work with Samuel Palmer. Palmer's print shop was on Bartholomew Close, near to the church of St. Bartholomew the Great, a twelfth-century structure built shortly after the Norman Conquest. Meanwhile, in the anonymity of the city, James Ralph forgot about the wife and child he had left behind in Philadelphia. Franklin too had left behind a fiancée named Deborah Read. He had courted her before his departure. They had discussed marriage, but Deborah's mother insisted that they should postpone until after Ben returned. Deborah faded from Franklin's mind in the metropolis. He wrote her just one letter from London, which advised her that he was not likely to return home soon. (Even after he did return home, it would be some years before Ben would resume this relationship.) Ralph found no steady work, but they both kept spending money at theaters and "other places of amusement." They were living hand to mouth and accumulating no money to get back to Philadelphia.[21]

In spite of the city's temptations, the topic of faith had not fallen from the young printer's thoughts. At Samuel Palmer's modest shop, Franklin set the type for a new edition of William Wollaston's popular *The Religion of Nature Delineated*. Wollaston, who died only months before Franklin's arrival, had produced one of the eighteenth century's most influential works on "natural religion." It ran through many editions and became a recommended text in American education. Many eighteenth-century writers sought to base religion on nature and reason, rather than revelation alone. Wollaston posited that the "great law" of natural religion was that "every intelligent, active, and free being should so behave himself, as by no act to contradict truth; or, that he should treat everything as being what it is." Immoral acts were wrong because they contradicted truth. People had access to the truth through reason.[22]

William Hogarth, A Just View of the British Stage, *London, 1724 (detail).*
Courtesy Wikimedia Commons.

Thinkers as varied as the Calvinist pastor-theologian Jonathan
Edwards and the great Scottish skeptic David Hume would deci-
mate Wollaston's naive rationalism. In spite of their differences on
religion, Hume and Edwards agreed that morality entailed much
more than acting on truth. Behavior sprung from desires, passions,
and affections, they said. Wollaston's natural religion also seemed
like a ripe target to the bright Franklin. Setting the type for
Wollaston allowed him to read the book closely, giving him an en-
tryway into contemporary debates over ethics. Franklin entered
those learned discussions himself by writing a "little metaphysical
piece" entitled *A Dissertation on Liberty and Necessity.*[23]

This pamphlet promised to give Franklin's "present thoughts
of the general state of things in the universe." But there is some
debate about whether the book was a satire, a straightforward argument, or a combination of both. This uncertainty is a common

feature of Franklin's philosophical writings. As an admirer of great ironical writers like Jonathan Swift, Joseph Addison, and Daniel Defoe, Franklin could shift into satire at any moment, but he did not always make those moves obvious to his readers. The relative immaturity of Franklin's polemical capabilities added to the confusion. He was hesitantly radical. Still, Franklin wished to skewer common assumptions, including those of the widely discussed Wollaston. Franklin longed to become a topic of debate too.[24]

In the *Dissertation*, Franklin joined skeptics like Hume (in those years a student at the University of Edinburgh) in taking a dim view of human nature and free will. As Franklin explained, his treatise was meant "to prove the doctrine of fate, from the supposed attributes of God." Skeptics like Franklin and Hume were not optimistic about people's moral capabilities. Indeed, they shared more in common with Calvinist thinkers on these topics than with optimistic natural religionists such as Wollaston. The teenager was still working through his reaction against his Reformed upbringing. Calvinist overtones would color Franklin's ideas about human nature, Providence, and morality throughout his career.[25]

Franklin opened the *Dissertation* by noting that it "is said" that God exists and that he is "all-wise, all-good, all powerful." That passive voice suggests the question of why a benevolent, all-powerful God allows evil. For his answer, Franklin advanced an argument that, while logical, would strike most readers as ridiculous. He contended that if God is all powerful and all good, then whatever he permits must be good. Therefore, "evil doth not exist." He intended this provocative thesis to force readers to engage the logical problem of how a good, sovereign God could oversee such a malevolent world. You cannot have it both ways, Franklin insisted. Either there is no evil, or God is not completely good and powerful. If evil exists, it proves that God is either not all powerful or not all good. Some Christian apologists postulated that God *permitted*, but did not cause, evil. Franklin dismissed this distinction. If God permitted evil actions, then he was either unable to stop those actions or he was not good. Franklin preferred the (presumably satirical) conclusion that evil did not exist.[26]

The apprentice then turned to Wollaston, who said that evil actions went against the truth. This was nonsense to Franklin.

Wollaston posited that a horse-stealer was acting against the truth when he presumed to treat the stolen horse as his own property. But, Franklin countered, the horse-stealer *was* acting according to the truth that he was "naturally a covetous being." That covetous nature produced an overwhelming temptation to steal. These facts were also true, Franklin said. The horse-stealer was acting in compliance with the truth of his natural inclinations.[27]

Further, if God had created the universe perfectly, and if all worked according to his will, then people could never act outside of his will. Thus, there was nothing good or bad about any action. Because of this, Franklin wrote, "every creature must be equally esteemed by the Creator." At this juncture, all traditional readers must have been indignant. Surely there must be some kind of distinction between the just and unjust! Yet Franklin posited that all of our actions are based on the "natural principle of self-love," which seeks to alleviate and avoid all "uneasiness." No behavior was good or bad. Every act was born out of self-preservation. Franklin concluded by acknowledging that most people would reject any philosophy that did not exalt humans "above the rest of the creation." But he thought what he had proposed accorded with "common sense." Truth was truth, he wrote, even if it sometimes proved "mortifying and distasteful."[28]

Franklin must have known that he was avoiding some of the strongest Christian explanations for why God permitted evil. In particular, he did not engage with the belief that when God created humankind (Adam and Eve), he made them free moral agents who could sin. The effects of Adam and Eve's "fall" into sin explained the existence of suffering, illness, and evil. God would ultimately resolve and eliminate the problem of evil, but not before the full number of the redeemed had come into God's Kingdom. God had already begun to deal with sin in Christ's death and resurrection. Destroying evil instantly, though, would require instant judgment against sinners. Thus, God's mercy forestalled his elimination of sinful people. Even if Franklin failed to acknowledge these ideas, he was raising tough questions about the existence of evil, God's superintending role over the world, and our ability to be good.

All told, the *Dissertation* was a bold but immature production. Franklin quickly had second thoughts about the volume. It is not

clear what bothered him about the *Dissertation*, though printer
Samuel Palmer berated him about its "abominable" principles.
Perhaps Franklin thought it was overly irreverent, or perhaps he
worried that Palmer would hold it against him (though Franklin
said that it helped convince Palmer that he was a young man
of some "ingenuity"). In the end, Franklin came to regard the
Dissertation as an "erratum" committed by his youthful self. He
claimed that he collected and burnt most copies of it. This seems
unlikely, as there are seven copies surviving today out of a hundred
originally printed, an unusually high survival rate for any imprint
of the time. The treatise became something of a cult classic, with
figures such as the English scientist and pastor Joseph Priestley
querying him about it more than fifty years later.[29]

Whether Franklin burned the copies or not, the *Dissertation*
garnered attention from some of London's prominent writers.
Franklin, still not twenty years old, was drawn deeper into the city's
rationalist and skeptical circles. Most immediately, the work came
to the attention of the surgeon and liberal Christian William
Lyons, best known for his *Infallibility of Human Judgment* (1719).
Infallibility was a typical anti-Calvinist treatise that took a high
view of human rationality. Lyons reviled the doctrine of predestination, for instance, as a "monstrous barbarity." Although God
could create people destined for eternal torment, such a system
made God out to be a "fool or a madman," Lyons insisted. His optimism about human judgment did not complement Franklin's pessimism. Still, Lyons was impressed by the teenager's potential.[30]

Lyons introduced Franklin to Bernard Mandeville, the celebrated author of *The Fable of the Bees*. Franklin had likely read the
Fable already and used it as a resource for the *Dissertation*. Like
Franklin, Mandeville closed the gap between sin and virtue by
claiming that all vocations, including "Parasites, Pimps, Players,
and Pick-Pockets," had something to contribute to society. The
Fable criticized the clergy, too, saying that

> Some few were learn'd and eloquent,
> But Thousands hot and ignorant:
> Yet all passed Muster, that could hide
> Their Sloth, Lust, Avarice and Pride.

The "scandalously cynical" Mandeville presided over a literary club at London's Horns Tavern. Franklin found Mandeville a "facetious entertaining companion."[31]

Such companions were abundant in London's radical circles. Franklin soon encountered the mother-son tandem of Jane and Jacob Ilive, two of the century's most exotic religious speculators. Jacob, who would serve jail time for his beliefs, publicly questioned the Bible's credibility. He "maintained that earth is hell and that human beings are embodied pre-existent spirit beings whose destiny is to inhabit and rule other planets." Decades later, Franklin told his sister Jane Mecom about meeting the Ilives. Mecom was one of Ben's most consistent correspondents, and her evangelical convictions helped tether Ben to the Calvinism of his upbringing. She was also one of his most engaging conversation partners on religion. Sending Mecom a couple of unnamed, apparently heterodox books from London in 1770, Franklin recalled that Jane Ilive's spiritual notions were like those of the books in the parcel. Mrs. Ilive died soon after Ben left London in the 1720s. By her will she instructed her son Jacob to give a public address which would demonstrate that "this world is the true hell or place of punishment for the spirits who had transgressed in a better state, and were sent here to suffer for their sins in animals." Man was one of those animals.[32]

Ben regarded the Ilives' theories as intriguing explanations for why people often acted like brutes. They could help to solve the question of why a good God would create humans who behave like "devils to one another." Humans were living out punishment incurred in an earlier life. This theory might clarify the contradiction between God's goodness and the "general and systematical mischief" in the world. That sinful "mischief" was both an empirical fact and a belief Franklin derived from the Reformed faith of his parents. However, Ben acknowledged to his sister (who found the Ilives' speculative theology disturbing) that the Ilives had had little evidence to go on from the Bible, history, or science.[33]

Religion could never just be speculative, of course. Faith was to be lived out in love. Endless speculation was one of religion's chief problems, Franklin believed. He later professed to have become

disgusted with the "endless disputes" in metaphysics that had intrigued him in his youth. His taste of London's temptations convinced him that he needed a practical moral code to live by. Like
many people entering adulthood, Franklin was realizing that personal freedom did not necessarily lead to a fulfilling life. Indeed, he
noted in his autobiography that an "erratum" he committed in
London wrecked his friendship with the wastrel James Ralph.
Ralph met a charming milliner (a hatmaker) at his and Ben's lodg-
ings, with whom James started reading plays in the evenings. Soon
they "grew intimate" and moved in together. The milliner needed
support for a child from a previous relationship, so James got a
job in a village outside of London. (He apparently began using
Franklin's name on his accounts at the same time.) While he was
away, Ralph asked Ben to look after his girlfriend. Ben complied—
but gave her a bit too much attention. He enjoyed visiting with
her, and, "being at this time under no religious restraints," Ben
tried to become intimate with her as well.[34]

"Under no religious restraints," he wrote. That phrase is an important signal that his *Autobiography* was, among other things, his
personal conversion testimony. His "want of religion" had nearly
wrecked him in London, and only "the kind hand of Providence, or
some guardian Angel" kept him out of the gutter. Written in sections during the 1770s and 1780s, the *Autobiography* was Franklin's
way of securing his public image, defending himself from his
political enemies, and explaining his religious journey. Leaving his
regrets about London behind, he converted from amoral licen-
tiousness to pragmatic morality. The teenager in London could not
help himself from acting like that fool James Ralph. Here was the
vulnerable milliner, a young single mother, taken advantage of by
Ralph. Franklin doubled the sin by exploiting the duress under
which Ralph put her. Thankfully, she "repulsed" his overtures and
advised Ralph that Ben had tried to seduce her. When Ralph
learned about it, he denounced Franklin. He told Ben that his infidelity had rendered all of Ralph's debts to him null and void.
Franklin figured that this was no big deal, since Ralph was not
likely to ever pay him back anyway. Additionally, their friendship
was fatally damaged, but Franklin considered that the relief of an
unwanted burden.[35]

The record of the scurrilous seduction attempt is an example of the kind of honesty (stylized honesty, to be sure) that makes Franklin's *Autobiography* so accessible. Most of us have memories of our immature past that make us wince. Franklin was contributing to a genre of autobiography chartered by John Bunyan and (soon) George Whitefield, whose life story would become a source of great profit for Franklin's printing business. Rather than casting themselves as pristine saints and heroes, these writers readily admitted failings in order to connect with their audience. But Bunyan and Whitefield, like Franklin's parents and sister Jane, pointed to the saving power of Christ as the only way out of sin's trap. How would Franklin escape the snare?

One method that appealed to him was simple: moral effort. In particular, he recommended the disciplines of temperate behavior. (Recall his earlier experiments with vegetarianism.) The value of temperance became clearer to him when he began working for a larger print shop in London. While Franklin chose to drink only water, his fellow workers were "great guzzlers of beer." They mocked his abstinence, calling him the "Water-American." One of his friends drank six pints of beer a day, starting with one before breakfast. Franklin regarded this as a "detestable custom." But his friend insisted that if he did not drink so much beer, he would not have the strength to perform the arduous duties required at the press. Franklin scoffed—the nutritional value of beer was the equivalent to a penny's worth of bread. His buddies disagreed and kept binging on alcohol. They often borrowed money from Franklin, who never missed work because of hangovers. Some saw the light, however, and dropped their usual "muddling breakfast of beer and bread and cheese," realizing that they could have a more satisfying breakfast with Franklin and keep their heads clear, too.[36]

Some of Franklin's experiences while laboring in London had lasting educational value. These included meeting people of non-Protestant faiths. When he switched employers, he moved into a home "in Duke Street opposite to the Romish Chapel," he wrote. This was likely London's Church of Saints Anselm and Cecilia, which in the early eighteenth century was attached to the Portuguese and Sardinian embassies. Saints Anselm and Cecilia was a rare, officially operating Catholic church during a time of

immense hostility toward Catholics in England. Franklin lodged at
the house of a Catholic widow. She was an elderly shut-in, but she
was an "amusing" conversation partner. Another Catholic woman
also lived at the lodging. She was seventy years old and single, having planned in her youth to enter a nunnery. Unable to find a suitable one abroad, she returned to England where nunneries had
been abolished, thus she vowed to live in monastic fashion on her
own. Franklin admired how the disciplined woman gave almost all
her money to charity and sustained herself on water gruel.[37]

Meeting these pious Catholic ladies helped to temper the strident prejudice of his upbringing. His anti-Catholicism would
resurface from time to time, of course. Many "Enlightenment"
writers indulged such sentiments as virulent as those of any traditionalist Protestant. The Enlightenment was often hotly anticlerical
too. The French philosopher Denis Diderot classically proposed
that "men will never be free until the last king is strangled with the
entrails of the last priest." But Franklin watched as a living priest
visited the nun-like woman to hear confession every day. The in-
credulous Franklin (knowing how many gross sins of his own he
could readily list) asked the landlady how the woman, "as she lived,
could possibly find so much employment for a confessor?" The
landlady figured that though the nun rarely sinned outwardly, it
was "impossible to avoid vain thoughts."[38]

Franklin once visited the ascetic's room, which he detailed with
a curious Protestant eye. "She was cheerful and polite, and conversed pleasantly. The room was clean, but had no other furniture
than a mattress, a table with a crucifix and book, a stool, which she
gave me to sit on, and a picture over the chimney of St. Veronica,
displaying her handkerchief with the miraculous figure of Christ's
bleeding face on it, which she explained to me with great seriousness. She looked pale, but was never sick." Franklin was definitely
not convinced about that miraculous figure of Christ, but he reckoned that she was a fine example of frugality and temperance.[39]

In the end, these Catholic ladies could serve as no more than
instructive curiosities for Franklin. Yet even Catholics could benefit from serious piety if it inculcated healthful, disciplined habits.
He needed more than better habits to break out of his rakish ways
in London, however. Help came in the person of his old patron,

the Philadelphia Quaker Thomas Denham. When yet another "in-genious young man" like James Ralph invited Franklin on a grand tour of the European Continent, Franklin told Denham about the plan. Denham urged him to refuse. Get serious about your life and business, he told Ben, and come back to America.[40]

The sturdy patron invited Franklin to join him as a clerk. Upon their return, Denham promised to send Franklin to the slave islands of the Caribbean with a consignment of foodstuffs. All this would be "profitable," Denham assured him, and "if I managed well, [it] would establish me handsomely." Franklin jumped at the offer. After eighteen months, he had grown tired of London. Although he had seen amazing things, read many new books, and met fascinating people, London (and James Ralph) had left him in financial distress and grasping for focus. He was ready for a new start on the smaller stage of Philadelphia, where he might have more control over his own fortune. Taking a pay cut and leaving the print business, he began helping Denham to prepare for departure.[41]

They left London in July 1726. On board, as he kept musing about his future, Franklin drafted a personal "Plan of Conduct." He admitted that he had "never fixed a regular design in life." Thus, he had stumbled through a "variety of different scenes," and it left him dissatisfied. Now was the time for a new set of "resolu-tions" by which he might live as a "rational creature." In the ver-sion of the plan that survives, Franklin resolved to get out of debt by living frugally. He vowed to be truthful and never promise more than he could deliver. Sincerity was "the most amiable excellence in a rational being," he noted. He would work hard and avoid get-rich-quick schemes. "Industry and patience are the surest means of plenty," he reminded himself. Finally, he committed to overlooking the faults of others, and to speaking "all the good I know of everybody."[42]

The Plan of Conduct was Franklin's declaration of moral seri-ousness. It was a key moment in his journey to maturity and virtue, or at least his aspirations toward them. He unabashedly described the plan as "remarkable," since it was drawn up when he was so young. He later figured that he had stuck to it "pretty faithfully" into old age. At the time, as he sailed back to his future in

Philadelphia, he set down markers of a new self. He wanted to be prosperous, useful, virtuous, and rational. No longer did he wish to feed the James Ralph–like tendencies of the flesh. The future was devoted to what he saw in Thomas Denham. Emerging from his London sojourn, Ben Franklin had gone through his conversion experience. Now he would fashion himself into a virtuous, enlightened individual.[43]

CHAPTER THREE

Philadelphia Printer

EN FRANKLIN KNEW THAT he should go to church, or, at least, that he should be the sort of person who goes to church. Church attendance had "its utility when rightly conducted," he admitted. But he did not go that often. Claiming that he could not find a pastor who preached authentic Christian virtue, he rarely went for more than a Sunday or two in a row. He did give money to support the Presbyterian church in Philadelphia. And one of its ministers, Jedidiah Andrews, sometimes visited Franklin and urged him to appear on Sundays.

Franklin tried. Once he went for five straight weekends. Had Andrews been "a good preacher perhaps I might have continued," Franklin lamented. But instead the pastor peddled stupefying doctrine and polemics. The sermons were "dry, uninteresting, and unedifying. . . . Not a single moral principle was inculcated or enforced, their aim seeming to be rather to make us Presbyterians than good citizens," Franklin surmised.

One Sunday, Andrews named Philippians 4:8 as his text: "Whatsoever things are true, whatsoever things are honest, whatsoever things are just, whatsoever things are pure, whatsoever things are lovely, whatsoever things are of good report; if there be any virtue, and if there be any praise, think on these things." Franklin perked up in his pew. Surely here was a text on virtuous, rational living, if there ever was one! But Andrews botched it. The pastor applied the verse by telling the congregation to keep the Sabbath, read the Bible, go to church, take communion, and respect their minister. Franklin "was disgusted, and attended his preaching no more."[1]

Franklin's Christianity was the religion of the enlightened individual. Doctrine and church attendance were valuable only if they inspired right living. Virtue was the main point, and virtue bred success. Franklin's doctrineless Christianity would not foster sectarian rivalry or bolster the institutional church. As often as not, he believed, churches detracted from real Christianity. Accordingly, Franklin created new outlets for benevolent fellowship and mutual improvement. Hidebound churches could not supply those outlets for the new enlightened man.

Franklin's shipboard journey in 1726 from London to Philadelphia took three months. He occupied himself by composing the "Plan of Conduct" and by reading. He took notes on the fish that his companions caught and ate. The gregarious Franklin found the passage taxing, and his loneliness at sea turned his thoughts to the Bible's account of Noah and the flood: "When we have been for a considerable time tossing on the vast waters, far from the sight of any land or ships, or any mortal creature but ourselves (except a few fish and sea birds) the whole world, for aught we know, may be under a second deluge, and we (like Noah and his company in the Ark) the only surviving remnant of the human race." Delighted to see land again, his shipmates sailed up the Delaware River and landed at Philadelphia. "Thank God!" Franklin commented.[2]

Shortly after arriving back in Philadelphia, Franklin wrote to his "favorite" sibling Jane. Jane and Ben remained close throughout their lives, in spite of Jane's Calvinist convictions and her brother's religious wanderings. The letter—and their relationship—was rooted in the gender-specific conventions of polite English society. Having heard that his teenage sister was turning into a mature beauty, he wrote that he always knew she would "make a good, agreeable woman." Wanting to offer her a gift on his return, Ben thought at first of giving her a tea table. Tea and all of its accoutrements were new consumer products in the colonies, and still reserved primarily for the homes of the wealthy. In any case, Ben did not aspire for Jane to become "only a pretty gentlewoman" but to grow into the "character of a good housewife." Thus, he wished to give her a spinning wheel. This was the perfect gift for the household economy of women in New England, as the majority of eighteenth-century homes there owned a spinning wheel. Colonists saw spinning thread and yarn as women's work in the 1700s, more so than in earlier decades. Ben hoped that Jane would accept the wheel as "a small token of my sincere love and affection."[3]

Franklin—writing Jane on his twenty-first birthday—concluded the letter with Puritan-hued moral advice. He exhorted her to remember that modesty "makes the most homely virgin amiable and charming," but "the want of it infallibly renders the most perfect beauty disagreeable and odious." When virtue was paired with intellectual and physical beauty, however, it could render a woman "more lovely than an angel." Jane was indeed headed for matrimony, as that summer she married her next-door-neighbor Edward Mecom. He was twenty-seven; she was fifteen. As Ben catapulted to fortune and fame, Jane struggled with a difficult home life. Edward Mecom's dissolute habits kept him constantly at risk of debtors' prison. Eleven of Jane's twelve children would precede her in death, yet she remained steadfast in her evangelical beliefs.[4]

As promised, Franklin and the Quaker merchant Thomas Denham established a shop on Water (now Front) Street in Philadelphia, where Franklin worked as a salesman and bookkeeper. The general store sold everything from hardware and clothes to coffee and garlic. The men lodged together. They had a kind of father-son relationship, which Franklin needed due to his separation from Josiah. Denham "counseled me as a father, having a sincere regard for me," Franklin recalled. "I respected and loved him." Denham modeled the kind of honesty and diligence to which Franklin aspired.[5]

This happy period came to an abrupt end in early 1727 when both Franklin and Denham fell ill. Franklin called his sickness a "pleurisy," likely a lung infection. He feared it would become terminal (and indeed, it was a condition that would recur throughout Franklin's life). For a time he was disconsolate, so much so that he was almost disappointed when he began to recover. He regretted "in some degree that I must now some time or other have all that disagreeable work" of preparing for death "to do over again."[6]

His suffering with pleurisy may have prompted Franklin to compose his epitaph, which he imagined would be engraved on his tombstone:

> The Body
> of
> B. Franklin Printer;
> (Like the Cover of an old Book
> Its Contents torn out
> And stript of its Lettering and Gilding)
> Lies here, Food for Worms.
> but the Work shall not be lost:
> For it will, (as he believed) appear once more,
> In a new and more elegant Edition,
> Revised and corrected,
> By the Author.

This was classic Franklin. With its unsettling glimpse of the fate of our earthly bodies ("food for worms"), the epitaph compares his life to a book's. Like the imprints he produced, his body was subject to decay. Like his Puritan ancestors, Franklin believed that it was healthy to reflect on one's death. Doing so, he felt, helps you live as you will wish you had lived when you come to the end.[7]

But not all was grim. Some former Calvinists who turned skeptics during this era, like the Scottish biographer James Boswell, obsessed over their fate in the afterlife. Franklin, befitting his cheery nature, retained optimism from his Christian upbringing. The epitaph ends with the hopeful note that his body would not be lost but would appear in a "new and more elegant edition." This spoke not just to hope for heaven but to the new body the saints would receive at the resurrection of the dead. The Bible described this moment in passages like I Corinthians 15:52: "In the twinkling of an eye ... the dead shall be raised incorruptible, and we shall be changed." A number of Anglo-American deists, including London's Jacob Ilive, denied the bodily resurrection of Christ and the saints.

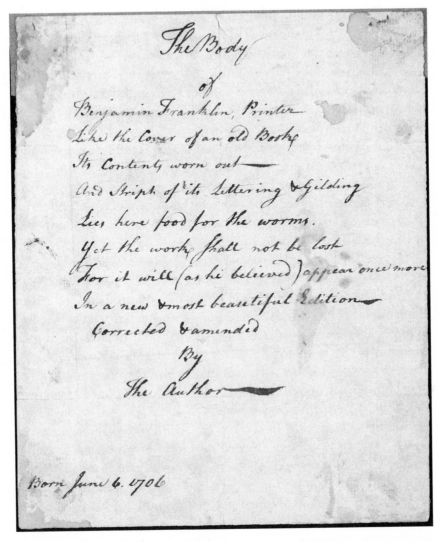

The Body

of

Benjamin Franklin, Printer
Like the Cover of an old Book,
Its Contents worn out—
And Stript of its Lettering & Gilding
Lies here food for the worms.
Yet the work shall not be lost
For it will (as he believed) appear once more
In a new & most beautiful Edition
Corrected & amended
By
The Author—

Born June 6. 1706

Benjamin Franklin's epitaph (the original draft in his handwriting). Circa 1727. Courtesy Beinecke Rare Book and Manuscript Library, Yale University.

Franklin differed from more radical deists on this issue. Lest anyone doubt it, Franklin inserted parenthetically that "he believed" in the resurrection of the body. As short breaths rasped in his infected lungs, his thoughts lingered over this expectation.[8]

Franklin survived, but Thomas Denham's time had come. He passed away in 1728. Denham made small provisions for Franklin in his will, but Franklin felt that he had been left "once more to the wide world." Providence was not always kind to Franklin, and now it deprived him of a father figure, a source of prosperity, and a model of virtue. All Franklin knew to do was to return to printing. His former boss, the eccentric Samuel Keimer, offered him his old job back. Franklin was reluctant, but he found no other options, so he returned to Keimer.[9]

Keimer employed several apprentices and indentured servants. These servants, essential to America's unfree labor regime, typically agreed to work for a master for no wages in exchange for passage across the Atlantic. If he or she lived out the term of indenture (four or seven years), the servant could often expect more opportunity in the colonies than in Europe.

Franklin was especially surprised to meet George Webb, a former Oxford student whose four-year indenture Keimer had purchased. The teenage Webb was born and educated in Gloucester, England, the home of Franklin's soon-to-be friend George Whitefield. Webb's similarity to Whitefield did not end with their common hometown, for he was a talented play-actor. Webb also went to Oxford to study, but (unlike Whitefield) he lasted only a year before he dropped out of school. Leaving the university town, Webb "hid his [scholar's] gown in a furz," or gorse bush, and "footed it to London." In the metropolis Webb fell in with a bad crowd, ran out of money, hocked his clothes, and began to starve. Homeless, he happened upon an advertisement for passage to America in exchange for indentured service. He immediately signed the papers and shipped out, telling none of his friends that he was leaving. Franklin regarded Webb as "lively, witty, good natured, and a pleasant companion." Webb was irresponsible, though: the latest charming rake whom Franklin befriended.[10]

The return to Keimer's shop did not last long. Working there did have its advantages. Franklin broadened his expertise in all aspects of the print trade, from casting type to making ink. He also appreciated not having to work on weekends. In addition to Sundays, they took off Saturdays, which Keimer observed as the Sabbath. This gave Franklin a luxurious second full day for reading each week. But Franklin found Keimer insufferable. The man was "an odd fish," Franklin wrote, "ignorant of common life, fond of rudely opposing received opinions, slovenly to extreme dirtiness, enthusiastic in some points of religion, and a little knavish withal." The tension between Franklin and Keimer escalated when Keimer, insisting that he was paying Franklin too much, began treating Franklin like a servant.[11]

Finally a "trifle snapped our connection," Franklin recalled. One day, a great noise boomed outside the shop, and Franklin stuck his head out the window to see what was going on. Keimer was standing there and began berating Franklin, telling him to go back inside and mind his own business. Keimer came in, continuing to yell at Franklin and giving him three months' notice. Franklin went one better: he quit on the spot, took his hat, and walked out the door. Keimer soon thought better of firing Franklin and persuaded him briefly to return. But Franklin and Hugh Meredith, another of Keimer's workers, were already planning to open their own print shop, which they did in 1728.[12]

Around the time of the Keimer fracas, Franklin, Hugh Meredith, George Webb, and several other men founded the "Junto," a semi-secret learned society. Members also called themselves the "Leather Apron" club, befitting their artisan occupations. The Junto focused its discussions on Franklin's favorite topics: philosophical inquiry and self-improvement. In Franklin's estimation, the group became the "best school of philosophy, morals, and politics that then existed" in Pennsylvania. Like Bernard Mandeville's club in London, philosophical societies were conventicles for the enlightened literati of America and Europe. The name "Junto" was a commonly used political term in English. Perhaps Franklin had also come across the word in Samuel Butler's oft-reprinted anti-Puritan poem *Hudibras*. There Butler sneered at the Puritan zealots' "midnight juntos, and sealed knots." Similarly, Robert Creighton's anti-dissenter sermon preached before King Charles II in 1682 explicitly denounced those Christians who broke off into "little juntos and conventicles." Franklin likely had his father's non-conformist meetings in mind when he picked the name.[13]

The dissenting and Puritan authors who had most influenced Franklin, including Daniel Defoe and Cotton Mather, had recommended similar assemblies for inculcating godliness and moral improvement. Although Franklin dispensed with Mather's prayer and catechizing, he resonated with the Puritan pastor's warning that the group should never discuss controversial theological topics. Instead, Mather urged, they should focus on "points of practical piety." Members of Mather's proposed societies would reflect on the simple question, "What good is there to be done?"[14]

The Junto met at a tavern on Friday nights. Under rules composed by Franklin, members were to contribute discussion questions "on any point of morals, politics or natural philosophy." They likewise read essays on those topics before the fellowship. Prioritizing the search for truth over winning arguments, the group fined any member who provoked disputes or spoke with undue "warmth."[15]

The inaugural Junto fellow whom Franklin admired most was the Quaker William Coleman, a clerk a couple of years older than Franklin. Reminding him of Thomas Denham, Franklin testified that Coleman had the "coolest clearest head, the best heart, and the exactest morals, of almost any man I ever met with." Ben still found himself drawn to good-time friends like George Webb, but he truly appreciated those like Coleman who lived out their faith in integrity and service. Coleman's and Franklin's friendship would last for forty years.[16]

The requirements and rules of the Junto borrowed from standards developed by the great English philosopher John Locke. Prospective members had to stand before the fellowship, place their hand upon their chest, and make four affirmations. First, they had to assure the Junto that they harbored no bad feelings toward any current members. For the next three statements, Franklin adopted language from Locke's own description of a society for "improvement in useful knowledge, the promoting of truth and Christian charity." Junto candidates had to affirm precepts tied to Locke's and Franklin's convictions about religion, truth, and freedom of thought. They had to swear that they loved "mankind in general; of what profession or religion soever." No one should suffer harm, they confessed, for "mere speculative opinions" or for their form of worship (or, presumably, for their lack of church attendance). Finally, society members had to affirm a love of "truth for truth's sake" and promise to investigate, accept, and communicate that truth to the Junto. Traditionalism and religious dogma, Franklin and Locke assumed, undermined the quest for truth.[17]

Cotton Mather also influenced the questions that Franklin used for Junto meetings. Among the points of discussion that Mather suggested for his "Reforming Societies" were instances of oppression that they could rectify, proposals for better laws, and relief of individuals under affliction. The Junto showed a similar concern for reform, but without Mather's emphasis on institutional religion. Franklin suggested that members discuss whether they knew of fellow citizens who had performed any "worthy action" to imitate or, conversely, those who had committed errors to avoid.[18]

Franklin focused on moral discipline when he proposed that the society contemplate the "unhappy effects of intemperance," imprudence, passion, and any other vice that they had observed. They should also reflect on the "happy effects of temperance," prudence, moderation, and other virtues. For Franklin and the Puritans, "temperance" did not mean abstinence from alcohol. Those "puritanical" strictures would not come until after the era of the Puritans had passed, as nineteenth-century crusaders battled the ill effects of drunkenness. Temperance, to the Junto, meant moderation. Franklin had seen too many friends waste their money and health on worldly pleasures. In this emphasis on moral discipline, Franklin's enlightened philosophy and Puritan ethics aligned.[19]

Franklin and his Junto colleagues reflected the new ambitions of middle-class artisans. Neither gentlemen nor commoners, these urban service providers blurred traditional lines between aristocrats and working people. In Franklin's America, the middle-class businessman would become the driver of a new capitalist society. Traditionally, social mobility for poorer men had required the aid of patrons, elite older men who helped them to become established. Such patronage was usually the domain of men, not women, to whom most business, political, and religious vocations were not open. The artisan Junto members wished to serve as patrons too.

Junto members monitored the streets of Philadelphia for strangers whom they might "oblige." They advised each other of any "deserving young beginner . . . whom it lies in the power of the Junto any way to encourage." Such patronage would assist young men trying to establish themselves in a trade, but it would also put those workers in debt to the better-established artisans of the Junto. Members agreed to connect one another with "any man whose friendship" an individual coveted. Franklin understood that good business depended on cultivating these kinds of personal connections. The Junto sought out gentlemen who could secure the right kinds of projects and contracts the artisans needed. Franklin was a man of many gifts. Most importantly, he was a relational genius.[20]

The Junto was explicitly political. Members sought to influence the public good via legislation (as Mather's Reforming Societies had). "Have you lately observed any defect in the laws of your country?" they asked one another. Assuming that the "leather aprons" had the right to influence policymaking, they discussed possible legal reforms. In addition, they cast a suspicious eye on government in an era when authorities expected people's deference. Believing with Locke that government ruled by the consent of the people, and knowing from the history of ancient Greece and Rome that a people's freedoms could vanish in a moment, the Junto carefully watched for "any encroachments on the just liberties of the people."[21]

The Junto was a social experiment, gathered outside of normal government or church circles. Members would help one another cultivate the arts of sociability. For example, Franklin knew that he needed to discipline himself to engage in good conversations. Tending to be chatty, and overly eager to make a joke, he needed to learn to be silent, to listen, and to probe the thoughts of others. This was not only good for learning, but it secured the favor of one's conversation partners. Listening made you more friends, whether they were above or below you on the social ladder.

In the *Pennsylvania Gazette*, the newspaper he would establish, Franklin wrote a piece titled "On Conversation" several years after founding the Junto. According to Ben, most people believed that they were good conversationalists. They usually were wrong, he noted. Charming people showed more interest in what their partner had to say than what they wanted to say themselves (or, at least, they showed a "seeming preference" for what others had to say). They were willing to overlook the annoying habits of colleagues. A person who mastered these habits would gain the "good opinion" of those with whom they interacted "and make them fond of us." Good humor and intelligent commentary were appealing, but only in small doses. First and foremost, a good conversationalist had to demonstrate a willingness to listen.[22]

Franklin tried to find a middle way between purposeless friendship and outright manipulation. "Would you win the hearts of others?" he asked. Then you must not "seem to vie with, but admire them." You should even indulge their "vanity," he advised. Then they will prefer you above other friends. Let others have their full turn to speak and guard against "talking overmuch." (Franklin was undoubtedly preaching to himself.) When you get *two* people together who talk too much, sparks fly. "The vexation they both feel is visible in their looks and gestures; you shall see them gape and stare, and interrupt one another at every turn, and watch with the utmost impatience for a cough or a pause, when they may crowd a word in edgeways: neither hears nor cares what the other says; but both talk on at any rate, and never fail to part highly disgusted with each other." If one of these chatterers would defer, it would result in lasting endearment. But did Franklin recommend conversational deference because it was right? Because it was profitable? Or both?[23]

Since his return from London, Franklin had been trending away from radical deism and amoral license. He "began to suspect" that while deism "might be true, [it] was not very useful." A man unable to control his lusts could expect no prosperity. Although he would never revert back to his parents' traditional doctrines, Franklin knew that unchecked deism was insufficient for good living. This emerging conviction accounts both for the precepts he developed in his "Plan of Conduct" and for his view of God's Providence in an essay he presented at the Junto meeting.[24]

Junto members commonly explored topics related to religion, since Franklin believed that learning happened best in conversations like those at Junto meetings, not by a minister or teacher delivering a unilateral homily. His essay "On the Providence of God in the Government of the World" (1732) expanded on the society's discussion at a previous meeting. He began with self-deprecation, a technique designed to win the affection and hearing of his conversation partners. Making clear that he held his religious views lightly, he called his address a "rash undertaking." He admitted that the Junto had already heard him "say a 1000 silly things" before. Thus, they should not afford him the veneration that one might give to a pastor on such topics. They knew him too well to indulge "reverence for my habit" or the "sanctity of my countenance." He was definitely not "inspired or divinely assisted." He assumed his Junto colleagues would disagree with him, but he chose to revisit the topic anyway.[25]

Could Junto members understand the ways of God without recourse to superstition and rigid tradition? Franklin felt there was hope. Eschewing the techniques of the ministers with their rhetorical flourishes, "deceitful science," and "glosses of oratory," Franklin promised to depend on "sound argument" and "plain reasoning, devoid of art and ornament." Junto members might have grinned upon hearing this, realizing that everything Franklin had said thus far was artful rhetoric. Still, Franklin continued, saying that he would depend on no books and no men, no matter how sacred, for his argument. No Bible was needed, for in the Junto, reason reigned supreme. But reason did tell him many things about God and his attributes. There was no need to address the "first principle" of God's existence and his creation of the universe, for this was obvious and something that "mankind in all ages have agreed in." Whatever objections they might have about Christian theology, the theistic underpinnings of Franklin's and his circle's philosophy would go unquestioned.[26]

Not only did reason affirm that the Creator God existed, but it indicated that God was wise, good, and powerful, Franklin told the meeting. Adapting a strategy common to followers of Isaac Newton, Franklin discerned God's attributes by an argument from design. The complexity of the universe, from the stars to the structures of earthly bodies, suggested God's incomparable wisdom. In his goodness, God gave life to creatures, who demonstrated the preciousness of life by their unwillingness to die. God provided everything needed for sustaining life, and made "those things that are most useful, most common and easy to be had," such as water, air, and light. The vastness of the universe, combined with its controlled order, spoke to God's supremacy. "What power must he possess who not only knows the nature of everything in the universe, but can make

things of new natures with the greatest ease and at his pleasure!"
Franklin exclaimed. None of these beliefs contradicted Franklin's
moderate deism. They remind us that eighteenth-century deists often acknowledged God's glory displayed in creation.[27]

Stipulating God's goodness, wisdom, and power was only a
prelude to Franklin's main point: God ruled the world by
Providence. Here he refuted the argument he had made in his puz-
zling *Dissertation on Liberty and Necessity*. In that piece, he had contended that since God decreed everything, there was no good and
evil, and no free will. Franklin now asserted that given the
Creator's immutable nature, there were four possibilities for how
God related to the world. First was that God had decreed and appointed everything that happened, leaving humans without free
will (the argument of the *Dissertation*). Second was that God had
decreed nothing, leaving all up to the free will of his creatures, including humankind. Third was that God had unalterably decreed
some things and left others up to free will. Fourth—Franklin's
preference—was that God "sometimes interferes by his particular
Providence and sets aside the effects which would otherwise have
been produced by any of the above causes." He asserted that the
first three options were unreasonable. Therefore (striking the ten-
tative tone preferred in Junto discussions), Franklin concluded that
point four, God intervening by particular Providence, was "most
probably true."[28]

Franklin demonstrated the ridiculous implications of points
one through three in order to establish the reasonableness of God's
Providence. Mocking the fatalistic view he once defended in the
Dissertation, Franklin asserted that if God decreed all things once
for all, it would leave God with nothing to do. (Franklin saw
position three, in which God only decreed certain things while
leaving others to free will, as raising virtually the same problem.) If
God foreordained everything, then God "has tied up his hands,
and has now no greater power than an idol of wood or stone."
Furthermore, if God fixed all that was to happen, then he had decreed the coming of sin. That was contrary to God's immutable
goodness. The *Dissertation* had solved this problem by denying that
good and evil existed, but we are not sure if Franklin seriously
meant this. If he did mean it, he had come to realize that few

would accept such an outlandish proposition. That is why he supposedly burned extant copies of the *Dissertation*.[29]

Franklin thought that an absence of contingency made the
concept of prayer especially absurd. Would God have decreed that
people should say millions of prayers, which could never change
anything or prompt God to act? "It is not more difficult to believe
the world was made by a God of wood or stone, than that the God
who made the world should be such a God," he concluded.
Franklin showed an enduring fascination with the efficacy of
prayer—or its lack thereof. In one childhood instance, Franklin
requested that his father go ahead and pray over a whole barrel of
salted meat, instead of saying grace over each meal. Would that not
be more efficient, the boy asked saucily? Then there was his proposal for prayer at the Constitutional Convention, five decades
after his discourse on Providence before the Junto.[30]

Franklin's Junto address argued *against* the idea, classically associated with "deists," that God had set the universe in motion but
was now uninvolved. Franklin found it implausible that "he would
make so glorious a universe merely to abandon it." Would God
really watch a virtuous person pray for justice and refuse to intervene because of a pointless commitment to nonintervention? Does
he watch impassively as people commit acts of evil, with no inten-
tion of ever bringing judgment? Would God observe the innocent
taken captive by cruel oppressors and casually say, "I cannot help
you, 'tis none of my business nor do I at all regard these things"? If
God was passive in the face of such urgent scenarios, then what
was left of his power, wisdom, and goodness?[31]

As with the *Dissertation*, it is reasonable to wonder if Franklin's
"On the Providence of God" was advancing a position he really
believed. Was he just trying to provoke discussion? Maybe he was
advancing a flawed argument in order to flesh out the problem in
conversation? It was certainly a flawed argument: good people's
prayers do often go unanswered, or at least they do not seem answered in obvious ways. Evil actions often go unpunished in this
life. Innocent victims suffer oppression and exploitation with no
divine deliverance. So it may be that Franklin's opinions remained
closer to those of the *Dissertation* than an initial reading of this
Junto treatise might suggest.

Whatever his concrete convictions regarding the Junto treatise, Franklin defended the concept that God allowed contingency and free will, but that God also sometimes "interferes by his particular Providence." God could *both* impart freedom of action and reserve the right to intervene in human affairs. Other philosophers, such as the German mathematician G. W. Leibniz, had argued that if God had made the world in the best possible way, then God would not need to keep tinkering with the world after creation. (Leibniz tended to downplay the level of suffering in the world, earning him the scorn of more skeptical philosophers such as Voltaire.)[32]

Without naming him, Franklin rejected Leibniz's line of thinking. The world needed divine intervention. The printer did not explain why there was suffering in the world, but he likely attributed it to God's granting people free will, which they sometimes used to commit sin. If God does not interfere in the face of the world's crying needs, Franklin reasoned, it could only be because he could not, or would not. If he could not interfere, then he was not all-powerful. If he would not interfere in the face of evil and injustice, then he was not completely good. Thus, " 'tis highly reasonable to believe a Providence because 'tis highly absurd to believe otherwise," Franklin declared. Assuming that God intervenes, we can pray with confidence. We also have assurance that God will reward virtuous living. The belief in Providence would "render us benevolent, useful, and beneficial to others."[33]

Most of his thoughts in "On the Providence of God" remained theoretical. But the key to Franklin's musings about religion was the usefulness of faith. He did not need absolute certainty about its truth, as long as faith was reasonable, practical, and made people act selflessly. The world could not do without some kind of transcendent basis for benevolent behavior. Religion held our worst inclinations at bay and offered the most time-tested grounds for ethical actions. There might be good reasons for skepticism, even about God's intervention in human affairs. But skepticism did not fuel altruistic living. Franklin was backing away from his radical teenage deism, not to embrace Christian particularities, but out of pragmatic concern for virtue. That practicality would become one of the enduring qualities of American Christianity and American spirituality.[34]

In the summer of 1728, Franklin and Hugh Meredith opened their print shop in a rented, three-story brick house in Philadelphia. It was the third printing business in the city, and few thought that Philadelphia could support so many. But Franklin vowed never to be outworked. Unlike his old boss Keimer, he labored late into the night to get jobs done in a timely fashion. Still, town merchants whispered that Franklin had no chance to succeed. A Scottish physician, Dr. Patrick Baird, stuck up for Franklin, citing the young man's "industry." It was "superior to anything I ever saw of the kind," proclaimed the Scot. "I see him still at work when I go home from club; and he is at work again before his neighbors are out of bed."[35]

Even as his good reputation spread, Franklin wrestled to get his bearings in devotion to God. He still rarely went to church. He had fresh memories of his desperate illness in 1727, and of the sickness that carried off Thomas Denham. Trying to find an outlet for practical devotion, Franklin wrote his unpublished "Articles of Belief and Acts of Religion" in late 1728. Franklin scholar Kerry S. Walters regards this piece as the "most important religious document" that Franklin ever wrote.[36]

It is also one of the most perplexing of Franklin's religious writings, because of its affirmation of multiple "gods." The piece opens with an epigraph from Joseph Addison's "Cato," one that encapsulated Franklin's view of religion: "If there is a power above us (and that there is, all nature cries aloud, through all her works), he must delight in virtue, and that which he delights in must be happy." Note the "if": we do not ultimately know if there is a supreme God, but nature (aside from revelation) suggests that there is. Assuming that there is a God, he must be good, not evil. God's code of virtue must be for the benefit of his creatures. Benevolent actions, not passive veneration, are the essence of true religion.[37]

Franklin postulated that there "is one supreme most perfect Being," who is the "Author and Father of the Gods themselves." "Gods," he wrote. In the *plural*. This statement has generated much commentary and confusion among students of Franklin. Some have argued that Franklin was affirming full-blown polytheism, meaning that the one supreme Creator God had created other gods. Other interpreters have contended that this was yet another satire. Polytheism was an exotic notion in the eighteenth century. There is always a possibility that Franklin was being facetious. But there are reasons to believe that in "Articles of Belief," he was being serious. He did not publish the piece but instead used it as a personal devotional guide, perhaps on those Sunday mornings when he was absent from church. Why would he write something for private use in a satirical mode? Maybe he was just speculating about God—or the gods. Franklin made few definitive conclusions about God's nature, other than that God existed and that he favored virtue.[38]

Nevertheless, Franklin wrote that in some sense there were created gods who stood above people in the so-called Chain of Being. The Chain of Being theory held that all of creation ranked in a hierarchy from God the Creator down to the lowest life forms. Traditionally, Christians believed that only the angels stood between humans and God in this hierarchy. Franklin suggested that there were many beings above humankind, just as there were many animals and plants below them. When Franklin cast his mind's eye across the universe, with its immense complexity, he concluded that God must be far, far above us. Even the earth seemed to be "almost nothing, and myself less than nothing, and of no sort of consequence." Whatever Franklin meant by the "gods," the majestic Creator still stood high above the creation. This may have been a point where the notion of an inaccessible, supreme watchmaker God did resonate with Franklin.[39]

Franklin proclaimed that it was vanity to think that God, the "supremely perfect," would "regard such an inconsiderable nothing as man." Surely God was not interested in man's worship and praise. Here Franklin was thinking of Psalm 8:3–5: "When I consider thy heavens, the work of thy fingers, the moon and the stars, which thou hast ordained; What is man, that thou art mindful of him? and the son of man, that thou visitest him? For thou hast made him a little lower than the angels, and hast crowned him with glory and honour." Although Franklin shared the scripture's sense of wonder at the heavens, he did not share the confidence that the Creator God really showed attention to humankind. He further doubted that people could understand God's attributes. How could a finite mind fathom the infinite qualities of the divine?[40]

Still, people had an inborn inclination to worship. While good religion must produce virtuous actions, prayer and adoration were also natural desires. Franklin even regarded it as his "duty" to "pay divine regards to SOMETHING." The Supreme Being accommodated this inclination by creating "many Beings or Gods" who could better understand God's qualities than humans can. These created beings could "return him a more rational and glorious praise." Each of these was, like the one Supreme God, enormously good and powerful. Each of these gods had also created his own solar system. Thus, the God whom Christians and Jews know as "God the Father" was one of the lower gods, above and behind whom stood the ultimate Creator God. The god who was the "author and owner" of our solar system was humanity's proper object of "praise and adoration." While the Supreme God (the deistic God?) was unconcerned with human affairs, the god of our solar system was personable enough to care about individuals, "being pleased with our praise, and offended when we slight him, or neglect his glory." Our lower god had ordained that happiness came through virtue and the pursuit of "innocent delights." Therefore, Franklin loved the god we know for his goodness and adored him for his wisdom.[41]

Franklin seemed torn between his deistic belief in God's inscrutability and the lingering Christian conviction that people could know God. The "Articles of Belief" split the difference. The god we worship is not the final, mysterious Creator God. In making this peculiar argument, Franklin was following polytheistic-sounding musings that Isaac Newton and others had similarly advanced. Maybe he also remembered the Bible's occasional references to the "gods," such as Psalm 82, which speaks of the supreme God who "judgeth among the gods," or John 10:34, when Jesus asked Jewish critics, "Is it not written in your law, 'I said, Ye are gods?'"[42]

Franklin did not make clear how he arrived at his concept of multiple created gods, other than through his own reason. The god we can approach, he contended, is finite, created, and not sovereign over the universe. Yet this god is much like God the Father in the Bible. If our god is approachable and able to be worshipped, he must be a lower god, Franklin reasoned. Traditional Christians, like his parents and sister Jane, would find this proposal an unnecessary tradeoff. God the Father was transcendent yet had made himself approachable. This approachability was demonstrated most clearly in the incarnation of the eternal Son of God as a man. These would have been familiar theological options to Franklin, but in the "Articles of Belief" he took a solitary path of speculative theology.[43]

Franklin gave another hint of what he might have meant by these multiple gods in one of his 1729 "Busy-Body" essays, which appeared in Andrew Bradford's *American Weekly Mercury* newspaper. This piece was a classic Franklin exaltation of virtue. It posited that "virtue alone is sufficient to make a man great, glorious and happy." It was better to control one's passions, to be just, honest, and prudent, and to be temperate in indulging the pleasures of the flesh, than to master all the book learning in the world. People longed for the esteem of others, but they chose the wrong paths to get it, he wrote. Some pursued great learning, beauty, wealth, or wit, but what were these when compared to virtue? Through virtue alone, people took on godlike qualities: "We love the handsome, we applaud the learned, and we fear the rich and powerful," Franklin noted, "but we even worship and adore the virtuous." By "worship" he may have just meant deep veneration. But Franklin may have meant that humans exalted the most virtuous people among them—such as Jesus of Nazareth—as objects of worship. Such paragons of benevolence were so rare that we could easily mistake them for gods.[44]

People should and would worship a god they can know, Franklin insisted. Thus the "Articles" supplied directions for proper devotion and prayer, beginning with six short affirmations of God's goodness. "O Creator, O Father, I believe that thou art good, and that thou art *pleased with the pleasure* of thy children," he prayed. "Praised be thy name forever." (Each stanza closed with that refrain of praise.) The next prayers struck a Newtonian chord on God's rule over nature: "By thy power hast thou made the glorious sun, with his attending worlds; from the energy of thy mighty will they first received their prodigious motion, and by thy wisdom hast thou prescribed the wondrous laws by which they move." True worshippers understood God's attributes and the immutable laws

that revealed God's power and wisdom. The final prayer emphasized God's abhorrence of vice, and delight in virtue, concluding
with the affirmation that God was Franklin's "friend, my Father,
and my Benefactor."[45]

After reciting these prayers, Franklin's "Articles of Belief" suggests readings from prominent natural theology writers. Although
many of them also believed in scripture, natural theologians sought
to understand God from sources outside of revelation, and to use
contemporary scholarship to demonstrate God's superintending
power over the physical world. Among Franklin's suggested texts
was the influential *The Wisdom of God Manifested in the Works of the
Creation* (1691) by Anglican minister John Ray. *The Wisdom of God*
came out in seventeen editions in the century after its publication,
and remained well-known enough to merit a reference in Herman
Melville's *Moby-Dick*. Cotton Mather was a great admirer, praising
Ray as a "modern Pliny." Ray proclaimed that the "vast multitude
of creatures, and those not only small, but immensely great, the
sun and moon, and all the heavenly host, are effects and proofs of
[God's] almighty power." In Franklin's hands, Ray and other works
of "physico-theology" became aids to personal devotion.[46]

After the natural theology readings, Franklin proposed to
"sing" a poem of John Milton, the "Hymn to the Creator" from
book 5 of *Paradise Lost*. Milton was a critic of the English monarchy and state church who nearly lost his life when King Charles II
took back the English throne in 1660. Milton's epic poem *Paradise
Lost* was first published in 1667, and by the eighteenth century it
was regarded as one of the greatest English works ever written.
Franklin's beloved Joseph Addison wrote an important series of
commentaries on *Paradise Lost* in *The Spectator* in 1711–1712, which
boosted the fame of the poem. Addison's studies may have helped
introduce Franklin to Milton, whom Franklin regarded as one of
"the two best English Poets that ever were." Milton's fame continued among a wide spectrum of Anglo-Americans in the eighteenth
century. Methodist evangelist John Wesley, for instance, always
carried an annotated copy of *Paradise Lost*. Wesley also published a
popular abridgement of it, and recommended that his followers
memorize sections from it. There were about 120 reprintings of
Paradise Lost during the eighteenth century.[47]

Franklin quoted from Milton in a passage extolling God's works in creation:

These are thy Glorious Works, Parent of Good!
Almighty: Thine this Universal Frame,
Thus wondrous fair! Thy self how wondrous then!
Speak ye who best can tell, Ye Sons of Light,
Angels, for ye behold him, and with Songs,
And Choral Symphonies, Day without Night
Circle his Throne rejoicing. You in Heav'n,
On Earth, join all Ye Creatures to extol
Him first, him last, him midst and without End.
Fairest of Stars, last in the Train of Night,
If rather thou belongst not to the Dawn,
Sure Pledge of Day! That crown'st the smiling Morn
With thy bright Circlet; Praise him in thy Sphere
While Day arises, that sweet Hour of Prime.
Thou Sun, of this Great World both Eye and Soul
Acknowledge Him thy Greater, Sound his Praise.

It is not clear what Franklin meant by "singing" Milton's verses. Perhaps he put a tune to them and sang quietly during morning devotions.[48]

At the beginning and end of this section of *Paradise Lost*—which was a prayer uttered by Adam and Eve before their fall into sin—Franklin cut some lines that addressed God's inscrutability and anticipated the couple's coming temptation by the serpent (whom Christians traditionally identified as the devil). Franklin's Supreme God was remote, to be sure, but the god whom Ben addressed in his devotions was not. In Franklin's large body of writings on religion, he did not grapple much with fundamental questions of evil or sin, except what the existence of sin told us about God's foreordination of all things. He only made occasional serious references to the devil. In an atypical note in one of the Busy-Body essays, Franklin compared people's cringing admiration for rulers to the "worship paid by Indians to the Devil." His lack of interest in these malevolent forces was another example of Franklin's departure from his Calvinist inheritance.[49]

After Milton's hymn, Franklin's devotional program had him reading from books (he named no examples) related to "MORAL VIRTUE." Then he entered the "Petition" section of his prayers. Franklin professed confidence that God would never withhold earthly blessings "if by a VIRTUOUS and HOLY life I merit his favour and kindness." Although the Bible speaks routinely of the righteous receiving God's approval, Ben's parents would have winced at this quid-pro-quo relationship with God. That word "merit" was noxious to traditional Calvinists: the only thing people "merited" from God was wrath. But to Franklin, a virtuous life was its own blessing. It also brought earthly goods such as prosperity and happiness.[50]

Franklin's short petitions began with the plea that God would preserve him from "Atheism and Infidelity, Impiety and Profaneness." In spite of a few scholars' efforts to paint Franklin as a "stone-cold atheist," atheism contradicted Franklin's religious convictions. Franklin was unquestionably a theist. He and his contemporaries connected atheism not so much to refuting God's existence but to the "denial of God in deed or thought arising from immorality and ignorance." Even Voltaire, the strident opponent of France's institutional church, derided atheism and dreaded its social consequences. Franklin knew that traditional Christians (like his friend George Whitefield) regarded deism and atheism as virtual synonyms. John Adams once sullenly placed Franklin's own faith among "Atheists, Deists, and Libertines." But Franklin's brand of deism venerated God through virtuous living. Worship through moral actions was more central to Franklin's deism than it was to traditional Calvinism, since he gave little attention to grace (the idea that God shows the saints favor in spite of their sins). Franklin also prayed—on a theme that did complement his Puritan heritage—that in his devotions he would avoid all "ostentation, formality and odious hypocrisy." He concluded that prayer, and all these petitions, with "Help me, O Father."[51]

For Franklin, moral behavior included duty to one's nation. As of 1728, that country was Britain, not something called "America." Thus he prayed in the "Articles" that he would be "loyal to my Prince" (the recently acceded King George II) and "faithful to my Country." A dutiful citizen abhorred both tyranny and treason.

Critics of the Patriot rebels in the 1770s would contend that they forgot about the evils of treason, putting all their attention on the fear of British tyranny. But that was five decades in the future for Franklin. It would take most of those intervening years for Franklin to lose his attachment to Britain and its monarch.[52]

Righteous living also required humble acceptance of one's station in life. Franklin remained a modest tradesman, so he asked God in the "Articles" to help him to be "dutiful, humble, and submissive" to his social superiors. But he also prayed that he would be kind to his inferiors, "avoiding cruelty, harshness and oppression, insolence and unreasonable severity." We may be surprised to see Franklin's British, hierarchical mindset. Too often, biographers have rushed to find evidence of Franklin becoming an egalitarian, middle-class American. True, he did represent the emergence of a new middle class of tradesmen who stood between the ranks of the gentry and the poor. Yet in the late 1720s, he was also a young artisan, one with ravenous social ambitions. Only a couple of years earlier, he had languished as an apprentice, a condition from which he had literally run away. As a free man, he kept on running—or climbing, as it were. The opening of his print business was soon followed by marriage and growing signs of gentility, such as the "China bowl with a spoon of silver" that appeared, supposedly to his surprise, on his breakfast table one morning in the early 1730s. (He blamed his wife, Deborah, for buying the extravagances "without my knowledge.") As early as the mid-1730s, Franklin had also acquired a "negro boy" as a servant, or possibly as a slave. Franklin was intimately familiar with social ranks and their respective responsibilities.[53]

The rest of his prayers in "Articles of Belief" concerned an exemplary list of vices and virtues, qualities one could derive from the Golden Rule, the "fruit of the Spirit" in the book of Galatians, and Christ's Sermon on the Mount. He asked the Father to help him "be honest and openhearted, gentle, merciful and good, cheerful in spirit, rejoicing in the good of others." The prayers concluded with thankfulness, focusing on his supply of daily provisions. "For peace and liberty, for food and raiment, for corn and wine, and milk, and every kind of healthful nourishment, *Good God, I Thank thee*," he wrote. He thanked God for knowledge, literature, and "every useful

art"; for friends, reason, and for "every pleasant hour." Echoing
sentiments from "On the Providence of God," Franklin acknowledged that the goods of life came from God's hand. Thanking God
for these gifts was right, and doing so put him in the kind of benevolent mindset that would keep eliciting God's blessings.[54]

However often Franklin uttered the prayers of "Articles of Belief,"
it was a private program of devotion. Private behavior was only a
fraction of real religion. Full devotion to God, for Franklin, was
found in what we might call "moral sociability," and that had to be
lived out in relationship with others. His Puritan forebears emphasized Christian sociability and "sympathy" as well, but they saw the
local church as the locus of such loving service. In his influential
Vindication of the Government of New England Churches, published
while Franklin was still a boy in Boston, Puritan pastor John Wise
argued that "sociableness" grew *both* out of people's desire for self-
preservation and out of their humane inclination to serve the common good. The Puritan emphasis on moral sociability was one of
the reasons why Franklin felt bad about not going to church. His
guilt spurred him to pursue alternatives. The Junto was one major
outlet for Franklin for ethical service and self-advancement. But he
found perhaps the epitome of social religion in the Freemasons.[55]

The Freemasons flourished in early eighteenth-century
England as part of the new trend for social clubs. The Masons emphasized principles that Franklin enshrined in the Junto: nonsec-
tarianism, mutual support, and virtue. Freemasonry had
quasi-religious qualities. Members enjoined brother Masons to es-
pouse only "that religion in which all men agree, leaving their particular opinions to themselves." Freemasons took theism for
granted, but specific Christian doctrines remained a matter of private conscience. The Freemasons' unifying principles included a
commitment to virtue and belief in the Creator God, whom they
called the "Grand Architect." No Mason in good standing would
ever "be a stupid atheist, nor an irreligious libertine," an early
Masonic document asserted.[56]

Franklin did not get off to a good start with Philadelphia's
Masonic lodge. When Masons founded it in 1730, as probably the
first lodge in America, they did not invite Franklin to join. So he

borrowed and updated an anti-Masonic spoof from a London newspaper and ran it in the *Pennsylvania Gazette*. The Freemasons already had a dubious reputation as a secret society. In his version of the mock piece, Franklin added the punch line that "their Grand Secret is, that they have no secret at all." The Philadelphia Masons voted to admit Franklin several weeks later, and he joined in February 1731. The young printer had made it clear that he could make life rough for the Masons if they continued to ignore him.[57]

Subsequently, Franklin ran a positive piece on the Masons in May 1731, in order to "give the reader what information we can concerning the society called Free Masons." In spite of its affirmative tone, the excerpt still focused on the brotherhood's secrecy, which enhanced its news value.

> FREE or ACCEPTED MASONS . . . are now very considerable both for numbers and character; being found in every country in *Europe*, and consisting principally of persons of merit and consideration. As to antiquity, they lay claim to a standing of some thousand years; and, it is said, can trace up their original as early as the building of Solomon's Temple. What the end of their institution is, seems still, in some measure, a secret; though as much of it as is known, appears truly good and laudable, as it tends to promote friendship, society, mutual assistance, and good-fellowship. The brethren of this family are said to be possessed of a great number of secrets, which have been strictly from age to age: Be their other virtues what they will, 'tis plain they are masters of one in a very great degree, viz. secrecy.

Freemasons were typically people (all men) of some means, but the fraternity also fostered the mingling of wealthier tradesmen—the new middle class—with gentlemen.[58]

The Freemasons elected Franklin a warden of the lodge in 1732, and in 1734, the Philadelphia fraternity chose him as their Grand Master. Franklin publicized these events in the *Pennsylvania Gazette*, making news items out of both himself and the Masons. Franklin also became a key player in America's network of lodges.

He reprinted the most important text of Freemasonry, *The Constitutions of the Free-Masons*, in 1734, just before his election as Grand Master. *The Constitutions* began with a biblical history of architecture, contending that "Adam, our first parent, created after the image of God, the great Architect of the Universe, must have had liberal sciences, particularly geometry, written on his heart; for even since the Fall, we find the principles of it in the hearts of his offspring." Deistically inclined as many Freemasons were, they still traced their history to the biblical record, and interwove the history of Masonry with events such as the construction of Solomon's Temple. Franklin printed *The Constitutions* not just for Pennsylvania lodges but sent copies to South Carolina, Massachusetts, and Rhode Island.[59]

Because of its religious character and international scope, Freemasonry became like an alternative church for many members. Although Freemasons were often affiliated with traditional churches, too, the organization offered fellowship, exchange of ideas, and the inculcation of virtue outside the bounds of established congregations. It attracted a number of other prominent Founding Fathers, including George Washington. But in spite of Franklin's long membership and service in the society, we should not overemphasize its significance in Franklin's personal life. He did not often discuss it in his papers or in the *Autobiography* (a skeptical observer might suggest this was to ensure secrecy). The Junto was more significant for Franklin's daily friendships.[60]

Franklin kept experimenting in moral sociability, though. Just months after he joined the Masons he was brainstorming about yet another secret club, which he called the "Society of the Free and Easy." He thought that there was "great occasion for raising an united party for virtue, by forming the virtuous and good men of all nations into a regular body, to be governed by suitable good and wise rules, which good and wise men may probably be more unanimous in their obedience to, than common people are to common laws." Perhaps he had found Freemasonry somewhat unsatisfying, as the description of the Society of the Free and Easy's purposes sounds quite similar to it.[61]

The name "Free and Easy" signaled that the fellowship's industrious members—all unmarried young men—would be free from the burdens of vice and debt. In spite of its nonsectarian character, Franklin proposed a "creed" for the society, to which prospective members would have to assent. It contained "the essentials of every known religion, and [was] free of everything that might shock the professors of any religion." Its tenets were theistic but avoided particular Christian doctrines:

That there is one God who made all things.
That he governs the World by his Providence.
That he ought to be worshipped by Adoration, Prayer and Thanksgiving.
But that the most acceptable Service of God is doing Good to Man.
That the Soul is immortal.
And that God will certainly reward Virtue and punish Vice either here or hereafter.

Wishing to avoid any "shocking" topics, Franklin's essentialist statement did not broach topics such as multiple created gods. But it was striking that Franklin still assumed that this enlightened society *needed* a creed. Worship of God, and belief in God's coming judgment, undergirded virtue.[62]

The twenty-five-year-old printer wanted a new religion of worshipful theism, personal integrity, selfless service, and mutual improvement. His dream of the Society of the Free and Easy would never materialize, however, as he never got around to forming it. His relentless joining of clubs reflected his quest to find an enlightened substitute for the Calvinist congregations of his parents' faith. Even as he sloughed off his family's religion, its frameworks and categories shaped him. He represented a type of "Calvinist *malgré lui-même*": a Reformed Christian in spite of himself. Abandoning Puritan doctrine was not enough. He needed a discipline and a creed to replace it.[63]

CHAPTER FOUR

Poor Richard

B EN FRANKLIN FOUND HIS "way to wealth" in publishing. He
was so successful that he retired from printing in 1748, at
the age of forty-two. One of his most lucrative ventures
was his almanac, published under the pseudonym "Poor
Richard." There was a huge market for almanacs in early America.
If a colonial American family owned any printed item besides the
Bible, it was usually an almanac, and Poor Richard's typically sold
ten thousand copies a year.[1]

We often remember Poor Richard's pithy sayings on industriousness: "Haste makes waste," "a penny saved is twopence clear,"
and "no gains without pains." These were moralistic, practical aphorisms stripped of any specifically Christian content. But standing
alongside these proverbs were other religious references that
reflected Franklin's idiosyncratic views and the buying public's demands. On the first line of Poor Richard's first calendar—January
1, 1733—was the solitary word "Circumcision." This was a reference to the Church of England's liturgical calendar, as January 1
was traditionally the Feast of the Circumcision of Christ. Jesus was
understood to have been circumcised eight days after his birth on
Christmas. Further down, other references to the church calendar
dotted the list: "Epiphany," "Septuagesima," "Ash Wednesday,"
and more.[2]

Faith ordered time in eighteenth-century America. We properly emphasize Franklin's skepticism about faith, yet Poor Richard's year was interwoven with the festivals and seasonal markers of Christianity. His Puritan parents would not have acknowledged the Anglican church calendar, but Franklin's Philadelphia had a strong Anglican presence. Indeed, Franklin himself maintained a rented pew at the city's Christ Church. Most of the people mentioned in Poor Richard's calendars were either saints or British monarchs. The latter spoke to the colonists' deep commitment—as of the 1730s—to the king of England. It was a distinctly Protestant calendar, too, with notes like "Luther Nat. 1483" for Martin Luther's birthdate of November 10.[3]

Deism was not the whole story of Franklin's religion. Franklin and his fellow Founders lived and breathed Christian culture, whatever their quibbles with specific Christian doctrines. Yet hints of Poor Richard's unorthodox views did appear in the almanac's pages. August 1733's poem spoke of climate, noting how "the Gods assign'd" the weather patterns of the most habitable climes. A traditionalist reader of the only extant copy of this first almanac (now held at the Rosenbach Museum and Library in Philadelphia) was bothered by this rendering, which hinted at Franklin's notions about multiple created gods. The reader blotted out "the" and the plural "s," and added a singular "hath"—"*God* hath assign'd," the faithful reader corrected it. Franklin's concept of plural gods would not have received a warm reception from many Americans, in his time or later. But he still lived in a world where a January 1 reference to circumcision needed no explanation.[4]

Even before becoming Poor Richard, Franklin kept laboring for financial security and independence. He had established his own press in 1728 with Hugh Meredith. But like his London pal James Ralph, Meredith turned out to be unreliable and undisciplined. Franklin's sturdy Junto friend William Coleman warned him that people often saw Meredith staggering about "drunk in the streets, and playing low games in alehouses, much to our discredit." Franklin arranged to buy Meredith out of the business, and in 1730, Ben became its sole proprietor.[5]

The next obvious move, for someone of Franklin's age and station, was to get married. But he could not easily find a spouse. Franklin already had a child, William, whom he would bring to the marriage. The identity of the mother, and the birthdate of Franklin's son, have always been mysteries. William was apparently born in Philadelphia in 1728 or 1729; his mother might have been a prostitute. Silence Dogood had commented on women in the colonial cities who, seeking to "revive the spirit of love in disappointed bachelors . . . expose themselves to sale to the first bidder." In one of the most frank passages of the *Autobiography*, Franklin confessed that before his marriage, the "hard-to-be-governed passion of youth, had hurried me frequently into intrigues with low women that fell in my way, which were attended with some expense and great inconvenience." He knew he should stop going to prostitutes. He worried about catching venereal disease, "a distemper which of all things I dreaded, though by great good luck I escaped it." Paying for sex was a dangerous and undisciplined habit, just the kind of thing he had vowed to avoid.[6]

Still, Franklin struggled to reconcile his stated commitment to rational virtue with his habit of visiting prostitutes. Indeed, Franklin's "low intrigues" came while he was composing some of his most important spiritual writings, such as "Articles of Belief and Acts of Religion." Had they known, his parents and sister Jane would have suggested that he was reaping what he had sown. No faith in Christ meant no power over sin. But Franklin's experience was hardly unusual. He was in his early twenties, with growing financial resources and no structures of church or marriage to rein him in. It might be more surprising if he had avoided illicit escapades, especially in London. Franklin's experiences paled in light of the exploits of the Scottish biographer and former Calvinist James Boswell. Boswell's European tour of the 1760s led him to contract multiple cases of venereal disease. He also cuckolded Jean-Jacques Rousseau, as Boswell traveled with and bedded Rousseau's wife Thérèse. Like Franklin, Boswell tried to swear off prostitutes, even as he pestered the Continent's greatest philosophes with inquiries about the afterlife.[7]

There are good reasons to think that William's mother might not have been a prostitute, though. If she was, how would Franklin have known that he was the father? Perhaps the mother was the wife of one of Franklin's friends or business associates. Maybe the husband had gone away on a long trip to the Caribbean, or to Britain. In any case, Franklin realized that he was the father and that he needed to take care of William. (This was unusual, as women have almost always carried the burden of raising children born out of wedlock in American history.) William added to Franklin's struggles in finding a spouse. In the *Autobiography*, Franklin dubiously blamed his lack of options on his status as an artisan printer. His tactics did not make things easier. Franklin injudiciously requested that one set of prospective in-laws pay off his debts with a dowry.[8]

After several failed wooings, Franklin returned to his on-and-off relationship with Deborah Read, whom he had courted prior to his London sojourn. He and Deborah had discussed marriage before he left Philadelphia in 1724, but he ignored her and only sent her one letter while in England. He later called this one of the great "errata" of his life. The jilted Read went on to marry a no-account potter named James Rogers. Franklin blamed this development on his negligence, but it is notable that Read married Rogers just nine months after Franklin left Philadelphia. Perhaps she forgot about Franklin as quickly as he forgot her.[9]

Regardless, Read was never happy with Rogers. She "soon parted from him," Franklin recalled. Refusing "to cohabit with him, or bear his name," rumors circulated that Rogers had taken another wife. "He was a worthless fellow," Franklin concluded. Debts prompted Rogers to run away from Philadelphia and go to the West Indies, where he died. Franklin regarded Read with pity, as she was "generally dejected, seldom cheerful, and avoided company. I considered my giddiness and inconstancy when in London as in a great degree the cause of her unhappiness," he wrote.[10]

Their "mutual affection" revived upon Franklin's return, but there were a host of complications facing them if they got legally married. Should Rogers reappear (it was not certain he was dead), Deborah could be charged with bigamy. Creditors could force Franklin to take responsibility for Rogers's debts. The couple avoided these potential difficulties by entering a common-law marriage in September 1730. In effect, they announced their intent to

cohabit together without going through the legal process of matrimony. Common law marriages were not unusual in colonial
America. Franklin figured that this all worked out for the best:
"None of the inconveniencies happened that we had apprehended,
she proved a good and faithful helpmate, assisted me much by
attending the shop, we throve together, and have ever mutually
endeavored to make each other happy." Referencing God's purpose
for creating Eve in Genesis 2, Franklin could not ask for more than
finding a good "helpmate" as a wife. Thus he "corrected that great
erratum" as well as he could.[11]

Although bits of evidence would suggest that Deborah harbored resentment toward Ben's child, William, the new couple's
early relationship was supportive and functional. Many marriages
in eighteenth-century America were more like business partnerships than companionate romances. Assisted by household slaves
and servants, "Debby" ran the general store on the ground floor of
Franklin's print shop, freeing him to oversee the press.[12]

A month after marrying, Franklin published a piece entitled
"Rules and Maxims for Promoting Matrimonial Happiness." The
principles he enshrined there amounted to instructions to Deborah.
Franklin combined an exalted view of marriage with a Puritan view
of human depravity. Marriage was the "most lasting foundation of
comfort and love; the source of all that endearing tenderness," and
"the cause of all good order in the world." But because of the "per-
verseness of human nature," marriage could become racked by the
"most exquisite wretchedness and misery." He addressed his maxims to women instead of men, not because women were the chief
culprits in marital strife, but because they were more likely than
men to adjust their behavior. "Good wives usually make good husbands," he posited.[13]

Most of Franklin's strictures related to women accepting their
husbands, warts and all. Wives should be patient and long-suffering. Avoid "all thoughts of *managing* your husband," he insisted. He
told women to "be not over sanguine before marriage, nor promise
yourself felicity without alloy, for that's impossible to be attained in
this present state of things." While engaged, remind yourself that
you are preparing to marry "a man, and not an angel." React to all
disappointments with cheerfulness and resilience, he advised. Do

not dispute with him, lest you "risk a quarrel or create a heart-burning, which it's impossible to know the end of." Remind yourself often of your matrimonial vows, and do not forget your sacred promise (from the Book of Common Prayer's marriage liturgy) to "obey" your husband. Always wear your wedding ring, a glance at which would help ward off any "improper thoughts" that might assault the mind. We do not know what Deborah thought about these recommendations.[14]

As Franklin's printing business expanded, religion was one of his steadily selling topics, as it was for most colonial printers. He marketed titles on a range of religious subjects. Besides the Freemasons' bylaws, Franklin printed the work of authors including one who sought to prove "that the Jewish or seventh-day sabbath is abrogated and repealed." Less polemical was the seventh edition of English hymn-writer Isaac Watts's influential *The Psalms of David, Imitated in the Language of the New Testament, and Apply'd to the Christian State and Worship*. Watts's hymns would be crucial for the new congregational music of the Great Awakening of the 1730s and 1740s.[15]

Franklin's ongoing personal writings about religion often tackled controversial issues. But his sarcastic or indirect prose frequently obscured Franklin's own conclusions. One of his favorite targets was religious or mystical superstition. Sometimes he mocked superstition by comically threatening to employ its tactics. He once did that in the voice of "The Busy-Body," a self-appointed moral censor for Pennsylvania society. The Busy-Body would act as a "terror to evil-doers," he thundered. But as a gesture of goodwill, the Busy-Body in 1729 announced an "Act of General Oblivion" for all crimes and sins committed by Pennsylvania residents. This absolution lasted from the founding of the colony to the date of the first Busy-Body essay. To show that he had the wherewithal to enact serious moral reformation, the Busy-Body printed a letter from a fictional assistant who had the gift of "second sight." This person claimed to be descended from John Bunyan, the author of *Pilgrim's Progress*. Just as a number of people in Europe and America were rumored to possess powers of special knowledge and witchcraft, this clairvoyant said that he had "not only a faculty of discovering the actions of persons that are absent or asleep; but even of the Devil himself in many of his secret workings, in the various shapes, habits and names of men and women."[16]

Readers at the time would have realized that this second-sighted Bunyan descendant was based on Duncan Campbell, a sensational mute clairvoyant in London in the 1710s. Although Campbell had convinced many of his special powers, Joseph Addison's *The Spectator*, Franklin's favorite publication, called Campbell a fraud. *The Tatler*, a brief-lived English journal founded by Addison's colleague Richard Steele, likewise scoffed at how credulous people came to Campbell, "full of expectations, and pay his own rate for the interpretations they put upon his shrugs and nods."[17]

Franklin also spoofed the case of the "Tedworth drummer," the best known supernatural mystery in seventeenth-century England. (Arthur Conan Doyle wrote two centuries afterward that the case was still "probably too well known to require elucidation.") In a 1661 encounter, a man named John Mompesson had exposed a fraudster, William Drury, who was playing a drum in town, ostensibly to raise funds to help the poor. Drury was arrested, and Mompesson took the drum to his home in Tedworth. The house was immediately struck by a poltergeist: inexplicable drumming and banging, furniture flying around rooms, and children assaulted in their beds. The poltergeist threw a Bible into the fireplace on Christmas Day. American colonists knew the case well. Increase Mather had written about it in his *Illustrious Providences*, which catalogued various episodes of witchcraft, demon possession, and poltergeists.[18]

The 1730 "Letter of the Drum," a sarcastic anonymous account in the *Pennsylvania Gazette* attributed to Franklin, told a similar (presumably fictional) story. Franklin claimed that religious belief of any kind was at stake in the plausibility of the phantom drummer accounts. Supernatural truth was under attack by "Spinosists, Hobbists, and most impious freethinkers, who despise revelation," referencing Benedict de Spinoza and Thomas Hobbes, the most radical skeptics of the era. Indeed, with his notorious materialism and anti-providential views, Spinoza was the "supreme philosophical bogeyman of early Enlightenment Europe," according to one historian of the era. Such skeptics denied the "existence of the Devil" and biblical stories such as Saul and the witch of Endor (from I Samuel 28), Franklin warned. Worse, his letter lamented, the new skeptics denied accounts such as the "well-attested one of the Drummer of Tedworth." As popular as the drummer tale was, any devout reader would know that one should not put *more* weight on that story's authority than on scripture's.[19]

Franklin's fictional letter-writer said he had once started to doubt the existence of witches, spirits, and apparitions. For some years he even stopped living in fear of "Demons and Hobgoblins." That all changed because of this story: a pastor and some of his clerical colleagues had gathered at an inn to discuss how to prevent the "growth of atheism." That night, sounds of drums under their bed awoke the pastor and his companion, though the other two pastors said they heard nothing. The next night, the same thing happened, and one of the pastors was almost pulled out of bed by his big toe. In the midst of the racket, they recognized the voice of one of their "brethren." He had come into the room intending to scare them, he said. But now he heard the mysterious noise, too! The prankster was frightened out of his wits. (Franklin did not address an obvious question: was the companion in the tale not just extending the trick he had started playing the night before by feigning fear?) The letter-writer admitted that some still might deny that the devil had pulled the prank, but he was convinced.[20]

The "Letter of the Drum" satirized people's gullibility about the supernatural. But it also raised questions about biblical authority. If we regard stories like the Tedworth drummer as silly folktales, where did that leave comparable accounts in the Bible? Scotland's great skeptic (and future correspondent with Franklin) David Hume argued against "miracles," which depended solely on the testimony of witnesses. For example, if someone proposes that a dead man was raised to life, Hume suggested that we ask ourselves if it is "more probable, that this person should either deceive or be deceived, or that the fact, which he relates, should really have happened." We should always go with the more likely explanation. Hume believed that the witnesses to the resurrection were deceived.[21]

This was a dangerous line of thought. Franklin, more affable and less dogmatic than Hume, always liked to work out his opinions

David Hume, *lithograph by Antoine Maurin, Paris, 1820 (detail). Courtesy
New York Public Library.*

in conversation. So he discussed his skeptical satire on the drummer's tale by writing an opposing letter to the editor, meaning himself. (It is difficult to follow the logic because Franklin is the author
of both letters, one a satire, and the other a criticism of satire.
Neither is written in Franklin's own voice. What position, we wonder, does Franklin actually take?) Writing in the voice of a concerned Christian reader, "Philoclerus," Franklin warned against
satirizing religious authority. The "Letter of the Drum" would not
do "good to any one creature living." Again we see the primacy of
"doing good" in Franklin's thought. It might be fun to mock those
who believed in poltergeists, or even in the Bible's miracle stories,
but what *good* did it do? No one should ridicule "things serious
and sacred." Even though the "Letter of the Drum" had feigned
concern about Spinoza, Hobbes, and the freethinkers, the point
of the piece was actually to denigrate pastors and the scriptures,
Philoclerus insisted. This was unworthy of an honest man,
"even though he was of no religion at all." Whether or not a person

adhered to its doctrines, attacking institutional Christianity could do considerable harm.[22]

What kind of harm? Philoclerus said he would not bother to address the similarity of the Tedworth drummer to the Bible's witch of Endor. Arguments about revelation, he assumed, would not convince the skeptical editor Franklin. (Even after he repudiated radical deism, revelation per se carried no weight for Franklin.) Appealing instead to the social utility of faith, Philoclerus reminded Franklin that "wise governments have always thought religion necessary for the good of mankind; and, that wise governments have always thought religion necessary for the well-ordering and well-being of society." Thus, they have afforded clergy and the Bible great public respect.[23]

In a breathtaking passage, Franklin's letter-writer proposed that even "if there were no truth in religion, or the salvation of men's souls not worth regarding," ministers and biblical revelation still deserved special honor. They are the indispensable guides to virtue and morality, "without which no society could long subsist." People of good sense should do nothing to unnecessarily bring the clergy "into contempt." In defending this functionalist view of religion, Franklin made an implicit argument for agnosticism. In the voice of Philoclerus, Franklin projected a basic lack of certainty about eternal verities. We do not know whether religion is true, or whether the soul has an immortal destiny. But we should act as if these things are true, because collectively we cannot bear to live as if they are not true.[24]

In the end, Franklin's personae stepped back from the agnostic edge. Making an argument for the reality of unseen spiritual forces, Philoclerus contended (against Hume) that we should believe testimonies about supernatural episodes when the character of witnesses warrants it. Thus, we can trust accounts of the supernatural, like those fictionalized in the "Letter of the Drum," when they come from "men of probity, learning and sound good sense." The pastors in the "Letter of the Drum" concurred about the details of the story of the drums under the bed, and they had nothing to gain by fabricating it. In Franklin's winding conversation with himself regarding the phantom drummer, the reliability of the scriptures and the testimony of the apostles were at stake. Franklin was asking whether we can really believe accounts of supernatural phenomena if the witnesses are trustworthy. Franklin was not sure of the answer, but he liked raising the question.[25]

Poltergeists and other eerie phenomena suffused Franklin's world. Rumors of witchcraft did too, but that topic was a bit sensitive for a Massachusetts boy. The Salem witchcraft trials and executions had racked Massachusetts fourteen years before Franklin's birth. His aunt and uncle, Bathsheba and Joseph Pope, were among the accusers in Salem Village. After 1692, no colonial Americans would be executed for witchcraft again, although many people in Britain and America still believed in the existence of witches. In 1730, the same year as the "Letter of the Drum," a Richmond County, Virginia, court convicted a woman for practicing magical arts. The charges against her included "enchantment, charm, witchcraft or conjuration, to tell where treasure is, or where goods left may be found." Because these offenses fell under a "lesser" species of witchcraft according to English law, the convicted woman received a "reduced" sentence of thirty-nine lashes.[26]

Franklin also tackled the subject of witchcraft in 1730, with the newspaper account of "A Witch Trial at Mount Holly." Most historians have assumed that Franklin fabricated this trial, but he could have based it on a real witchcraft episode in rural New Jersey. Witchcraft accusations, if not convictions, remained common in the first half of the eighteenth century. It is hard to imagine why Franklin would have chosen that moment to invent the account, with no obvious provocation. A simpler explanation would be that the trial—or something like it—did happen. Another account of the Mount Holly trial exists, from the pen of an indentured servant named William Moraley. The two accounts differ in details, but they match up enough to demonstrate that they are describing the same event. That also suggests that the trial was real, although Franklin may have fabricated some elements for greater effect.[27]

In any event, Franklin found the folk practices for discovering witches contemptible. The setting of his story, Mount Holly, New Jersey, was about forty miles from Philadelphia, in the countryside, where doubts regarding folklore had hardly penetrated. As Franklin told it, three hundred people gathered in early October

1730 to watch officials test two defendants accused of witchcraft. The accusers insisted that the witches had made their "neighbors' sheep dance in an uncommon manner." They had also caused pigs to speak and sing psalms.[28]

In order to prove the accused (a man and a woman) were really witches, the Mount Holly accusers proposed two tests. The first was that if "weighed in scales against a Bible, the Bible would prove too heavy for them." The second was that if they were bound and thrown into a river, they would float. The accused agreed to the tests, but only if two of their accusers (also a man and a woman) were tried by the same means. Officials brought out a "great huge Bible" and placed a large set of scales atop a gallows built for the occasion. Then "a grave tall man carrying the Holy Writ before the supposed wizard" stepped forward. "The wizard was first put in the scale, and over him was read a chapter out of the Books of Moses, and then the Bible was put in the other scale, (which being kept down before) was immediately let go; but to the great surprise of the spectators, flesh and bones came down plump, and outweighed that great good Book by abundance." Then they weighed the accusers, and "their lumps of mortality severally were too heavy for Moses and all the Prophets and Apostles."[29]

Not satisfied by this seeming exoneration, the "mob" called for the trial by water. This also turned into a farce when both accused and accusers floated. An angry sailor then jumped on the back of the accused man, trying to drown him—disrupting the point of the test. The accusing woman, dismayed that she was floating, claimed that the witches had "bewitched her to make her so light." She proposed that she should be dunked as many times as needed to drive the Devil out of her body. The "more thinking part of the spectators" decided that anyone would float unless they choked and their lungs filled with water. Others said, in a bawdy conclusion to the account, that the women's shifts were keeping them afloat, and that they should resume the test on the next warm weather day, when the women could be tried "naked."[30]

Franklin's satirical targets in "A Witch Trial at Mount Holly" were, again, popular superstition and belief itself. Franklin knew that the Bible was littered with stories about talking animals and demon-possessed pigs. It occasionally discussed witchcraft, too. If it was absurd to believe in popular tales of superstition today, what about believing similar stories in the Bible? Franklin had something like this question in mind when he related how their "lumps of mortality" outweighed all the Law and the Prophets. He was not making up the fanciful-sounding Bible weight test either: accusers occasionally employed that trial against witches using huge church Bibles. Evidence of Bible weight tests for witches appeared in England and Ireland, if not in New Jersey.[31]

Franklin's skeptical and anticlerical views enraged Philadelphia's traditional believers. He crossed another line with a note he included when publishing a handbill advertising a ship preparing to sail for Barbados. It was a mundane topic but an important one for Franklin's thriving business. "Job printing" of items such as handbills was a core business for any colonial publisher. Thinking a humorous jab would make this particular advertisement "more generally read," either Franklin or the ship captain added a warning that "*No Sea Hens nor Black Gowns will be admitted on any Terms*" on the boat. Sea hens were cantankerous birds, but the term was also sometimes used for prostitutes. "Black gowns" meant ministers, especially Anglican clerics, but it was also the common Native American name for Jesuit missionaries. The term was not endearing. Paired with the reference to sea hens, the note was quite rude, and Franklin caught an earful from local pastors.[32]

The firestorm prompted Franklin to write his 1731 "Apology for Printers," one of the most important defenses of a free press in American history. The "Apology" was a justification of a printer's vocation, rather than an admission of fault. Profitable printing always entailed controversy, he wrote. Of all jobs, publishing came with the most risk of offending people, because the business had "chiefly to do with men's opinions." (Franklin did not distinguish between opinions and comments that were simply rude.) A typical merchant might trade with "Jews, Turks, Hereticks, and Infidels of all sorts," Franklin noted wistfully, "without giving offense to the most orthodox." No one could reasonably expect that they would always like everything printed.[33]

If the publishing business thrived on controversy, Franklin blamed the audience, not printers. If he and his brother publishers "sometimes print vicious or silly things not worth reading, it may not be because they approve such things themselves, but because the people are so viciously and corruptly educated that good things are not encouraged." Copies of popular chapbooks like *Robin Hood's Songs* flew off the shelves, he claimed, while his edition of Isaac Watts's hymns languished. (He spoke from experience regarding Watts, but no prerevolutionary American edition of *Robin Hood's Songs* has survived, if one ever existed.) Still, Franklin argued that printers did prevent the publication of many bad pieces, stifling "them in the birth." Franklin positioned himself as a moral gate-keeper who refused to print items promoting vice.[34]

Franklin contended that if he only catered to the "corrupt taste of the majority," he could make far more money. But he would not print pieces that he knew would injure people. He had been of-fered large sums of money to do so yet had maintained his princi-ples. Indeed, *he* was a long-suffering victim because of his journalistic integrity: it had made enemies out of many disaffected customers. "The constant fatigue of denying is almost unsupport-able," he moaned. But did the "publick" care about his fastidious management of the press and newspaper? No. They only saw occa-sional indiscretions that got through Franklin's moral filter, and censured him "with the utmost severity" for each slip-up.[35]

Following this overture, Franklin addressed the matter of the "sea hens" and "black gowns." Those words had precipitated more "clamor" against him than anything else he had ever printed, he claimed. Some said that Franklin knew just what he was doing by inserting the crass insult against ministers, and that it sprung from Franklin's "abundant malice against religion and the clergy." These critics had canceled their subscriptions to the *Pennsylvania Gazette*. Of more concern to the up-and-coming Franklin, they swore not to do any more business with him. "All this is very hard!" he exclaimed.[36]

Admitting that he should not have printed the advertisement, Franklin insisted that he did not intend to offend. He had business dealings and friendships with many clergymen in Pennsylvania, Delaware, and New Jersey. He would have to be "stupid" to go out of his way to insult them. Anticlericalism was a tempting and fruit-ful topic, he acknowledged, but he said that he had never indulged anticlerical vitriol. In the thousands of advertisements and handbills he had produced before, this was the first mention of "sea hens or black gowns." Given his record, he thought he could expect more grace from the pastors. You cannot please everyone, especially as a printer. Trying to do so could drive you to despair, but he vowed to keep publishing. "I shall not burn my press or melt my letters," he concluded.[37]

In spite of the controversy, his print enterprise was getting on "swimmingly." In addition to books, the newspaper, and numerous print jobs, Franklin became the official printer for Pennsylvania in 1730. Meanwhile, his old boss Samuel Keimer had to sell his printing business to pay off debts. Franklin, still in his mid-twenties, cultivated the image of a thrifty, respected businessman. Image meant a lot. "In order to secure my credit and character as a tradesman," he recalled, "I took care not only to be in *reality* industrious and frugal, but to avoid all *appearances* of the contrary. I dressed plainly; I was seen at no places of idle diversion; I never went out a-fishing or shooting; a book, indeed, sometimes debauched me from my work; but that was seldom, snug, and gave no scandal." If he had an enduring vice, it was reading. That was not so bad, as vices went. Moreover, "to show that I was not above my business, I sometimes brought home the paper I purchased at the stores, through the streets on a wheelbarrow." He displayed the best character traits of both gentlemen and commoners. Franklin was an independent man of means, yet not too proud to push a wheelbarrow.[38]

Franklin's cultivated image of independence, however, did depend on some ugly realities of unfreedom for others. In his business, Franklin often dealt with servants and slaves who were much less likely to achieve personal independence. He advertised these people in his newspaper, he purchased them and used their labor, and he may have sold them himself. For example, in 1731, the *Pennsylvania Gazette* advertised "A *Likely Negro Wench*, about fifteen years old, has had the smallpox, been in the country above a year, and talks English." Those interested in buying her could "enquire of the printer hereof." In 1738, he advertised an indentured servant, a "LIKELY young *woman*, well clothed, can sew and do household work." She could be purchased for eight pounds, the price of her passage to America. The buyer could negotiate the length of her service. The same ad listed a *"Breeding Negro Woman* about 20 years of age, can do any household work." Again, anyone interested could "enquire of the printer hereof." He published many ads for slaves and servants, as well as notices about runaways. Franklin seems to have had less than ideal relationships with some of his own slaves. In a 1750 letter to his mother, he vowed to sell a slave couple he owned, for he and Deborah did "not like Negro servants."[39]

The consummate entrepreneur, Franklin constantly probed for business opportunities. Most of them revolved around the print market. He returned often to religious texts as some of his bestsellers, whether he printed them himself or imported them for sale at his store. Seizing on the flood of German immigration into the Middle Colonies, he produced the first German-language hymn book printed in America. His customers were part of the Ephrata Community, west of Philadelphia. This monastic "Camp of the Solitaries," as they called themselves, sought to give up earthly attachments in order to achieve mystical union with Christ. Franklin began learning German in order to work with immigrants at Ephrata and elsewhere. In 1732, he started publishing the colonies' first German-language newspaper, the *Philadelphische Zeitung.* Not everything he touched turned to gold, of course. The German newspaper never caught on and soon folded.[40]

A 1744 retail catalogue of hundreds of books Franklin had for sale ("for ready money only") illustrated that while Franklin experimented in skeptical thought, his book business depended on traditional Protestant texts. Heading the sale list was a "Fine large Folio BIBLE, complete, Oxford 1727." Another Bible came with maps and notes, and he also sold various biblical Greek texts. Some titles were historic standards from the Calvinist tradition, including a French-language edition of Calvin's *Institutes.* Puritan author Daniel Rogers's *Lectures on Naaman the Syrian* appeared in the catalogue; it weighed in at almost nine hundred pages in some editions. Franklin also had recent titles by the English Calvinist Baptist John Gill. Some items were key texts in the new evangelical

movement, to which Franklin was one of the prime suppliers of
books. These included Henry Scougal's *The Life of God in the Soul
of Man* (1677), a book that evangelist George Whitefield credited
with convincing him of the need to be born again. Other Franklin
standards included the Book of Common Prayer and the works of
John Bunyan, Franklin's childhood favorite. The sale list contained
rationalist and skeptical sources such as Shaftesbury, Hobbes,
Locke, and *The Spectator*, too. But those Enlightenment texts were
few compared to the number of Bibles, devotional guides, Calvinist
treatises, and Greek and Roman classics Franklin retailed.[41]

For a voracious reader like Franklin, buying books imported
from London was expensive. The kinds that sold well in
Philadelphia, and the kinds that he wished to read, did not always
overlap. So he and his Junto friends opened a lending library. Since
they often discussed particular books, they figured that "it might be
convenient to us to have them all together. . . . It was liked and
agreed to, and we filled one end of the room with such books as we
could best spare." Unfortunately, this trial run at a library did not
work well. "The number [of books] was not so great as we expected; and though they had been of great use, yet some inconveniencies occurring for want of due care of them, the collection
after about a year was separated, and each took his books home
again."[42]

Franklin remained convinced, though, that mutual intellectual
improvement would necessitate a viable Philadelphia library.
Requiring a subscription fee was essential to its success. So he drew
up a proposal by which people could get an initial library membership for forty shillings, followed by an annual fee of ten shillings.
Fifty subscribers signed up in 1731. "This was the mother of all the
North American subscription libraries," Franklin wrote. Although
colleges like Harvard and Yale, as well as many pastors, had sub-
stantial private libraries, the Library Company was the first in
America to operate on a public subscription model. Franklin regarded it as a significant boost to his autodidactic education. It
"afforded me the means of improvement by constant study, for
which I set apart an hour or two each day; and thus repaired in
some degree the loss of the learned education my father once intended for me. Reading was the only amusement I allowed," since

he avoided "taverns, games, or frolics." The organizers soon sent off a book list, and forty-five pounds in cash, to London in order to obtain their first shipment of titles.[43]

By the time that Franklin printed the library's catalogue in 1741, it contained 375 books. In comparison to his retail catalogue of 1744, the Library Company's collection was weighted toward newer volumes on science, law, and history, and less toward theology and the classics. The balance reflected the subscribers' interests and Franklin's sense of what books were expensive and harder to get in Philadelphia. But there was plenty of religious-themed material in the library's holdings, some of it gifts from members. Robert Grace, the Junto's host and probably its youngest member, donated a copy of the Bible (with the Apocrypha, a standard inclusion in the King James Version) and of the great anti-Catholic compendium *Fox's Acts and Monuments of the Church*. The library also held copies of an English Bible commissioned during the time of Henry VIII, a Latin translation of the Bible, and Richard Blackmore's 1721 English version of the Psalms.[44]

Contemporary religious treatises also peppered the collection. Members could peruse John Locke's works, including his writings on religion. Franklin commented on Locke's *Essay Concerning Human Understanding* in the catalogue, saying that it was "esteemed the best book of logic in the world." The library possessed William Wollaston's *The Religion of Nature Delineated*, the book that had prompted Franklin's 1725 *Dissertation on Liberty and Necessity*. Boston pastor Cotton Mather was part of the collection with his *Christian Philosopher*. The "physico-theologians" were well represented, including *The Wisdom of God Manifested in the Works of the Creation* by John Ray, one of the books Franklin recommended for devotional reading in his personal prayer guide. There were texts on comparative religion, such as Henri de Boulainvillier's *The Life of Mahomet*, which cast Islam's prophet as a seventh-century anticlerical reformer reacting to corrupt Christian churches of the Arabian Peninsula. The library contained a few straightforward devotional texts, such as William Law's *A Serious Call to a Devout and Holy Life*, a standard among evangelical Christians. The collection reflected a cross-section of religious titles from the period, in accord with the members' "different sects, parties, and ways of thinking," which Franklin noted in his description of the Library Company.[45]

Business and civic affairs dominate Franklin's own accounts of his life, but matters related to his young family remained on his mind in these years. His exodus to Philadelphia meant that he was remote from the day-to-day lives of his Boston parents and siblings. A letter to his sister Sarah (Franklin) Davenport in 1730 lamented that he had heard from none of his family, save his parents, for two years. Franklin expressed relief that Sarah's family had weathered an outbreak of smallpox, the great scourge of colonial American society. Then, a year and a half later, Franklin found himself writing to his sister Jane, who had informed Franklin of Sarah's recent death. He lamented her loss not only as a sister but as a "good woman." He believed that Sarah was in heaven. Her family and friends ought "to be comforted that they have enjoyed her so long and that she has passed through the world happily ... and that she is now secure in rest, in the place provided for the virtuous." Jane would have expected to hear this kind of hope for the afterlife, and there is no reason to think that Ben was being insincere. What could it hurt to hope for future rewards, anyway? Jane might have quibbled with his concept of heaven as the home of the virtuous, though. In the Puritan tradition, the question was not how good you were but whether God had forgiven your sins through Christ.[46]

   The rituals of life and death pervaded Franklin's world. Even the affluent could do little to control their timing. In late 1732, Deborah gave birth to a son, Francis Folger Franklin. Franklin's son William seems never to have received the ritual of baptism as a child, likely because doing so would have made the question of his mother's identity more conspicuous. Franklin may not have been keen on baptism anyway. Deborah, however, was a practicing Anglican, a fact that muted some of Franklin's skepticism. She had baby Francis baptized at Christ Church, eleven months after his birth, though Ben was away in New England at the time. Presumably Deborah notified him that she was going to have Francis baptized in his absence. A decade later, the Franklins would similarly have their baby Sarah baptized at Christ Church a month after her birth. A humorous piece of evidence suggests that Deborah attended the church regularly in the intervening years. In 1737, someone took her prayer book from the family's rented pew. The book was good quality, "bound in red, gilt, and letter'd DF on each corner." Franklin scolded the thief in the newspaper: "The person who took it, is desired to open it and read the *Eighth* Commandment ["thou shalt not steal"], and afterwards return it into the same pew again; upon which no further notice will be taken." In 1741, he repeatedly noted in the *Gazette* that someone had borrowed, but not returned, books by popular devotional writer William Law. The owner (Deborah) now had the "leisure to read them" and wanted them back.[47]

Deborah undoubtedly took solace in her decision to have had "Franky" baptized, and thus (to Anglicans) put on the path of grace, for the boy passed away in November 1736. He died of

William Russell Birch, Second Street North from Market St. with Christ Church—Philadelphia, *Philadelphia, 1800 (detail). Engraving. Courtesy Library of Congress.*

smallpox, which Franklin emphasized that the boy had contracted "in the common way." Some whispered that Franky had died from a botched smallpox inoculation, but Franklin insisted that this was not the case. Although he had planned on inoculating the sickly child as soon as his health was up to it, Franklin never got the chance. Recalling his brother's battles with Cotton Mather over inoculation in the early 1720s, Franklin urged parents to give their children this preventative treatment. It carried less risk than going without, as Franklin bitterly learned. The Franklins commissioned a posthumous portrait of Franky, an unusual choice. Few people, especially in tradesmen's families, sat for paintings in early America, and it was rare to have an individual child painted, much less after the child's death. In the portrait Franky's face looks incongruously old; in fact, he looks a lot like Ben.[48]

Through the joy and suffering of family life, work was a constant for Franklin. As Max Weber observed, Franklin never abandoned the Puritans' commitment to industry. Father Josiah had constantly reminded him of Proverbs 22:29: "Seest thou a man diligent in his business? He shall stand before kings; he shall not stand before [lowly] men." So Ben labored feverishly, looking for new business opportunities. Just before the end of 1732, shortly after Franky's birth, the *Pennsylvania Gazette* announced the publication of "POOR RICHARD: AN ALMANACK." The almanac contained "the Lunations, Eclipses, Planets' Motions and Aspects, Weather, Sun and Moon's rising and setting, Highwater, &c. besides many pleasant and witty Verses, Jests and Sayings." Cotton Mather, in his own 1683 almanac, reckoned that these popular imprints came "into almost as many hands" as the Bible. In spite of their popularity at the time, much of the almanacs' content seems obscure today. Almanac makers mixed traditional Protestant beliefs, British politics, astrology, and eighteenth-century astronomy. Poor Richard delivered what readers expected to find in almanacs. But his fine-tuned sense of humor helped Poor Richard dominate the almanac market in the Middle Colonies.[49]

   Poor Richard illustrated, as much as any of Franklin's publications, the way that religious beliefs saturated the printer's world. As we have seen, faith gave order to Poor Richard's calendar, which

> ## Poor Richard, 1743.
>
> ### AN
> # Almanack
> For the Year of Chrift
> # 1 7 4 3,
>
> Being the Third after LEAP YEAR.
>
> | *And makes fince the Creation* | Years |
> | --- | --- |
> | By the Account of the Eaftern *Greeks* | 7251 |
> | By the Latin Church, when ☉ ent. ♈ | 6942 |
> | By the Computation of *W. W.* | 5752 |
> | By the *Roman* Chronology | 5692 |
> | By the *Jewifh* Rabbies | 5504 |
>
> *Wherein is contained,*
>
> The Lunations, Eclipfes, Judgment of the Weather, Spring Tides, Planets Motions & mutual Afpects, Sun and Moon's Rifing and Setting, Length of Days, Time of High Water, Fairs, Courts, and obfervable Days.
>
> Fitted to the Latitude of Forty Degrees, and a Meridian of Five Hours Weft from *London,* but may without fenfible Error, ferve all the adjacent Places, even from *Newfoundland* to *South-Carolina.*
>
> By *RICHARD SAUNDERS,* Philom.
>
> PHILADELPHIA:
> Printed and fold by *B. FRANKLIN,* at the New Printing-Office near the Market.

Benjamin Franklin, Poor Richard, 1743. An Almanack, *Philadelphia, 1743.*
Courtesy Library of Congress.

was the core of any almanac. The title page of Poor Richard throughout the late 1740s featured five different calculations regarding the number of years elapsed since the creation of the world, from 7,241 ("By the Account of the Eastern Greeks") to 5,494 years ("By the Jewish Rabbies"). While we might look for skeptical implications in this indeterminate range of dates since creation, we should remember that these numbers were not original to Franklin. As with much of the almanacs' contents, he borrowed the creation dates from other sources. Titan Leeds, Franklin's primary competitor, placed several of the same calculations on his title page for 1733. Fifty years earlier, Cotton Mather's almanac had given only one option for the years since creation

(5,632), a reckoning that Franklin categorized as the "Roman Chronology." To the conventional range of options, Franklin added the "computation" of English almanac maker William Winstanley (5,742 years since creation). It was not just sacred history dates he took from Winstanley and other almanac makers. He also derived the name "Poor Richard" from a combination of Winstanley's character "Poor Robin" and the actual English almanac maker Richard Saunder (spelled without a final "s," unlike in Franklin's pen name).⁵⁰

"Poor Richard" Saunders's introductory essay followed the title page of the first edition. Richard said that he could try to convince the public that all he intended the almanac to do was serve the public good. But really, he just needed the cash. "The plain truth of the matter is, I am excessive poor, and my wife, good woman, is, I tell her, excessive proud; she cannot bear, she says, to sit spinning . . . while I do nothing but gaze at the stars; and has threatened more than once to burn all my books and rattling-traps (as she calls my instruments) if I do not make some profitable use of them for the good of my family. . . . I have thus begun to comply with my dame's desire." The real Franklin was not "excessive poor," but perhaps this story reflected some tension in Ben's and Deborah's relationship.⁵¹

Blaming your wife for virtually anything was a standard comic move. What came next was the real explosion, one that Franklin needed to properly launch the first issue. He explained that he had been reluctant to cut into Titan Leeds's almanac business, but that obstacle was soon to be removed. Why? Because Leeds's time was up. "That ingenious man must soon be taken from us. He dies, by my calculation made at his request, on Oct. 17. 1733. 3 hr. 29 m. *P.M.*" Poor Richard claimed to base the prognostication on an upcoming conjunction of Mercury and the sun. Franklin had gotten the idea for using mock-astrology to predict someone's death from a 1708 satire by Jonathan Swift, the Anglo-Irish minister and author of *Gulliver's Travels*. Leeds angrily replied to Franklin in his 1734 almanac: I am still alive! he thundered. Poor Richard had "usurped the knowledge of the Almighty . . . and manifested himself a fool and a liar." Leeds signed his retort at four minutes past his supposed appointment with death.⁵²

Leeds's response was fatal (pun intended), because it took Poor Richard seriously. This was just what Franklin wanted. He had already drafted a response to Leeds, which he dashed into print. It was one of the great satirical performances of Franklin's career. Poor Richard opened with an innocent-sounding update on his progress since publishing the first almanac, ignoring the feud with Leeds. Because his audience had bought many copies of the almanac, Poor Richard wrote, his grumbling wife had been able to purchase some new clothes and "a pot of her own." This had pacified her. "I have slept more, and more quietly within this last year, than in the foregoing years put together."[53]

After this throat-clearing, Franklin sprung his trap. Reviewing the prognostications about Leeds's death, Poor Richard noted that "at which of these times he died, or whether he be really yet dead, I cannot at this present writing positively assure my readers." He wished he could have attended Leeds's passing, but family business had detained him. Thus Poor Richard could not "be with him in his last moments, to receive his last embrace, to close his eyes, and do the duty of a friend in performing the last offices to the departed." Expanding on previous musings about Providence, Franklin noted that the movement of the heavenly bodies only predicted the natural course of events. Astrology could not anticipate special interventions of God's hand, such as an episode in which God preserved the life of someone whom the stars had marked for death. The best evidence that Leeds was dead, Poor Richard concluded, came from "Leeds's" supposed 1734 almanac, "in which I am treated in a very gross and unhandsome manner; in which I am called *a false predicter, an ignorant, a conceited scribbler, a fool, and a liar.*" This could not have been the voice of Titan Leeds! "Mr. Leeds was too well bred to use any man so indecently and so scurrilously, and moreover his esteem and affection for me was extraordinary: So that it is to be feared that pamphlet may be only a contrivance of somebody or other, who hopes perhaps to sell two or three year's almanacs still, by the sole force and virtue of Mr. Leeds's name." An impostor was using Leeds's almanac to carry on a feud with Poor Richard.[54]

Franklin kept having fun—and selling almanacs—at Leeds's expense, even after Leeds actually died in 1738. In the 1740 edition,

Poor Richard reasserted that Leeds had indeed died in 1733. The Bradford family, Leeds's printers, kept publishing the almanac and pretending that he had not died until they could no longer hide the truth. "These are poor shifts and thin disguises," Poor Richard admonished, "of which indeed I should have taken little or no notice, if you had not at the same time accused me as a false predictor; an aspersion that the more affects me, as my whole livelihood depends on a contrary character." To prove his case, Poor Richard said that the ghost of Leeds had visited him and left him a letter explaining everything. The letter confirmed that he "did actually die at that time, precisely at the hour you mentioned, with a variation only of 5 min. 53 sec. which must be allowed to be no great matter in such cases."[55]

Franklin could not resist a dash of mock ghost-lore in this parody. How could Leeds's ghost leave him a handwritten note? "You must know that no separate spirits are under any confinement till after the final settlement of all accounts," the ghost informed him. "In the mean time we wander where we please, visit our old friends, observe their actions, enter sometimes into their imaginations, and give them hints waking or sleeping that may be of advantage to them." Coming upon Poor Richard as he drowsed, the ghost said that he "entered [Richard's] left nostril, ascended into your brain, found out where the ends of those nerves were fastened that move your right hand and fingers, by the help of which I am now writing unknown to you; but when you open your eyes, you will see that the hand written is mine, though wrote with yours." Striking the same theme as the "Letter of the Drum," Poor Richard confessed that "the people of this infidel age, perhaps, will hardly believe this story." Few besides Franklin could so deftly weave together skepticism and satire, all while producing a bestselling series of almanacs. Poor Richard became an outsized Franklin persona well before Franklin's transatlantic celebrity began to ascend. Soon Franklin would meet a real-life persona, George Whitefield, whose fame and friendship took Franklin's business to a new level.[56]

CHAPTER FIVE

Ben Franklin's Closest Evangelical Friend

I N THE LATE 1730s, the *Pennsylvania Gazette* began covering the phenomenal field meetings of the young English preacher George Whitefield, who was becoming the most-discussed person in Britain and America. Importantly for Franklin, Whitefield would also become the most widely *read* author in Anglo-America, and the most controversial personality in the news. Picking up information from London newspapers, Franklin recognized the value of Whitefield's rising star. He reprinted accounts of the itinerant's preaching as soon as he could—typically two months after the London papers ran them.

The crowds Whitefield was drawing were mind-boggling. One report from London noted that "in the evening [Whitefield] preached at Kennington Common to about 20,000 people, among whom were nearly forty coaches, besides chaises, and about one hundred on horseback; and though there was so great a multitude, an awful silence was kept during the whole time of singing, prayers and sermon." Further accounts—which Franklin found dubious—had the evangelist preaching before as many as eighty thousand.[1]

All these people, in an age with no electric amplification? Franklin suspected the man must be a charlatan. When Whitefield came to Philadelphia, Franklin figured he would investigate. To his surprise, Franklin came away impressed. Yes, Whitefield preached the gospel of salvation through Christ, which held little interest for Franklin. But Whitefield thought creatively about doing good. The great benevolent project of Whitefield's career was an orphanage outside of Savannah, Georgia. Franklin, always fascinated with applied Christianity, was intrigued. He also saw in Whitefield the biggest printing opportunity he had encountered since Poor Richard.

Something about Whitefield's preaching helped Franklin stay tethered to the faith of his youth, even if he resisted embracing all of Whitefield's doctrines. As Franklin recalled in his autobiography, Whitefield's incredible oratory had "a wonderful power over the hearts and purses of his hearers, of which I myself was an instance." He went to one of Whitefield's Philadelphia sermons, curious to see the minister in action but knowing that he would ask for donations for the orphanage. "I silently resolved he should get nothing from me," Franklin wrote. Few could withstand Whitefield's appeals, though. "I had in my pocket a handful of copper money, three or four silver dollars, and five pistoles in gold," Franklin said. "As he proceeded I began to soften, and concluded to give the coppers. Another stroke of his oratory made me ashamed of that, and determined me to give the silver; and he finished so admirably, that I emptied my pocket wholly into the collector's dish, gold and all."[2]

Franklin called his relationship with the great preacher a "mere civil friendship." But it represented more than that, in spite of their enduring differences over faith. It began as a business connection, with Whitefield employing Franklin for his expertise in the new media of the time. Franklin would make a great deal of money from publishing tracts by, about, and against Whitefield. During the height of the Great Awakening, in the early 1740s, more than half of the books that Franklin published were related to Whitefield. Franklin's newspaper would also increase its coverage of religion by 14 percent between 1735 and 1740. Franklin hitched his wagon to Whitefield's star, since Whitefield was far more famous. Franklin would become a celebrity too, and the printer and evangelist empathized with one another amid their common experience of fame. Together they were instrumental in founding the

University of Pennsylvania, although Whitefield worried that Franklin's plan for the college was not Christian enough. Whitefield also kept quietly pressing Franklin to accept Jesus as his Savior. Still, Franklin kept Whitefield and Jesus at bay. "He used indeed sometimes to pray for my conversion," Franklin recalled, "but never had the satisfaction of believing that his prayers were heard."[3]

Like all newspaper publishers, Franklin needed to generate material to put into the *Pennsylvania Gazette.* Any controversial topic would do, and religion normally worked well. He produced several key religious essays in the years following his marriage to Deborah Read. How much we know about the background to these essays varies. Sometimes the precipitating circumstances are obvious (a recent church fracas or something Franklin read). Sometimes we know so little that we are not even sure that he wrote the piece in question. The latter is the case for the satirical "Meditation on a Quart Mugg," which he published in the *Gazette* in July 1733. Franklin scholar J. A. Leo Lemay, unlike the editors of Franklin's papers, designated the piece as one of Franklin's.[4]

Franklin's "Meditation" was based on Jonathan Swift's "Meditation upon a Broomstick." Both mocked the contemplative writing of Robert Boyle, an early physico-theologian in whose hands virtually any occurrence could occasion lyrical musings. Among Boyle's eclectic topics were a milkmaid singing to her cow and Boyle's dog fetching his glove. Swift thought such poetic flights were silly. So did Franklin, even though he had recommended prayerful reflection on other physico-theologians' writings. Franklin was so action-oriented that he worried that the popular literature of "sensibility" could amount to all feeling and no benevolence. Franklin and many traditional Christians worried that the priority of feeling sympathy for the sufferings of others could transform into faux moralism.[5]

The "Meditation on a Quart Mugg" lamented the "wretched, miserable, and unhappy" fate of the humble mug, the sort used at taverns. "Because of thee are tears made frequently to burst from my eyes," the author declared lugubriously. In his hands, the mug turned into a Christ-like figure who did not protest his maltreatment by sinners: "How often is he forced into the company of boisterous sots, who lay all their nonsense, noise, profane swearing, cursing, and quarreling, on the harmless mug, which speaks not a word!" There was no way for this "unpitied slave" to seek redress for his grievances, leaving it as the constant victim of "arbitrary power." Mock it as he might, this kind of moral sentimentalism—and emotional appeals on behalf of victims—became foundational to reform movements such as the campaign against the slave trade and to the Patriot appeals for liberty in the Revolution.[6]

Morose musings on the futility of life also came into Franklin's crosshairs in his anonymous "Parody and Reply to a Religious Meditation." In this instance, Franklin reprinted a poem from English pastor Joshua Smith in order to parody it. Newspapers in London and Boston had already printed the poem before the *Gazette* did, so it was receiving transatlantic attention, making it an even more appealing target for Franklin's humor. Smith had reflected, Job-like, "UNHAPPY we, children of the dust! why were we born to see the sun? / Why did our mothers bring us forth to misery; and unkindly rejoice to hear us cry?" The pleasures and vain pursuits of this life, Smith concluded, were bound to terminate with our deaths. Only our good works and God's favor would go to the grave with us.[7]

With typical indirection, Franklin responded to Smith's "melancholy" meditation by writing letters to the editor. As with the "Letter of the Drum," he was writing letters to himself and publishing them. This mode makes it difficult to follow Franklin's point, but it enabled him to mock Smith, and those who liked Smith's kind of poetry, without directly offending subscribers. Smith's poem would appeal to the "gloomy and splenetick part of your readers," the letter said, but "as for me, I do not love to see the dark side of things." Here Franklin showed more ambivalence about the Calvinist view of the world. He asserted that the "world is a very good world," not the vale of tears that Smith made it out to be. Franklin denied Job's view that man's days are "few and full of trouble." You cannot logically complain about your days being both few and troubled, he wrote. If your "days are full of trouble, the fewer of 'em the better." (Three decades later, his view of the world's goodness had sobered a bit. Consoling Jane Mecom on the death of a child, Ben wrote that her departed daughter was "doubt-less happy: which none of us are while in this life.")[8]

Franklin contended that Joshua Smith was like a child "who laments that he cannot eat his cake and have his cake." (This proverb was not made up by Franklin; it dates to the sixteenth century in English.) Franklin ran with the cake analogy, interspersing the pastor's lines of poetry with new ones of his own. Where Smith had written "All the few days we live are full of vanity; and our choicest pleasures sprinkled with bitterness," Franklin countered that "All the few cakes we have are puffed up with yeast; and the nicest gingerbread is spotted with flyshits!" Smith was being whiny, Franklin suggested, so "away with all such insignificant meditations." He recommended Solomon's advice from Ecclesiastes 9:7: "Eat thy bread with joy, and drink thy wine with a merry heart." God had not made us oysters, hogs, or horses—we have the power of reason and choice. God had also not made us angels. Somehow the troubles we encountered fit into God's providential plans. Enjoy what God gives us, instead of lamenting what he has not, Franklin advised.[9]

After the parody, Franklin composed a reply to Smith concerning the pleasures of life. Those pleasures were this-worldly. By using our God-given reason and pursuing virtue, we could "spend our days in gaining and enjoying the blessings of life, which are innumerable." Difficulties were but as "sour sauce to the sweet meats we enjoy" and made our blessings that much more satisfying. Hope for eternity was the natural end of a virtuous life. "If we have done all the good we could, we have done all that we ought, and death is no terror to a good man." As usual, hope for our future state depended on our righteous living on earth. Righteous living was also the most pleasant and satisfying way to live. Borrowing a phrase from Shakespeare, Franklin envisioned the end of life as the "sweet sleep of death," which would be like settling into bed after a long journey. Franklin did not explain whether this eternal "sleep" would be conscious, but it would certainly be restful for those whose bodies had worn out in doing good.[10]

Franklin had doubts about the eternal fate of souls. Eminent philosophers such as John Locke argued that because of God's righteousness, God must address the world's ills in an afterlife.

Franklin himself mused on the subject in the grimly serious 1734 *Pennsylvania Gazette* essay "The Death of Infants." Few marriages in early America were spared from the pain of losing children in infancy. Jane Mecom had seen her first child, Josiah, die in 1730, and eleven of her twelve children died before she did. Ben and Deborah would soon lose Franky, who was sickly even as Franklin wrote his reflection on infant mortality. He cited seventeenth-century English economist William Petty's *Political Arithmetick* to the effect that half of all children die before they are sixteen.[11]

In light of these horrible realities, Franklin asserted that the afterlife was essential. Why would God create these children only to have them endure brief lives of suffering, then go to a permanent grave? He followed others such as Locke in admitting that the unresolved crimes and unrelenting suffering in this world made his heart long for a future reckoning. There the "just and the unjust will be equally punished or rewarded by an impartial judge." Dying babies made a compelling case for the afterlife, too. Human bodies, even in infancy, were a marvel of intricate construction. Why would God give so much care in "framing an exquisite piece of clock-work" only to "dash it to pieces" at birth? If there was no future existence for these dead children, then "every wise man [would] naturally infer, that [God's] intense application had disturbed his brain and impaired his reason." The possibility that the grave was the end for dead infants was unnerving. Maybe God really had lost his mind?[12]

Still, Franklin made a common theistic case for belief in the afterlife, whatever nihilistic undertones the essay contained. The recent death of a child he had known prompted him to write the piece. His sympathy for the fate of the young one drove his conclusion about children's souls. Franklin employed humanitarian feeling as part of his reasoning. The beauty of that dead child was "now turning apace into corruption." He could not accept the idea that the child would simply be annihilated. "Reason should despise" the prospect of the destruction of body and soul as "shocking and absurd." Instead, we should believe that when they departed this life, children became "inhabitants of some more glorious region." But Franklin speculated, on an unorthodox theme, that the dead might populate worlds elsewhere in the galaxy. They might become "our better *Genii*, our Guardian Angels [and] watch round our bed and our couch." He admitted that this was just a theory, for those matters belonged to the "provinces of light and immortality, and lie far beyond our mortal ken."[13]

As the essays from the 1730s suggest, Franklin was becoming an important authority on religion in Philadelphia. His prominence as a printer permitted him to weigh in on church politics, too, so he became a key figure in a controversy over the orthodoxy of Philadelphia Presbyterian minister Samuel Hemphill. The city was the center of early American Presbyterianism, whose churches served new immigrants from Ulster, or Northern Ireland. More than 100,000 Scots-Irish immigrants came to the colonies in the first eight decades of the eighteenth century. (The Scots-Irish were the century's largest cohort of European immigrants.) Many of these immigrants settled in, or at least passed through, Philadelphia. Jedidiah Andrews, the minister whose preaching so displeased Franklin, had become Philadelphia's key Presbyterian pastor and organizer by the early 1700s. In 1717, Andrews helped to form the Synod of Philadelphia, which oversaw Philadelphia-area presbyteries. These in turn helped to govern the local churches. Andrews was an enormously busy pastor (and an "old man," wrote the twenty-nine-year-old Franklin).[14]

In the early 1730s, Andrews received an assistant minister, Samuel Hemphill, who presented credentials from a presbytery in Northern Ireland. Hemphill said that he adhered to the doctrines outlined in the Westminster Confession of Faith, the 1646 classic articulation of Reformed beliefs and a common creedal requirement among Presbyterians. When Hemphill began preaching, Andrews became convinced that the minister was a proponent of deistic moralism. Writing to Boston pastor Benjamin Colman, Andrews lamented that "free-thinkers, deists, [and] nothings, getting a scent of him, flocked to" Hemphill.[15]

Franklin was among those whom Andrews classed as "free-thinkers, deists, and nothings." He loved the preaching of Hemphill, who delivered his practical, extemporaneous sermons "with a good voice." Although George Whitefield's Calvinist doctrine differed from Hemphill's, an excellent pulpit performance could always hold

Franklin's attention. The printer became one of Hemphill's "constant hearers, his sermons pleasing me, as they had little of the dogmatical kind, but inculcated strongly the practice of virtue, or what in the religious style are called Good Works." This was just the kind of preacher Franklin had been waiting for. So when Andrews and the Philadelphia Synod brought Hemphill up on charges of heterodoxy in 1735, Franklin rushed to his defense.[16]

Franklin's advocacy for Hemphill produced his greatest outpouring of religious writings in any one year. Franklin's "Dialogue between Two Presbyterians" appeared in the *Pennsylvania Gazette* a week before Hemphill's trial. In it, a critic and a defender of "Mr. H" squared off. The critic complained that the "new-fangled preacher" taught only moral duties, a topic that was not "fit to be preached in a Christian congregation." Hemphill's defender wondered how the critic could object to morality since it was so central to the teaching of Christ and the apostles. Citing Matthew 7, the defender noted that Jesus had taught that only those who did "the will of my Father" would enter heaven. Advancing a position that would have horrified his Calvinist family, Franklin (in the voice of the defender) contended that the Bible recommended faith as "a means of producing morality, and morality of salvation." Virtuous heretics had a better claim on salvation than wicked Christians, he asserted. The idea of faith alone leading to salvation was "neither a Christian doctrine nor a reasonable one." Surely the synod did not intend to "persecute, silence and condemn a good preacher, for exhorting [people] to be honest and charitable to one another"? The critic retorted that Presbyterians had the right to remove pastors who did not support the Westminster Confession. Franklin countered that, for all the good they did, even the revered Reformers did not recognize all the corruption in Christian teachings. The Westminster divines were not infallible. For Franklin, right living took precedence over right belief. "Peace, unity, and virtue in any church are to be more regarded than orthodoxy," he admonished.[17]

Franklin did not help Hemphill by denying the doctrine of salvation by grace alone. Indeed, one of the main charges brought against Hemphill was that his teachings were "subversive of the Scripture doctrine of justification by faith." Andrews and others unfriendly to Hemphill controlled the trial, and it concluded with his suspension for teachings that were "unsound and dangerous, contrary to the sacred Scriptures and our excellent confession." The synod delayed a final determination on Hemphill's standing for several months, which opened the door for Franklin to attack the methods used against Hemphill. First he produced *Observations on the Proceedings against Mr. Hemphill,* which sold out in two weeks, necessitating a second edition. In it, Franklin sought to clear Hemphill of "false aspersions" and to expose the synod's unjust approach.[18]

Scholars attribute *Observations* to Franklin although the printer chose to maintain anonymity in most of his contributions to this debate. Not revealing his identity allowed him to vent his rage with impunity while protecting his social status in Philadelphia. The *Observations* and subsequent publications illustrated his ability to engage in high-level doctrinal disputes. In *Observations,* he tackled the complicated relationship between faith and works in Protestant theology. He commented on a series of extracts from Hemphill's sermons that had become part of the trial evidence. In one passage, Hemphill challenged the way that certain ministers used Christ's name like a "charm" in order to "work up the hearers to a warm pitch of enthusiasm." Franklin glossed this section by noting that Hemphill was teaching against antinomianism. The term "antinomian" harkened back to New England controversies a century earlier, when Anne Hutchinson and her devotees ran afoul of Puritan authorities. They accused Boston ministers of teaching morality at the expense of grace. (Anti-revivalist critics in the Great Awakening would charge Whitefield with antinomianism because he ostensibly emphasized emotional outbursts and dramatic experiences over obedience.) Antinomianism was the "most impious doctrine that ever was broached," Franklin wrote. It suggested that "Christ came into the world to patronize vice, and allow men to live as they please." This was a strong point for Franklin. No one in Presbyterian circles would have a good word to say about such a doctrine, and all would agree that free grace did not sanction licentious living. One wonders if Hemphill might have coached Franklin on what to write in the theological sections of his tracts. Whatever the case, the production was another example of

Franklin's remarkable capacity for becoming conversant in fields of knowledge from soteriology to the science of electricity.[19]

Franklin followed up the *Observations* with a furious anticlerical piece, *A Letter to a Friend in the Country*. Franklin certainly wrote the preface to this letter, though he and Hemphill may have collaborated on the body of it. *A Letter* posited an enduring clash between the power of priests and the freedom of the people. It called on the people to assert their "natural rights and liberties in opposition to [the ministers'] unrighteous claims." The problem was not that Christian beliefs were false, but that power-hungry ministers had hijacked the faith. Whenever "men blindly submitted themselves to the impositions of priests, whether Popish, Presbyterian or Episcopal, &c. ignorance and error, bigotry, enthusiasm and superstition, more or less, and in proportion to such submission, most certainly ensued." The Hemphill case represented a new instance of that old priestly threat. Unchecked clerical power fed enthusiasm and superstition, two of Franklin's great religious foes.[20]

Hemphill and Franklin also railed against creeds as tests of orthodoxy. Although the Quaker-founded government of Pennsylvania honored liberty of conscience, many Presbyterians wished to require adherence to the Westminster Confession for their pastors. Creedalism had not snuffed out differences of opinion, though; it just made those differences more fractious. *A Letter* pointed to the diversity of Pennsylvania as a model for religious liberty: "Even in this city we have half a dozen, for aught I know half a score, different sects; and were the hearts of men to be at once opened to our view, we should perhaps see a thousand diversities more." Why should church authorities squelch those differences? Why not let love be the rule for Christians, and permit honest disagreements "as we do in astronomy or any other part of natural philosophy?" Franklin and Hemphill asked.[21]

Drawing on pervasive anti-Catholic sentiments, Franklin and Hemphill reminded Pennsylvanians that Catholics were arch-imposers: "The greatest absurdities and falsehoods are supported by this goodly method of imposing creeds and confessions: Such as cringings, bowings, mortifications, penances, transubstantiations, praying to saints and angels, [and] indulgences. . . . If the church has a power of imposing at all, she has a power of imposing everything she looks upon to be truth." Generous Protestants should not need to force uniformity of doctrine.[22]

The Hemphill case took an unexpected turn in the summer of 1735, when it became apparent that Hemphill had borrowed unattributed passages from other authors to produce some of his sermons. The clerical commission charged him with plagiarizing from writers including the London Anglican minister Samuel Clarke. Admirers of Clarke considered him "the foremost metaphysician in England." Critics, by contrast, viewed Clarke as a proponent of Arianism, or the idea that Jesus was separate from and subordinate to God the Father. Although standards against plagiarism were looser in Franklin's era than today, Franklin still regarded the discovery as unfortunate. It "gave many of our party disgust, who accordingly abandoned his cause, and occasioned our more speedy discomfiture in the synod." But Franklin was not dismayed. Instead, he "rather approved [Hemphill] giving us good sermons composed by others, than bad ones of his own manufacture."[23]

Franklin extended this point in his final pro-Hemphill publication, *A Defense of the Rev. Mr. Hemphill's Observations.* Here Franklin took exception to *A Vindication of the Reverend Commission of the Synod,* believed to have been penned by evangelical pastor Jonathan Dickinson. Franklin mocked the hypocrisy of the learned pastors: "Are they beholden to no author, ancient or modern, for what they know, or what they preach? . . . If they preach from their own natural fund or by immediate inspiration, what need have they either of learning or books? Yet books they have, and must have, and by the help of them are their sermons composed." They were not so different from Hemphill, except that he had better taste. The traditionalists, Franklin charged, foisted the dullest conclusions of the dullest authors on their unfortunate audiences. It was as if the orthodox clergy "searched only for stupidity and nonsense" in their reading. At least Hemphill "gave us the best parts of the best writers of the age." Echoing (without citation) another analogy by Jonathan Swift, Franklin asserted that the differences between the imaginative Hemphill and backward pastors such as Andrews were like those between a bee and a fly. A bee "wanders from flower to flower, and for the use of others collects from the whole the most delightful honey; while the other (of a quite different taste) places her happiness entirely in filth, corruption, and ordure."[24]

Ratcheting up his onslaught, Franklin contended that instead of defending the gospel, the traditionalists were advocating doctrines that promoted "enthusiasm, demonism, and immorality." What was the "main design and ultimate end of the Christian revelation?" he asked. It was to "promote the practice of piety, goodness, virtue, and universal righteousness among mankind, or the practice of the moral duties both with respect to God and man, and by these means to make us happy here and hereafter. All the precepts, promises, threatenings, positive institutions, faith in Jesus Christ, and all the peculiarities and discoveries in this revelation tend to this end." Adding another dash of skepticism, Franklin concluded that "if God gives a revelation to mankind at all, it is this, and this only that can make it worthy of him."[25]

Moreover, "natural religion" complemented scripture by fostering the love of God and of neighbor. Hemphill had emphasized the congruence of natural and revealed religion, while the traditionalists emphasized the sharp disjunction between the two. Instead of focusing on the practice of righteousness, for example, they trumpeted the "imputed righteousness" of Christ for believers. This concept, in which God viewed the forgiven sinner through the perfect holiness of Jesus, was a staple of conservative Presbyterian and Puritan theology. Franklin raged against imputed righteousness as "abominably ridiculous and absurd," a notion subversive to natural religion and Christianity. The doctrine suggested that our moral behavior had nothing to do with faith. He further rejected the idea that because of original sin, the guilt of Adam has been imputed to all of his descendants. Each person should stand accountable for his or her own virtues and vices. The commission, for its part, responded to Franklin's "ignorant, impertinent harangue" by noting that saving faith "is necessarily accompanied with good works." God's regenerating power and the gift of faith were needed to produce true righteousness in any sinner, the traditionalists contended.[26]

Franklin's pamphlets placed him as the leading skeptical writer in the American colonies, his anonymity notwithstanding. He displayed deep familiarity with the technical details of anti-Calvinist polemics. This was a special interest he had cultivated in years of reading. Citing the English Baptist and skeptic James Foster, a follower of Samuel Clarke, Franklin argued that the "heathen" could share in salvation if they obeyed God as best they knew how, according to the light of nature. In a classic Protestant move (one he commonly employed), Franklin argued that the traditionalists' position was less biblical than his. How did they know that those with no exposure to Christianity could not be saved? Was Christ's death on the cross not powerful enough to extend to all people? Denying another Calvinist precept, Franklin insisted that Jesus died not just for the chosen elect but for everyone. Christ's mission, the Bible tells us, conveyed a "general benefit, a benefit which regards all men, and in fact, tells us that 'Christ died for all' [II Corinthians 5:14]." Would God damn people for eternity for not obeying a law, or believing a message that they had never heard? That doctrine was utterly irrational and cast God in a terrible light, Franklin argued. If we find that the "orthodox" give an irrational interpretation of scripture, then we should return to the text and find a rational reading of it. Reason and scripture could not possibly contradict one another.[27]

Although Franklin's writings contained much fodder for skepticism, Franklin maintained a rationalist approach to the scriptures. Rationality and the Bible would both lead to truth, Franklin assumed. In this belief, he joined legions of lay and clerical Bible interpreters from the colonial era to the American Civil War. Franklin's view of what doctrines were rational departed sharply from those of more traditional believers such as his parents and his sister Jane. Still, the reasonableness of faith was the keystone of Anglo-American theology long before and after Franklin's life.

Franklin painted Calvinism as irrational. If Calvinism was irrational, then it must not be biblical, he insisted. Although he did sometimes raise the question of whether God gave humankind a revelation at all, Franklin tended to assume that God had given the Bible to the world as a preeminent source of truth. In debates over theology, Franklin began with his contemporary sense of rationality and insisted that valid doctrines must match up with that standard. Traditionalists started with orthodox theology, as framed by the Westminster Confession of Faith and similar documents, and assumed that such doctrines *were* rational. Unlike more radical deists such as his revolutionary ally Tom Paine, Franklin did not devote much time to the question of whether the whole Bible was credible as true revelation.[28]

For Franklin, the Hemphill debate entailed far more than the pastor's career. Franklin was battling against the faith of his parents. The evidence of plagiarism had derailed hope of Hemphill saving his job anyway. The synod confirmed Hemphill's final dismissal in September 1735, and Hemphill left the colony. Franklin had directed his most venomous attacks against Philadelphia pastors who used Calvinism to maintain their power, and to exclude those like Hemphill who doubted the creed. Franklin's exasperation at the synod finally produced one of his classic aphorisms:

> *Asses are grave and dull Animals,*
> *Our Authors are grave and dull Animals; therefore*
> *Our Authors are grave, dull*, or if you will, *Rev. Asses.*[29]

How did the skeptical Franklin, who called the pastors "Rev. Asses," become close friends with George Whitefield, the greatest evangelist of the age? Part of the explanation is that Franklin never embraced his role as a public anti-Christian skeptic. He wished to portray—indeed, he wished to *construct*—himself as an advocate of ethics-centered, doctrinally minimal Christianity.[30] But events in the mid-1730s kept taking him off track. In the Hemphill case, he cemented a reputation as an antagonist of orthodoxy. Then a bizarre incident with the Freemasons implicated Franklin not just in irreligion but possibly in outright Satanism.

The controversy began when a naive apprentice named Daniel Rees approached his master, Evan Jones, and some of Jones's friends, whom he incorrectly believed could gain him admission to Philadelphia's Masonic lodge. Rees thought that joining the secret society was a step toward gentility and independence. Jones and his friends decided to have some fun at Rees's expense. They led him through a mock Masonic ritual in which they made him swear a diabolical oath and kiss the bare posterior of one of the bullies. The harassment continued another evening when Jones and his friends took Rees into a dark cellar and tried to convince him that they were demons. To do so, they ignited a pan of liquor and illuminated their faces with the flickering blue flames. The trick did not seem to frighten Rees, however. When he insisted that he was not afraid, Jones either spilled or threw the pan's burning contents on him. His clothes lit on fire and burned Rees. Three days later, he died.[31]

Trial records showed that when Jones and his friends told Franklin about the first humiliating rite, Franklin found it funny and laughed heartily. He asked for a copy of the Satanic oath and showed it around to friends. When this information came out during the investigation of Rees's death, however, Andrew Bradford's *American Weekly Mercury* accused Franklin of contributing to Rees's demise. It also reported that Franklin had added to Rees's humiliation by making Masonic signs to him and congratulating Rees on having joined the brotherhood.[32] Philadelphia's Freemasons took to the pages of Franklin's *Gazette* to defend themselves. The miscreants who tricked and killed Rees did not belong to the Philadelphia lodge, they insisted. No true Mason approved of what Jones had done. Given the secrecy of the Masons' proceedings, they could not afford to be tarred by association with Satanic rituals and murder.[33]

Franklin appeared as a witness in the trial of Jones and his accomplices. The alarmed Franklin thought that the newspaper attack on him was unfair, and he realized that the "aspersions" could injure his carefully cultivated reputation. A man who approved the bullying of a doomed apprentice was hardly a paragon of virtue. He admitted in court that Jones had told him about tricking Rees into thinking that they were initiating him. When Jones told him about the "ridiculous signs" they taught Rees, Franklin laughed ("perhaps heartily," he admitted). But as Jones's story proceeded to the mocking and the diabolical oath, Franklin insisted that he stopped laughing and grew "serious." He warned them that when Rees learned how they had deceived him, he would never forgive them. Franklin denied the charges that he had played along when Rees made the bogus Masonic signs to him or welcomed him as a new initiate. Meeting the printer at a tavern, Jones had tried to bring Franklin in on the joke, telling Rees that Franklin was a Freemason and that he should "make a sign to him." Franklin said he was embarrassed and stared out the tavern window instead. Franklin claimed that he tried to advise Rees privately of Jones's shenanigans—but he missed his chance. In the end, Franklin's reputation survived the killing of Rees mostly untarnished. The authorities convicted Jones of manslaughter, sentenced him to having his hand branded (a lesser version of Rees's excruciating ordeal), and released him.[34]

The coverage of the Rees incident humiliated Franklin, and it came hard on the heels of his efforts to defend Samuel Hemphill. Jones's trial also precipitated a remarkable exchange between Franklin and his aging parents (Josiah would pass away in 1745, Abiah in 1752), who still worried about their prosperous son's soul. Josiah and Abiah had read the Boston newspapers' accounts of the trial and were troubled to learn of Ben's involvement. They wrote to him, imploring him to avoid the heterodox Freemasons and to come back to the Calvinist faith of his youth. Franklin assured them that the Freemasons were "harmless," and that they promoted nothing "inconsistent with religion or good manners."[35]

As to their concern for his "erroneous opinions," Franklin pled guilty, after a fashion. He was confident that he was wrong about some of his convictions. Everyone believed in some false ideas, due to the "imperfection of human understanding." Although the Calvinist tradition was ambivalent about the reliability of human knowledge, Franklin indicted Calvinists for overconfidence. In a typical move, Franklin employed an aspect of Reformed thought (human frailty) to make an anti-Calvinist argument. We are so influenced by our cultural and intellectual surroundings, he warned, that no one should presume that they hold objective truth. At other times Franklin professed great confidence in unfettered reason, but to his parents he emphasized how corrupted reason could become under unreliable influences.[36]

Echoing themes from the Hemphill controversy, Franklin insisted that no pastor, church, or council—whether Protestant or Catholic—should pretend to infallibility. Neither should laypeople. "Opinions should be judged of by their influences and effects," he posited. He hoped that his parents would grant that his skepticism did not make him an immoral person. If it were possible to change one's opinions "to please others," he would do so for his beloved parents, he wrote. (Implicitly, he charged them with asking that he change his views merely to please them. In another draft of the letter, Franklin wrote that he believed it was wrong to be "angry with any one for differing in judgment from me.") Striking another Calvinist theme, Franklin contended that a person did not get to choose his or her own convictions. All he could do was weigh the evidence about God and believe what seems right. "If after all I continue in the same errors, I believe your usual charity will induce you rather to pity" than indignation, he told them.[37]

But parental charity was not forthcoming. "My mother grieves that one of her sons is an Arian, another an Arminian," he wrote to his parents. Presumably Abiah was thinking of Ben as the Arian, or a non-Trinitarian, with regard to the nature of Jesus. Franklin pressed on with his dismissal of doctrinal boundaries. He claimed to not even know what an Arian or Arminian was. "I make such distinctions very little my study," he wrote (a claim belied by his informed participation in the Hemphill debates). "At the last day," he told his parents, "we shall not be examined what we thought, but what we did," citing the Gospel of Matthew 25.[38] His parents might well have asked *how* Franklin knew that morality was more important than doctrine. How did he even know that Matthew 25 was reliable? If we have little basis for theological certainty, how can anyone know what God thinks about ethics? Or what God is like at all? In any case, he thanked them for their care and concern. But he made it clear that, intellectually and socially, he was now his own man.[39]

Franklin did not wish to be rude to his parents, but undue attachment to familial tradition was, to him, a common obstacle to truth. Sometimes Franklin used Poor Richard to comment on the tensions regarding the faith of one's forefathers. In the 1739 edition (prepared the same year as the exchange with his parents), Franklin printed an epigram found in a 1734 edition of London's *Gentleman's Magazine*, the first Anglo-American periodical to describe itself as a magazine. The lines explained how the gullibility of previous generations can lead to unbelief today:

What Legions of Fables and whimsical Tales
Pass current for Gospel where Priestcraft prevails!
Our Ancestors thus were most strangely deceiv'd,
What Stories and Nonsense for Truth they believ'd!

But we their wise Sons, who these Fables reject,
Ev'n Truth now-a-days, are too apt to suspect:
From believing too much, the right Faith we let fall;
So now we believe—'troth nothing at all.

Franklin added a proverb to bolster the point: "Let our fathers and grandfathers be valued for their goodness, ourselves for our own." We might honor them for their virtue, but we are not beholden to our parents and grandparents. Franklin then continued, "sin is not hurtful because it is forbidden but it is forbidden because it's hurtful. Nor is a duty beneficial because it is commanded, but it is commanded, because it's beneficial." The point of religion was to foster practical virtue. If one's religion did not do that, it was not true. It was no good defending one's beliefs by stubborn recourse to revelation, or by insisting "thus saith the Lord."[40]

Because of the Hemphill controversy and the Daniel Rees tragedy, Franklin endured many attacks about his heterodox views and allegedly immoral behavior. The thirty-three-year-old had sought to craft a public persona of virtue and industry, but these episodes threatened to undo his image. He was at risk of becoming known as a scandalous heretic. This would not do. The year 1739 marked a turning point, as Franklin began muting his skeptical opinions on religion. He started focusing on modeling the kind of ethical devotion he propounded, and sought to set aside his anticlerical, anti-institutional bombast. For example, in addition to his rented pew at Christ Church, Franklin listed himself as a subscriber who promised to help support expanded seating for the growing church.[41]

The key to Franklin's transition, however, was his encounter with George Whitefield. Whitefield went to Oxford in the 1730s and had become part of the "Holy Club" associated with John and Charles Wesley, founders of the Methodist movement. The Wesleys' recommendations of classic devotional books helped the anxious Whitefield break through to spiritual conversion in 1735. Whitefield had long displayed an aptitude for public speaking and stage acting, and he brought those gifts to the service of the evangelical gospel. Because churches could not hold the throngs that gathered to hear him, Whitefield went into the fields, drawing thousands more. The Wesleys recruited him to go as a missionary to Georgia in 1737, just as his fame began to flourish. He returned to England in late 1738, where his celebrity went stratospheric. Almost as soon as he landed back in England, Whitefield was thinking about returning to the colonies, this time for a preaching tour.

The gathering Whitefield storm began to resound in America in 1737, when the *Pennsylvania Gazette* and the *New-York Weekly Journal* printed a snippet regarding Whitefield's charitable investment in the new Georgia colony. "The sum of £80 was paid into the Bank of England, being the benefaction of a person unknown, by the hands of the Rev. Mr. George Whitefield; to be applied by the trustees for establishing the colony of Georgia in America, towards building a church at Frederica." The next year and early 1739 were quiet, as Whitefield traveled in Georgia. Then the

George Whitefield, *engraving by Elisha Gallaudet, New York, 1774 (detail).*
Courtesy Library of Congress.

media dam burst in mid-1739. In July, Franklin reprinted a London account of Whitefield preaching on consecutive days in May to audiences of ten and twenty thousand each.[42]

Franklin followed Whitefield's movements as the evangelist departed for his new American tour. The November 8 edition of the *Gazette* heralded Whitefield's arrival in Lewes Town, Delaware. Whitefield and his lead publicist, William Seward, immediately recognized Franklin as an important American media connection. In the same 1739 issue of the *Gazette* in which Franklin reported on Whitefield's arrival, Whitefield and Seward placed an advertisement of items for sale to finance the itinerant's journey and the construction of the Savannah orphanage. Aside from hardware goods, he was selling fabric from London: "Spun yarn, ruggs and blankets, duffills strip'd, brills for bed sacking … Scotch cloth, cotton romalls, seirsuckers, white dimities … buttons, buckrams, and sewing silk." From the start, Whitefield's ministry thrived on marketing. The business connections between Whitefield and Franklin ran in multiple directions, printing and selling Whitefield imprints, advertising Whitefield's goods for sale, covering Whitefield's events, and more.[43]

Franklin's competitor Andrew Bradford began printing Whitefield's sermons first, as the *American Weekly Mercury* advertised the publication of Whitefield's *The Marks of the New Birth* in November 1739. Whitefield and Seward seem to have approached Bradford and Franklin separately, within weeks of their arrival, giving them both materials to publish. Bradford got sermons. But Franklin also got copies of Whitefield's travel journals, probably Whitefield's most successful publications of all. Whitefield wrote that "one of the printers" in Philadelphia, undoubtedly Franklin, had told him that he had already taken more than two hundred subscriptions for the sermons and journals. In November 1739, Franklin announced the subscription program in the *Gazette*. The "Rev. Mr. Whitefield having given me copies of his journals and sermons, with leave to print the same; I propose to publish them with all expedition, if I find sufficient encouragement," Franklin wrote. "Those therefore who are inclined to encourage this work, are desired speedily to send in their names to me."[44]

Printers loved subscription programs because they guaranteed against overproduction of books. Taking subscriptions, and printing based on demand, was less risky than printing books first and then trying to sell them. But few authors generated the kind of demand that made subscription schemes worthwhile. A reader might have to wait months to get the book in question. Whitefield was unique, the perfect author for a subscription plan. Thousands of readers would prepay Franklin and his affiliated printers across the colonies in order to get early access to Whitefield materials. Indeed, Franklin struggled to keep up with the number of subscribers. By mid-1740, he announced that subscribers who had already paid, or who brought cash to his office, would get their copies first. People who bought on credit would have to wait.[45]

Whitefield was a publisher's dream come true. He and Seward helped sell subscriptions as much as any author's team could in the eighteenth century. Franklin's efforts complemented what Whitefield was already doing. Whitefield expertly promoted his ministry, and delivered products that catered to the tastes of a broad reading public. One of the biggest differences between Whitefield and other religious authors was that Whitefield wrote short manuscripts. His journals came out in brief, serial editions.

Franklin already knew that there was a steady appetite for theology among Anglo-American readers. But during the height of the Great Awakening, whatever Whitefield touched turned to gold, and a lot of that gold went into Franklin's pockets. Although most in Whitefield's audiences had basic familiarity with theology and the Bible, he avoided technical theological points in his revival preaching. As he said in one sermon, he came "not to shoot over your heads, but rather . . . to reach your hearts." In certain publications, Whitefield battled over high-level doctrinal concerns such as the difference between Calvinism and Arminianism. But even these polemical imprints sold well.[46]

Franklin realized that a decent percentage of the hundreds of thousands who attended Whitefield's meetings would buy his books. That guaranteed good results for Whitefield materials. No one had the kind of potential audience that Whitefield did, and Franklin did whatever he could to keep the momentum going. During the fourteen months of Whitefield's great campaign in the colonies, Franklin ran Whitefield-related content in forty-five of the sixty issues of the *Pennsylvania Gazette*. Many of these items were reports on Whitefield's meetings supplied by William Seward, accounts that Franklin and many other printers ran unattributed.[47]

Although their doctrinal differences were stark, Franklin found more to like in Whitefield's ministry than just money. Aside from his charitable work, Whitefield showed shocking disdain for clerical authority and for the denominational boundaries that divided Protestants. When the Anglican commissary of Boston chastised the itinerant for cooperating with non-Anglicans, Whitefield replied that he "saw regenerate souls among the Baptists, among the Presbyterians, among the Independents, and among the Church folks [Anglicans], all children of God, and yet all born again in a different way of worship, and who can tell which is most evangelical?" Franklin loved it. Nonetheless, the printer had to overcome doubts about the veracity of reported crowd sizes before he could promote Whitefield's work. The stories of crowds of up to eighty thousand people in London seemed outrageous (and indeed, William Seward did include some implausibly high crowd totals in his accounts).[48]

In classic Franklin manner, he decided to set up an experiment to test these numbers. When he went to hear the revivalist, two qualities struck Franklin about Whitefield and his assemblies. One was that Whitefield's "loud and clear voice" traversed great distances. The second was "the most exact silence" that the crowd maintained so that they could hear Whitefield. The revivalist "preached one evening from the top of the [Philadelphia] Court House steps," and the town's streets were "filled with his hearers to a considerable distance." This was Franklin's chance: "I had the curiosity to learn how far he could be heard, by retiring backwards down the street towards the river, and I found his voice distinct till I came near Front-Street, when some noise in that street, obscured it. Imagining then a semi-circle, of which my distance should be the radius, and that it were filled with auditors, to each of whom I allowed two square feet, I computed that he might well be heard by more than thirty-thousand."[49]

A recent study by acoustic scientists suggests that there were some problems in Franklin's calculations. He misunderstood the way that sound travels over space, and he probably gave people too little room in the crowd. Nevertheless, his experiment produced a decent estimate of Whitefield's effective acoustic range. The calculation convinced Franklin that the reports were real. It "reconciled me," he wrote, "to the newspaper accounts of his having preached to 25,000 people in the fields." Franklin was dazzled, as were most people who encountered Whitefield's preaching for the first time.[50]

Thus began one of the most profitable ventures of Franklin's publishing career, and a thirty-year friendship with the most recognized evangelical leader in the Anglo-American world. It was a step away from the fractious, skeptical mode that had threatened Franklin's reputation in the Hemphill affair. In spite of Whitefield's persistent pleading over the years, no evangelical conversion was on the horizon for Franklin. But since the day he counted up the crowd, Franklin defended Whitefield as "a perfectly honest man." Franklin wanted people to understand that his admiration for Whitefield endured *in spite* of their religious differences. "My testimony in his favor ought to have the more weight, as we had no religious connection," he assured readers of his *Autobiography*.[51]

CHAPTER SIX
Electrical Man

S TARTING IN THE LATE 1740S, Franklin's international celebrity soared because of his experiments in electricity. He set Europe and America to chattering about the possibility of harnessing lightning. Some even believed that electricity could heal people. Franklin soon had a steady stream of supplicants asking him to deliver shock cures. One of them, Joseph Huey, was convinced that Franklin's treatments had alleviated his partial paralysis. But Huey, an evangelical, cautioned Franklin: he should not expect to win salvation by his good deeds, medical or otherwise, Huey said. Franklin replied to the "impertinent" Huey and declared that we serve God best by serving others. Doing so paid debts of gratitude for the kindnesses others had shown him, as well as for the "numberless mercies from God, who is infinitely above being benefited by our services. These kindnesses from men I can therefore only return on their fellow-men; and I can only show my gratitude for those mercies from God, by a readiness to help his other children and my brethren."[1]

Charity was central to Franklin's concept of true religion. (The great historian Edmund Morgan said charity was "the guiding principle of Franklin's life.") Franklin told Huey that he did not, in fact, expect to "merit heaven" by his good works. There was nothing that he could do to earn that eternal happy state. He simply intended to submit to the "will and disposal of that God who made me," and trust that God would never consign his creatures to permanent misery. Huey countered by urging him to put his faith in Christ for salvation. Franklin conceded the value of belief, but only if it was "productive of good works," especially "works of kindness, charity, mercy, and publick spirit." Jesus himself preferred the doers of the Word to its mere hearers, Franklin reminded Huey.[2]

In Franklin's world, there were pervasive connections between faith and science. Joseph Priestley, an English Unitarian (non-Trinitarian) minister and scientist, had a profound influence on both Franklin and Thomas Jefferson. Priestley produced the most widely circulated account of Franklin's electrical experiment with the kite. Pastor Aaron Burr, Sr., inspired partly by Franklin's work, administered electric shock treatments to fellow evangelical Jonathan Belcher, the governor of New Jersey, seeking to alleviate symptoms of a "palsy." (The treatments led to no improvements.)[3]

The scientist and former Baptist minister Ebenezer Kinnersley also trumpeted the significance of Franklin's discoveries regarding lightning rods, which could protect buildings from lightning strikes. Kinnersley prayed that "this method of security from the destructive violence of one of the most [awful] powers of nature, [would] meet with such further success, as to induce every good and grateful heart to bless God for [the] important discovery. May the benefit thereof be diffused over the whole globe. May it extend to the latest posterity of mankind; and make the name of Franklin like that of Newton, *immortal.*"[4]

Unlike Kinnersley and Priestley, Franklin's French competitor, the minister and physicist Abbé Jean-Antoine Nollet, grumbled about the American's discoveries. Nollet "speaks as if he thought it presumption in man to propose guarding himself against the thunders of Heaven," Franklin wrote. Nollet quietly wished that his own electrical experiments were bringing him as much celebrity. For many followers, Franklin's experiments held spiritual significance. His discoveries proceeded in a community full of pastor-scientists.[5]

Before he became the electrical man, Franklin needed to secure his status as a gentleman. He pressed into his print business, the prosperity of which depended a lot on George Whitefield and the

B. Franklin of Philadelphia, *mezzotint by James McArdell, 1761 (detail).*
After a painting by Benjamin Wilson. Courtesy Library of Congress.

Great Awakening. In 1740, Franklin unleashed a flood of Whitefield-related publications, including at least six different segments of Whitefield's journals and autobiography. More than half of Franklin's publications from 1739 to 1741 were by or about Whitefield. And Franklin was hardly alone. The total number of publications in the colonies went up 85 percent from 1738 to 1741, with most of the growth resulting from works by or related to the minister. Franklin's ledger book filled with orders of individual titles, as well as subscriptions to the multivolume edition of Whitefield's journals and sermons. The *Gazette* covered the itinerant's travels, helping to boost sales. By 1742, Franklin was even selling "fine mezzotinto and grav'd pictures of Mr. Whitefield." Whitefield, as preacher, writer, and personality, sold unlike any product Franklin had ever known.[6]

"The alteration in the face of religion here is altogether surprising," Franklin reported in June 1740. "Never did the people show so great a willingness to attend sermons, nor the preachers greater zeal and diligence in performing the duties of their function. Religion is become the subject of most conversations. No books are in request but those of piety and devotion; and instead of idle songs and ballads, the people are everywhere entertaining themselves with psalms, hymns and spiritual songs [Ephesians 5:19]. All which, under God, is owing to the successful labors of the Reverend Mr. Whitefield." Business for religious books had never been better. This kind of newspaper report also helped to sell more products, by painting religion as fashion. *Everyone* was buying religious texts instead of more frivolous items, Franklin told his readers.[7]

In spite of their friendship, Franklin also helped to fan flames of controversy about the itinerant. He published Whitefield's notorious *Three Letters* (1740), which denounced Archbishop John Tillotson, the craze for whom Franklin had satirized in the Silence Dogood letters. Now Whitefield averred that Tillotson knew no more about true Christianity than did the Prophet Muhammad. *Three Letters* also indicted southern slave masters for their horrid treatment of slaves. Franklin seems to have published the Philadelphia edition of *The Querists* (1740), the first major anti-Whitefield attack printed in the colonies, and Whitefield's 1740 response to *The Querists*, too.[8]

The printer was personally intrigued by Whitefield. But first and foremost, Whitefield was business. Franklin and his customers juxtaposed items related to the itinerant with other kinds of products and advertisements, including ones related to slaves. Thomas Rogers, a Franklin client and shoemaker by trade, paid four shillings in 1740 for two Whitefield imprints and five shillings to place an ad selling a slave boy. The 1740 news story about the "alteration in the face of religion" appeared in the same issue as this announcement: "TO BE SOLD, a likely Negro Boy, about 10 years old, born in the town, has had the small pox and measles: Enquire of the printer hereof." Topics that may seem incongruous today reveal how much slavery was part of everyday life in Franklin's world. Slavery and the Great Awakening both brought the printer greater profits.[9]

For financial and personal reasons, Franklin was sympathetic to the religious "alteration" taking place in Philadelphia. Franklin did not

agree with Whitefield's Calvinist evangelical doctrine, but he figured that anyone who could bring about real moral change was
worth supporting. The printer even helped Whitefield and
William Seward in their attempt to shut down the city's dancing
school and concert hall, which had been started by Robert Bolton
in 1738. (Franklin had advertised its opening.) Seward procured
the keys to the school's dancing room and locked members out.
"May the Lord strengthen me to carry on this battle against one of
Satan's strongest holds in this city," Seward prayed. Some of the
gentlemen supporters of the school threatened to beat Seward with
a cane, and they broke open the door so meetings could continue.[10]

Seward, undaunted, supplied Franklin with a note for the
Gazette. After providing information about Whitefield's travels and
fundraising for the Georgia orphanage, Seward stated that "Since
Mr. Whitefield's preaching here, the dancing school assembly and
concert room have been shut up, as inconsistent with the doctrine
of the gospel." The passive voice made it unclear—*who* had shut up
the room? Had Bolton's dancing friends embraced Jesus as Savior
and become convinced of the sinfulness of dancing? That was not
the case, but Franklin ran Seward's account anyway.[11]

The dancing-school controversy precipitated a confrontation
between the dancers and Seward at Franklin's print shop on May 2,
1740. Bolton's associates "accosted me very roughly," Seward
wrote. They said he had lied about the closing of the school. The
lawyer and Anglican minister Richard Peters, who also served in
the Pennsylvania government, was one of Seward's accosters.
Peters was a couple of years older than Franklin, and had emi-
grated from England to Philadelphia in 1734. Peters would later
cooperate with Franklin on ventures such as the Philadelphia
Academy, the Library Company, and the American Philosophical
Society. But on Whitefield and the dancing school, Peters and
Franklin were enemies. Peters had already voiced his opposition to
Whitefield before Christ Church's congregation. At the shop,
Franklin watched as Seward challenged Peters to demonstrate that
Jesus or his disciples would have approved of dancing. Peters could
not do so, at least not to Seward's satisfaction. Seward insisted that
these pastimes were "odious in the sight of God, and did as effectu-
ally promote the Kingdom of Satan, as any of the heathen idola-

tries." Peters and the dancers thought Seward was wrong and was missing the point. They insisted that Seward, abetted by Franklin, had deceived people by claiming that the "gentlemen were convicted of their error by Mr. Whitefield's preaching."[12]

Bolton's friends pressured Franklin to allow them to respond in print to Seward. Whitefield's and Seward's enemies in turn claimed that "Mr. Whitefield had engaged all the printers"—most notably Franklin—not to criticize him. Only later would Franklin publish *The Querists'* attacks on Whitefield. Now Franklin needed to establish some journalistic distance from the evangelist. So he accepted a letter from the pro-dancing faction, headed by an editorial note explaining his reasons for printing it. Franklin registered concern that the gentlemen intended not just to defend their character but to denigrate Whitefield and Seward. They again cited Seward's dishonesty in the affair, and informed Whitefield that the "better sort of people" in the colony held "both him and his mischievous tenets in the utmost contempt." They also took a swipe at Franklin for printing the crowd numbers at Whitefield's meetings. Those numbers were double or triple the actual attendance, they claimed.[13]

Franklin had allowed Whitefield's and Seward's antagonists to have their say. Now Franklin would have his. Adopting the Puritan-sounding moniker "Obadiah Plainman," Franklin railed against Peters's "better sort of people" comment in the *Gazette's* next issue. Perhaps the choice of "Obadiah" held some biblical significance to Franklin. In that one-chapter book, the prophet warns the enemies of Israel that "though thou exalt thyself as the eagle, and though thou set thy nest among the stars, thence will I bring thee down, saith the Lord." Franklin was not convinced that the Seward account had damaged the dancers' reputations. "I cannot conceive," he wrote, "how any person's reputation can be prejudiced, though it should be reported, that he has left off making of legs, or cutting of capers." Franklin was fond of cheerful socializing, but this dancing club irritated him, not least because of their snooty attitude toward Whitefield's followers.[14]

Franklin pounced on that elitism, and the club's disdain for the "mob, or the rabble." The writers Franklin admired—the heroes of classical antiquity and the opposition writers of recent British history—never looked down on the people, he told readers. "Your

Demosthenes and *Ciceroes, your Sidneys* and *Trenchards* never approached us but with reverence. . . . They never took upon them to make a difference of persons, but as they were distinguished by their virtues or their vices." Judge people by the quality of their characters, not their social station, Franklin wrote. Here was another reason for Franklin's devotion to Whitefield. Franklin saw the minister as a champion of common people. Although he was well on his way to becoming an independent gentleman, he styled himself as a defender of regular folks too.[15]

The next issue of the *Pennsylvania Gazette* announced the publication of multiple Whitefield imprints, as well as Franklin's edition of pastor Gilbert Tennent's fiery sermon *The Danger of an Unconverted Ministry* (1740). Tennent called on supporters of the revivals to abandon ministers who showed signs of being unconverted. In this issue Franklin also promised delivery of the inaugural volumes of Whitefield's works to subscribers. He reported on the minister's travels through Pennsylvania, noting that at some stops "people were under such deep convictions, that by their cries they almost drowned his voice." By his defense of Seward and by these publications, Franklin became among the most active revival proponents in America.[16]

Still, Franklin allowed the dancing faction to print a rebuttal to "Obadiah Plainman" in the same edition of the *Gazette*. Controversy and sales went together. The author of the anonymous piece (likely Richard Peters) contended that Franklin fancied himself as the "prince and leader of a set of people," meaning the lowly folks who supported Whitefield. But this was hypocrisy: Franklin was no believer! The printer was "only a temporizing convert, drawn in with regard to your worldly gain, [who has] never understood Mr. Whitefield's spiritual doctrine of saving faith."[17]

Just how hypocritical was Franklin's support of Whitefield? Their subsequent friendship, which endured long after Whitefield's height of notoriety, suggests that Franklin sincerely appreciated the evangelist. But a correspondent in the *American Weekly Mercury*, replying to Obadiah Plainman as "Tom Trueman" (again likely Richard Peters), made the most pointed charges yet about Franklin's hypocrisy. Trueman implied that Franklin hid his skepticism now because he was making so much money off of Whitefield.

Everyone knew that Franklin had published skeptical views about Christianity in the past. Trueman even suggested that Franklin privately "sneered" at Whitefield and his gospel message, in settings where the printer "thought it would not hurt his interest." There was nothing more contemptible, Trueman concluded, than a "false fellow who carries two faces."[18]

If Franklin spoke ill of Whitefield in private, then the printer was indeed guilty of deep hypocrisy. One could imagine Franklin's sheer desire for profit overcoming his initial contempt for Whitefield. But however much Franklin disdained Whitefield at first, he warmed to the itinerant as time passed. Franklin responded as Plainman to Tom Trueman in the next issue of the *Gazette*, but the debate now centered around semantics in the various newspaper pieces more than the substance of the revivals. As for the charges of hypocrisy by Peters, Franklin declined to make "any return for those stagnant UNMERITED civilities, which I have received from your polite hand."[19]

Whatever Franklin's real personal view of Whitefield, Franklin always regarded the preacher's Calvinism as unacceptable. Franklin poked fun at the minister decades later when he commented on that "extraordinary influence of his oratory on his hearers, and how much they admired and respected him, notwithstanding his common abuse of them, by assuring them they were naturally *half Beasts and half Devils*." Franklin was not making up this line about "beasts and devils": it was a staple of Whitefield's preaching. Franklin found it befuddling that Whitefield remained so popular in spite of his Calvinism. Indeed, Whitefield's frankness made him many enemies, who banned him from a number of churches, including some Anglican parishes. These prohibitions, paired with the swelling throngs attending his sermons, sent Whitefield and his supporters looking for unconventional venues, including fields and town commons.[20]

In Philadelphia, Whitefield's supporters decided to erect an interdenominational preaching facility called the "New Building." It would serve as Whitefield's base when he visited the city. As Franklin recalled, "It being found inconvenient to assemble in the open air, subject to its inclemencies, the building of a house to meet in was no sooner proposed and persons appointed to receive contributions, but sufficient sums were soon received to procure the ground and erect the building which was 100 feet long and 70 broad." The so-called New Building was "expressly for the use of any preacher of any religious persuasion who might desire to say something to the people of Philadelphia, the design in building not being to accommodate any particular sect, but the inhabitants in general." Franklin embraced a fanciful view of the building's broad religious purposes. He claimed that "even if the Mufti of Constantinople were to send a missionary to preach Mahometanism to us, he would find a pulpit at his service." Whitefield disagreed—he was a pioneer of evangelical ecumenism, but that ecumenism had distinct limits. It did not include Muslims.[21]

To the New Building's supporters, the plan was to permit "such Protestant ministers to preach the gospel in the said house as they should judge to be sound in their principles, zealous and faithful in the discharge of their duty, and acquainted with the religion of the heart and experimental piety, without any regard to those distinctions or different sentiments in lesser matters which have to the scandal of religion unhappily divided real Christians." Franklin could affirm that last note against pointless divisions among Christians. Because of Whitefield's incessant travels, the New Building stood underused much of the time. Franklin found a more permanent function for it eventually, in creating the Academy of Philadelphia, which later became the University of Pennsylvania.[22]

Philadelphia's churches and pastors were split over Whitefield. At the city's Baptist church, Whitefield divided the pastoral staff, with long-term implications for Franklin's fame as a scientist. Baptist senior pastor Jenkin Jones welcomed Whitefield and radical itinerants such as the Presbyterian John Rowland to speak in his church. Rowland preached there in July 1740, with a forceful explication of the horrors of hell. A number of terrified people in attendance fainted, and some had to be carried out. Even Rowland's radical colleague Gilbert Tennent thought that Rowland was giving undue weight to the "terrors of the divine law," so Tennent interrupted the sermon and asked Rowland, "Is there no balm in Gilead?" Rowland changed tone mid-sermon and reminded the people that Jesus had the power to save.[23]

Rowland's performance was also too much for the Baptist church's assistant pastor, Ebenezer Kinnersley. The next Sunday, in Jones's absence, Kinnersley denounced Rowland and Whitefield's evangelical movement. He deplored Rowland's "enthusiastic ravings" and suggested that the revivals' chief supporters were common, ignorant people. Indeed, a group of these folks stormed out of Kinnersley's sermon against Rowland, headed by an outspoken woman and a "multitude of Negroes, and other servants." Kinnersley's address drew a public rebuke from Jones and the Baptist congregation. Kinnersley, incensed, approached Franklin about printing the text of his sermon against Rowland. As with Richard Peters's letters, Franklin was ambivalent. Where was the balance between journalistic fairness, and undermining his active support for Whitefield? Could printing Kinnersley's screed jeopardize his lucrative arrangement with Whitefield?[24]

Franklin adopted the same approach to Kinnersley as he had with Peters. Let the critic air his opinions, but Franklin would also weigh in. He prefaced Kinnersley's piece with a defense of his even-handedness. "It is a principle among printers," he wrote, "that when the truth has fair play, it will always prevail over falsehood." Printing opposing voices would allow the reading public to make their own decisions. Franklin was confident that truth, not bombast, would win out. Publishing antagonists' views deprived them of the complaint that the press was muzzling them. Critics (presumably including Kinnersley) had accused the "printers of this city" of partiality in favor of Whitefield and the evangelical cohort. Printing Kinnersley would demonstrate that this charge was "false and groundless." Franklin hoped readers would forgive him as the printer and blame Kinnersley alone for his invective. The *Pennsylvania Gazette* published another rejoinder from church members against Kinnersley, but after that, Franklin stayed clear of the Baptist church's controversy. He had made his point: he remained open to distributing anti-Whitefield content. For his part, Kinnersley managed to reconcile with the Philadelphia Baptist congregation and received ordination there in 1743. Later he became a teacher at the Philadelphia Academy and an evangelist in his own right—an evangelist for Franklin's electricity.[25]

Whitefield was constantly traveling through the colonies, but in November 1740, he returned to Philadelphia. He recruited

Franklin to help him with a plan to open a "Negroe school" on thousands of acres Whitefield had bought north of Philadelphia. The scheme fit into Whitefield's paternalistic sense of Christian responsibility toward African slaves with a focus on bettering the lot of African Americans and evangelizing them, not on abolishing slavery. Even as Whitefield procured the land for the Pennsylvania school, he was beginning to pressure Georgia's trustees to open that colony to slaves, where they were originally prohibited. Franklin, already a slave owner, loved the idea of the school. He helped to publicize it for fundraising. Franklin saw such strategies for charitable reform as the epitome of true religion. Thus Franklin announced in the *Gazette* that anyone wishing to contribute to the school could give money to a group of pastors and merchants including the evangelist Gilbert Tennent, or to Franklin himself.[26]

The school for African Americans never materialized. Franklin and Whitefield both had more ideas than they could feasibly implement. Whitefield in particular established almost no institutional legacy beyond the Bethesda Orphanage in Savannah (which struggled to stay afloat for much of the eighteenth century). Critics routinely charged Whitefield with raising vast amounts of money for charity but using the money for his own purposes. Franklin publicly denied this accusation.

Meanwhile, Whitefield was heading back to England. In a typical exchange between the men, Whitefield left Franklin with instructions about forthcoming publications. Franklin had requested to publish an autobiography of Whitefield's early life, which Whitefield granted. He asked Franklin to stay in contact with him, so they could coordinate plans from a distance. Then Whitefield inquired after Franklin's soul: "Dear sir, adieu. I do not despair of your seeing the reasonableness of Christianity. Apply to God; be willing to do the divine will, and you shall know it." Whitefield would make a number of such appeals in the coming decades, but to no avail.[27]

Whitefield's ministry was enormously profitable for Franklin, but still, not everything the printer tried was successful. As he expanded his business, Franklin had the idea of starting a magazine to supplement the *Gazette*. The *General Magazine* would mimic publications becoming popular in Britain, but it would focus on re-printing American news, including content related to the Great Awakening. The magazine stood somewhere between a newspaper and a book, and represented a new niche for Franklin. His rival Andrew Bradford heard of the plan for a magazine and preempted Franklin with one of his own, the *American Magazine*. Neither publication survived long. Franklin's suffered from a lack of clear distinction between the magazine and the well-established *Gazette*, and there was not enough of a market to support two new periodicals in Philadelphia.[28]

Still, the *General Magazine* offered Franklin another venue for disseminating news and publications he found interesting, as well as an outlet for occasional editorials of his own. One, written as "Theophilus," suggests that for all of his work with Whitefield, Franklin's theological interests had not shifted that much since his youthful sojourn in London. The essay defended the idea that "God concurs with all human actions," taking Franklin back to themes from his *Dissertation on Liberty and Necessity*. In the Theophilus essay, Franklin postulated that if God had eternally de-creed all things, then people did not have free will. Even if God simply foreknew everything that would happen, then nothing was contingent on human decisions. Either God had "immediate con-course with every action we produce," or God did not have com-plete foreknowledge. Franklin left implicit what he had made explicit in the *Dissertation*: if God was responsible for everything that happened, then he was either the author of sin or there was no such thing as evil.[29]

Franklin used the magazine to reprint news of Whitefield con-troversies elsewhere in the colonies. The same issue with the Theophilus essay printed a letter from the *South-Carolina Gazette* from Whitefield's supporter Hugh Bryan. Bryan blamed a recent fire, which had burnt much of Charleston, on the faithlessness of the city's pastors. The piece was so offensive that it earned both Bryan and Whitefield, who had edited it, a brief stay in jail. The juxtaposition of the Theophilus essay and the Bryan letter speaks to the eclecticism of Franklin's religious musings. As intriguing as he found the revivals, and as profitable as they were, his theological concerns ran in different channels. These non-evangelical concerns help explain Whitefield's routine pleadings with Franklin to believe in Jesus.[30]

The most controversial piece Franklin wrote in this period was, like the Theophilus essay, unsigned. It was titled "The Religion of the Indian Natives of America" and ostensibly records a response by a Susquehanna chief in Pennsylvania to a Swedish Lutheran minister's gospel preaching around the year 1700. Published in Bradford's *American Magazine*, Franklin scholar J. A. Leo Lemay argues that Franklin authored the speech's preface and translated the text. The content certainly accords with Franklin's opinions about the importance of virtue, and Franklin's authorship seems certain. Franklin revised the Native leader's speech, which he had acquired in a Latin version, to suit his essay's purposes. Franklin apparently knew enough Latin to make a workable translation of the piece, which came to him via Swedish ministers in America. How much of the Susquehanna chief's actual words remained is hard to say.[31]

The preface and speech were inflammatory stuff for traditional Christians. Although the piece affirmed monotheistic tenets such as a Creator God and an afterlife, it took a deistic approach to those who had not heard the Christian gospel. (Deism here meant anticlericalism, moralism, and a nonexclusive view of Christianity's truth.) When Franklin's New York associate James Parker republished an edition of the speech in 1752, local authorities charged Parker with heresy. People's happiness in the afterlife depended on their "good or bad behavior in this" life, Franklin averred. Because of the "depravity of human nature, mankind is vastly more prone to vice than to the pursuit of virtue." This fact made people anxious about their future state, an anxiety that deceiving priests exploited. They set up the false worship of idols to replace the "Religion of Nature." But Christianity had come as a "divine revelation" to restore the essence of natural religion in "its original purity and perfection."[32]

The crux of Christianity was what Christ had taught in the second greatest commandment: "Love your neighbor as yourself." This powerful but simple precept undercut the priests who had corrupted Christianity. "No wonder the Pope took the Bible out of the hands of the laity," Franklin wrote. But it was not Catholics alone who suffered from priestly deception. Others invented arcane theological systems and fostered "infinite wrangles on the meaning of sounds." (Here Franklin was recalling the Presbyterian controversy over Samuel Hemphill.) Still, some honest men sought to restore biblical interpretation to its original purity. "They interpreted Scripture by reason, and improved their reason by Scripture. The Religion of Nature was again revived." Virtuous teachers countered the abuses of priests who insisted on their "arbitrary interpretation of the Scripture." Among these arbitrary beliefs was the notion that God's mercy only extended to those who believed in Jesus.[33]

Franklin possessed an account of a Swedish missionary telling Indians that God's saving love only applied to Christian believers. The response of the Susquehanna chief illustrated how "palming such tenets on Christianity must necessarily obstruct the propagation of it," Franklin concluded. In his address, the chief said he could not accept the missionary's overtures because the Swede wanted the Indians to give up their own religion and accept Christianity. The Natives' religion sounded a lot like Franklin's. Their forefathers had taught them that good deeds in this life would be rewarded in the next according to a person's "virtue." The wicked would suffer punishment in the next life according to the severity of their crimes. As to the nature of religious truth, they regarded it the "sacred, inviolable, natural right of every man to examine and judge for himself."[34]

Franklin's chief posed rigorous questions to the missionary. Did he believe that their virtuous forefathers were now in hell? Why did God reveal himself to them only through nature, and not give them enough information to be saved? "Supposing our understandings to be so far illuminated, as to know it to be our duty to please God, who yet had left us under an incapacity of doing it; will this missionary notwithstanding conclude that we shall be eternally damned?" Should they be condemned for failing to do that which was impossible for them to do? Perhaps God dealt with "different races of people in a different manner," the Indian posited. Every person had sufficient knowledge in order to be saved, the chief argued. Salvation did not require possession of the

Christians' book. In spite of these skeptical views about Christian exclusivity, Franklin did not oppose missions per se, because they might "civilize" Native people. For example, in 1778, Franklin advised American ship captains to allow safe passage for a sloop carrying supplies to a Moravian mission in Labrador, which sought to convert "to Christianity the barbarians who live there." This was an "enterprise beneficial to humanity," Franklin wrote.[35]

In the magazine piece, however, the Indians' withering questions continued. Would God create people but block them from the path of salvation? Surely he would only damn those who merited it by some heinous crime. If one of their ancestors had indeed committed such an offense, would God hold a whole race accountable for it? (Here Franklin signaled his objection to the doctrine of original sin, in which the whole human family fell under judgment for Adam's transgression in the Garden of Eden.) God would never punish descendants for an ancestor's guilt. "Those who teach otherwise," the chief chided the missionary, "paint the Almighty, as a very whimsical ill-natured being."[36]

In such essays, Franklin sought to turn traditional Christians' arguments against themselves. You say you wish to evangelize Native Americans? Then why, he asked, impose extra-biblical doctrines on them, which present unnecessary obstacles to faith? The speech was a virtuoso performance, and it was frequently reprinted throughout the eighteenth and nineteenth centuries in both England and America. If we can be certain that it was written by Franklin, then the preface and speech give a strong indication of Franklin's enduring skepticism regarding the unique truth of Christianity, even as he facilitated Whitefield's ministry.[37]

Franklin returned to the account of the Swedish minister's encounter with the Susquehannas more than forty years later, in his Paris imprint *Remarks Concerning the Savages of North America*. There Franklin asserted that while Indians would listen politely to missionaries' overtures, they saw no reason to believe in the superior veracity of Christianity. To illustrate, Franklin related a story of the Swede and the Susquehannas swapping creation narratives. The missionary told of Adam and Eve's fall in the Garden of Eden, and Christ's redemptive work. An Indian orator replied drily that it was "indeed bad to eat apples. It is better to make them all into cider." Then the Susquehanna told how a kind woman, descending from the clouds, gave their original fathers maize, beans, and tobacco. The missionary did not care for this tale, calling it a "fable, fiction, and falsehood." The Susquehannas, taken aback, said that they had listened patiently and believed all the Europeans' stories. Why now did the Swedes refuse to believe theirs?[38]

In spite of his doubts about Christianity's exclusive truth, working with Whitefield tempered Franklin's outspokenness against traditional faith. Memories of his Boston upbringing also softened his views. In 1743, Franklin and his son William visited New England. They stayed in Boston with his sister Jane Mecom, at his childhood house. Jane remained a serious Calvinist and evangelical. They seem to have quarreled about religion while he was there, given a subsequent exchange of letters between them. She implored him to return to the faith of his upbringing. Her letter to him is lost, but it included an "admonition" about his lack of faith. Ben wrote back, saying that she had expressed herself as if he "was against worshipping of God, and believed good works would merit heaven." These were mere fancies of her mind, he commented. It seems unlikely that Jane accused Ben of being against the worship of God altogether. But Franklin did believe that works were the determinant of one's standing before God. Jane hardly made that up.[39]

Ben reminded Jane that he had composed his own book of devotions. Fifteen years after writing it, the prayer guide was still meaningful to him. At a minimum it served as a tool to counter Jane's charge that he was impious. But Franklin especially refuted the notion (at least in this conversation) that he believed anyone could *merit* God's favor by good works. He knew that traditionalists did believe that works were essential to the Christian life. Those good deeds could not earn God's favor, however, or resolve the problem of unforgiven sin. Few would imagine that our paltry good deeds could merit us eternal life in heaven, he told Jane. However God assesses people in the afterlife, all stood in need of grace.[40]

Still, good deeds were the core of authentic Christianity. To demonstrate this, Franklin again turned a Calvinist argument to his advantage. He conceded that there were aspects of "your New

England doctrines and worship" that he did not agree with. ("Your" New England theology is an interesting phrase. It was her theology, not his, as if they had not grown up in the same house. Here he postured as a sophisticated man to whom New England Calvinism was an object of analysis, not a personal legacy.) But he did not "condemn" those Calvinist beliefs, the Hemphill writings notwithstanding. Nor did he wish to turn Jane away from Calvinism. He just asked that she show him the same courtesy regarding his focus on good deeds. In a surprising move, he told Jane that even the great Calvinist theologian and Great Awakening leader Jonathan Edwards was on his side. He suggested that she consult Edwards on good works, providing a specific citation of seven pages from Edwards's tome *Some Thoughts Concerning the Present Revival of Religion in New England* (1742). This was not a book Franklin had published, so he must have consulted *Some Thoughts* closely if he was able to reference a passage on works deep within the text.[41]

In the passage Ben cited, Edwards contended that "moral duties" such as loving your neighbor were more important to God than external acts of worship, such as church attendance. What better authority to confirm Franklin's religious philosophy than the great Edwards? But Edwards had made clear elsewhere that the heart's love for God, not any external actions, was the core of true virtue. That did not concern Franklin. He told Jane that she should judge people by their fruit. If the fruit was good, she should not worry that the tree might be evil. He backed his admonition by citing Jesus from the Gospel of Matthew, where he taught that people would show their true nature by their fruit. "Do men gather grapes of thorns, or figs of thistles?" Christ asked. In spite of their disagreements, Jane's influence exerted significant pressure on Franklin, helping to set limits to his heterodoxy.[42]

While in Boston visiting Jane, Franklin attended an electricity demonstration by Dr. Archibald Spencer, a traveling Scottish scientist and fellow Freemason. Franklin was not impressed with the display itself, as Spencer was "not very expert." But Franklin was drawn to the promise of electrical research, which "surprised and pleased" him.[43] In his new scientific interests, Franklin was entering a field of study that had deep Anglo-American and Continental roots. One of the first colonial proponents of electrical theory was the religious dissenter and scientist Charles Morton, who came to Massachusetts in the 1680s to teach at Harvard College. (In England, Morton had been one of Daniel Defoe's tutors.) Morton also became minister at Charlestown, Massachusetts. For Morton, studying the natural world would inculcate wonder and "magnifye the Creator." Isaac Greenwood, another electrical theorist, was Harvard's first professor of mathematics and natural philosophy. Greenwood was also a childhood friend of Franklin's. Greenwood went to England in the 1720s and interacted with leading scientists, including Isaac Newton. Upon returning to Boston, Greenwood became one of the colonies' champions of experimental science, including that of "electrical attraction and repulsion." Typical adherents of experimental science did not promote religious skepticism. They emphasized people's ability to rationally discern the facts of nature by proper experiments, however. "All fanciful suppositions" would fall before this new experimental method. Its devotees, Greenwood insisted, would "take nothing for granted but what is shown to be really in nature."[44]

In 1735, Franklin reprinted an ode to Greenwood, which suggests the worship-inducing and superstition-killing effects of scientific knowledge (in this case, of astronomy):

Great GOD! what Voice could into Being call
These mighty Globes, and form this beauteous ALL!
What Power can all their various Motions guide?
And from what Hand but thine are they supply'd?

GREENWOOD, with what Delight we hear you prove
The hidden Laws by which those Bodies move. . . .
No more we'll gaze with superstitious Fear,
While you the secret Laws of Nature clear.

After Harvard authorities dismissed Greenwood in 1738 for drunkenness, Franklin helped the scientist get work in Philadelphia. He arranged for the Library Company to promote lectures by Greenwood in 1740, and he advertised them in the

Gazette in mid-1740, as the furor over Whitefield's ministry was at high tide. Franklin even loaned Greenwood twenty pounds to help the scientist get back on his feet. Franklin gave similar assistance to Archibald Spencer when he lectured in Philadelphia in 1744.[45]

At this stage, Franklin remained more of a scientific connector than an experimenter. This accounts for his work to create the American Philosophical Society. Botanist John Bartram of Philadelphia and New York's Cadwallader Colden joined Franklin in founding this society to link learned American colonists. Franklin was one of the best positioned people to facilitate communication among the colonies' top scientific minds. In a 1743 proposal for "promoting useful knowledge," he emphasized that correspondents of the society would advise one another of "experiments that let light into the nature of things, tend to increase the power of man over matter, and multiply the conveniences or pleasures of life." The American Philosophical Society, in Franklin's vision, would link people seeking to use science to do good.[46]

Colden, a leading politician and polymath, endorsed Franklin's proposal. Although the society was slow to start, Colden and Franklin exchanged dozens of letters in the coming decades regarding their common interests in science, politics, and social improvement. Bartram, Colden, and Franklin kept up a correspondence with the London-based Quaker Peter Collinson, a fellow of London's Royal Society for Improving Natural Knowledge and a prominent botanist. Colden, whose Scottish parents also once hoped for him to become a pastor, shared Franklin's views regarding Christianity's social usefulness. Colden told Collinson that scientific discovery should lead us to worship God. But worship only represented half of anyone's religious duties. Loving one's neighbor was the other half. "The practice of the second command," Colden declared, "gives no less pleasure to a good man than the speculations of" admiring God's creation.[47]

Between the years 1742 and 1745, as Franklin's interest in electricity escalated, business related to George Whitefield declined, with Whitefield in Britain for most of that time. Franklin devoted more attention to a burgeoning controversy over the Moravians, a German pietist sect that was drawing away a number of Whitefield's

Peter Collinson, *by J. S. Miller, [1768?] (detail). Courtesy Wellcome Library, London. Creative Commons attribution-only license, CC BY 4.0.*

converts. In 1742, Franklin printed nineteen pamphlets by or about the Moravians and their leader, Count Nicholas von Zinzendorf. After that, his publishing on the Great Awakening waned. The year 1744, however, saw renewed interest, prompted by reports of Whitefield's imminent return to the colonies. Franklin printed an attack on Whitefield by an anti-revivalist pastor in 1744. Late that year, the *Gazette* began to report on Whitefield's travels again. Then came word that the itinerant had come back, landing first in Maine. After recuperating from illness in New England, Whitefield arrived in Philadelphia in September 1745. He began preaching two or three times a day at the New Building to "large audiences."[48]

Among the most controversial news items about Whitefield was the status of the Bethesda orphanage in Georgia. The question of what Whitefield did with the funds he raised was tantalizing, even if Franklin was convinced that Whitefield was honest about money. Franklin admired Whitefield's benevolent work in Georgia. But he also published critics' claims that in Whitefield's absence, the orphanage had gone to ruin, with livestock wandering its ground floor. Franklin printed friendly assessments of Whitefield's work, too, including letters in 1746 from Whitefield about the condition of the orphanage. In a letter to Franklin, meant for publication, Whitefield shared an accounting report regarding Bethesda, which claimed that the minister had not converted any funds "to his own private use and property." Whitefield admitted that only thirty people were living at Bethesda, but he thought this was good: it reduced the cost of operations. Whitefield argued that if he "could have but six Negroes" (the colony still banned slaves), Bethesda would pay for itself. Whitefield would keep pressing the Georgia trustees to allow slaves, and he seems to have illicitly permitted slaves to work at Bethesda before the colony legalized slave labor in 1751.[49]

Franklin was so convinced of the orphanage's worthiness that he donated seventy-five pounds to it. Whitefield was grateful, but he discouraged Franklin from printing a list of donors to the orphanage. (Financial management was never Whitefield's strength.) He worried that a big fundraising push would bring in too much money, more than he or Bethesda really needed. He told Franklin that he preferred depending on God's provision. In a 1747 letter, Whitefield spoke to the printer as he might to an evangelical ministry partner. "Committing all my concerns to [God's] hands," he concluded, "I subscribe myself dear sir your very affectionate friend and servant." Franklin's contribution, and his ongoing schemes for promoting Bethesda, meant a great deal to Whitefield.[50]

Whitefield's influence, in addition to his parents' and Jane Mecom's, fostered Franklin's defensiveness about his faith. This defensiveness could appear at unexpected times, such as when he tried to read Scottish philosopher Andrew Baxter's *An Enquiry into the Nature of the Human Soul.* This popular book used Newtonian physics to demonstrate the reality of God and the soul. A number of Franklin's friends urged him to read it, but he hated Baxter's approach. Disliking the mix of hard science with proofs about God, he said that he could not finish reading Baxter because he stumbled at the "threshold of the building."[51]

Beyond his disagreements with Baxter's physics, what especially bothered Franklin was Baxter's notion that science could prove God's existence. Baxter asserted that divine truths were demonstrable from scientific facts, and that science represented a fundamental threat to atheism. Franklin countered that if God's reality was "demonstrable from no plainer principles, the Deist [by which Franklin meant a theist] hath a desperate cause in hand." Baxter was hurting the cause of theism by his incoherence. But Franklin made clear that he was still a deist/theist, not an atheist. Deism and atheism were opposites, he insisted.[52]

While writing a letter about Baxter, Whitefield's voice popped into Franklin's mind. Franklin knew that Whitefield saw his rationalism and scientism as a cloak for unbelief. Quoting the minister's journal (apparently from memory), Franklin recalled Whitefield saying that a certain Mr. B was "a deist, I had almost said an atheist." This association was totally wrong, Franklin insisted. Atheism and deism were not synonyms, but antonyms. They were as different as chalk and charcoal. Whatever Whitefield thought of him, Franklin would continue to insist that he was no unbeliever.[53]

Linking metaphysics and experimental science was no longer of interest to the printer. Franklin bore too many scars from theological battles with family members and Presbyterian authorities. Now he was reluctant to comment on matters in "the metaphysical way," he wrote, concluding his thoughts on Baxter: "The great uncertainty I have found in that science; the wide contradictions and endless disputes it affords; and the horrible errors I led myself into when a young man, by drawing a chain of plain consequences as I thought them, from true principles, have given me a disgust to what I was once extremely fond of." In a marginal note on this letter, Franklin made clear that by "horrible errors," he meant those he committed in *A Dissertation on Liberty and Necessity* two decades earlier.[54]

Understanding God through metaphysics seemed an increasingly futile pursuit. But everywhere Franklin turned, new scientific discoveries bloomed. They held major promise for helping people live better lives, and he wanted in on the action. Drawing on publications of the Royal Society, books at the Library Company, and equipment sent to him by Peter Collinson, Franklin began to study electricity. He learned about it in conversation with fellow Pennsylvania polymaths such as James Logan. The somber Logan

was a frequent officeholder in Philadelphia and a fellow biblio-
phile. While Franklin built the Library Company for public use,
Logan kept a large personal library (now also held by the Library
Company) that one historian calls "the greatest single intellectual
monument of colonial America." Logan mentored Franklin and
modeled the kind of multivalent knowledge to which Franklin aspired. In addition to expertise in science and history, Logan knew a
host of languages, including Greek, Latin, Hebrew, French,
German, and (extraordinarily for the time) Arabic.[55]

Remarks by Logan, naturalist John Bartram, and others would
suggest that Franklin began performing his own experiments sometime in 1746 or early 1747. Bartram told Logan about Franklin's
displaying a cork ball rotating around an electrified body. Logan
consulted his books and reports from the Royal Society, to check
what others had already done in this field. Franklin's experiments,
Logan concluded, "exceed them all."[56]

Finally Franklin wrote to his English friend Peter Collinson in
March 1747. He thanked Collinson for his "kind present of an
electric tube, with directions for using it." The gift had "put several
of us on making electrical experiments, in which we have observed
some particular phenomena that we look upon to be new."
Uncertain just how new these "phenomena" were, he sought news
from England that might confirm if he was breaking new ground.
Whatever the case, electricity had captured his imagination: "I
never was before engaged in any study that so totally engrossed my
attention and my time as this has lately done; for what with making
experiments when I can be alone, and repeating them to my
friends." The experiments were drawing audiences. They were
nothing like Whitefield's throngs, of course. But the printer had
gotten a taste of celebrity. "From the novelty of the thing, [people]
come continually in crowds to see them. I have, during some
months past, had little leisure for anything else." Those crowds had
started to envision him, in James Logan's phrase, as "that most ingenious man, Benjamin Franklin."[57]

CHAPTER SEVEN

Tribune of the People

B Y THE MID-1740s, the affluent Franklin began moving
away from printing. He focused on concerns that would
mark the rest of his career: science, charity, and imperial
affairs. There were wars and rumors of war with Europe's
Catholic powers. Franklin had grown up hearing about two great
enemies of godly religion: one was English persecutors who denied
liberty to dissenters. The other was Catholic power. If the Spanish
or French gained ascendancy, they might destroy Protestantism altogether. The fear of Catholicism was not mere paranoia either.
France had crushed its Protestant population, the Huguenots, in
1685 after the revocation of the Edict of Nantes, which had pro-
tected them under a canopy of tolerance. What if the French or
Spanish ever conquered the English colonies in America? Franklin
and his fellow Protestant colonists shuddered at the thought.

These matters were on Franklin's mind in 1745 as he watched
British colonial forces—without Pennsylvania's support—launch
an expedition against the French stronghold at Louisbourg, Cape
Breton Island, off the Canadian coast. Massachusetts led the
crusade, and George Whitefield addressed the troops as they
set out. Franklin knew that pacifist Pennsylvania Quakers
would never support the expedition. But he was still disgusted
when Pennsylvania legislators made a pretense of considering

Massachusetts's request for aid. It was a "farce," he grumbled. Some members had the gall to tell him they wished Massachusetts well in their fight against the French. The New Englanders were as "obliged to them for their good wishes as the poor in the Scripture to those that say 'be ye warmed, be ye filled' [James 2:16]," Franklin mused. Why could Pennsylvania not at least send supplies, Franklin asked? The Quakers replied, "that would be encouraging war."[1]

In spite of Franklin's advocacy for the Louisbourg attack, he still found time to joke with his brother John about the way that New Englanders spiritualized war. While the Pennsylvania Quakers' piety dissuaded them from conflict, some New Englanders seemed to think that faith was *all* they needed to win a war. The Massachusetts government appointed a day of prayer to back up the campaign. This got Franklin to thinking. Making some quick calculations, he figured that the total number of prayers by New Englanders probably totaled around 45 million. This flood of prayer, "set against the prayers of a few priests in the [French] garrison, to the Virgin Mary, gives a vast balance in your favor," he told John, who lived in Boston. The disparity was so overwhelming that a Massachusetts loss at Louisbourg would give him "an indifferent opinion of Presbyterian prayers." When besieging citadels, Franklin preferred works over faith. Citing the Gospel of Matthew, he noted that forts, like the kingdom of Heaven, "are to be taken by force and violence."[2]

In the summer of 1745, Franklin published a woodcut illustration of Louisbourg. This was likely the first time an American newspaper used a visual aid in a news report. In spite of his eye-rolling letter to his brother, Franklin concluded his account of the expedition by praying that the "God of Hosts grant success. *Amen.*" When news came of the remarkable defeat of Louisbourg by colonial forces, Franklin reprinted the *Boston Evening Post*'s statement that it "not only appears wonderful to us in America, but must surprise all the people of England. . . . It can scarce be paralleled in history." Starting in the mid-1740s, Franklin paid more attention to America's fate in European affairs, and to the way that Britons and Continental Europeans viewed American colonists. His own scientific experiments gave him greater notoriety in

Europe than any other American of his day. By the mid-1750s, he had become the emblematic American.[3]

Imperial concerns frequently interrupted Franklin's electrical tests and other experiments. In addition to Louisbourg, there was the suppression of Britain's Jacobite Rebellion in 1746. The Catholic "Bonnie Prince Charlie," who considered himself the legitimate (Stuart) successor to the British throne, led this revolt. He captured much of Scotland, but his army met its demise in April at the Battle of Culloden. As told in the August 28, 1746, *Pennsylvania Gazette*, Philadelphians celebrated this defeat. George Whitefield addressed a raucous Philadelphia crowd on the "mischiefs of Popery and arbitrary power," Franklin reported. Whitefield's focus had shifted, for the moment, away from the new birth. Now he gave greater scope to the threat of Catholic power, within and outside of Britain. The preacher won "universal applause," Franklin wrote, as he had "demonstrated himself to be as sound and zealous a Protestant, and as truly a loyal subject, as he is a grand and masterly orator." In 1748, his *Poor Richard* almanac memorialized Culloden, too, admiring how Protestant forces had conquered the Catholic rebels, who were backed by France, Spain, "the Pope and the Devil."[4]

The Jacobite revolt and Louisbourg seemed like important but distant concerns from a Philadelphian's perspective. The Catholic threat became much more immediate in 1747, however. French and Spanish privateers (state-sanctioned pirates) began attacking Pennsylvania settlements and farms along the Delaware River. The City of Brotherly Love was in peril. But the Quaker-dominated legislature refused to prepare defensive forces to counter the privateers, again citing their commitment to pacifism. Franklin and many other non-Quakers were indignant. Pennsylvania had failed to support the colonial campaign against Louisbourg; now it would not even protect its own people.[5]

The crisis inspired Franklin to launch a media campaign for a popular defense association. This effort was nearly unprecedented in American history. Acting outside of formal government channels, Franklin used multiple methods in print and in person to influence political decision-making. He promoted an extra-governmental militia to circumvent the legislature's recalcitrance. Printing broadsides

and newspaper pieces, Franklin argued that self-defense did not violate Quaker scruples against initiating war. The key to the campaign
was Franklin's decision to write and distribute two thousand copies
of the pamphlet *Plain Truth*. As Franklin recalled, this work "stated
our defenseless situation in strong lights, with the necessity of union
and discipline for our defense."[6]

This debate hinged on the question of a Christian's responsibility in the face of a threatening enemy. Franklin employed biblical and anti-Catholic arguments to cajole Pennsylvanians into
action. *Plain Truth* appealed to a relatively obscure passage in the

Non Votis, &c.

Frontispiece from Franklin's Plain Truth. *The woodcut depicts the fable of
Hercules and the wagoner; the partial quote, "Non Votis," is taken from a line
from Cato, which Franklin translated as "Divine assistance and protection are
not to be obtain'd by timorous Prayers and womanish Supplications." Courtesy
New York Public Library.*

book of Judges to explain why people needed to be vigilant against French and Spanish intrigues. Citing Judges 18, he recounted the story of how the impious, marginalized Danites sent spies to find more land on which to settle. They encountered an "idolatrous priest" who assured them of his god's blessing. Franklin asked readers whether they thought no similar priests lived in America who "might, in the like case, give an enemy as good encouragement?" There were plenty of Roman Catholic priests in the colonies, he warned. Such priests had (ostensibly) encouraged the Jacobite revolt. The Danites had conquered the slumbering land of Laish, even though the people of Laish greatly outnumbered them. God gave the Bible "for our reproof, instruction and warning," Franklin reminded his audience. "May we make a due use of this example, before it be too late!" If they underestimated the Catholic menace, they could find themselves reliving the experience of Laish. His appropriation of this passage again demonstrates Franklin's intimate knowledge of the Bible. He was prepared to use it in a range of theological and political conversations. Moreover, his reference to Judges 18 speaks to the salience of Bible passages as sources for framing conflict in Anglo-America. Under similar circumstances eight years later, Franklin would also justify a volunteer militia by references to passages in Deuteronomy 20 and Judges 7.[7]

Playing on colonists' religious and racial trepidations, Franklin forecast that if they continued to delay, Catholic forces would sack Philadelphia. If that happened, many would fall prey to privateers and their lecherous crews, which included Africans and mixed-race sailors. Then "your persons, fortunes, wives and daughters, shall be subject to the wanton, and unbridled rage, rapine and lust, of Negroes, Molattoes, and others, the vilest and most abandoned of mankind." If the Quakers' principles would not permit action against such scum, they should stand aside and let others do the fighting for them.[8]

Drawing ever deeper on his repertoire of ancient sources, Franklin cited the Jewish scholar and historian Josephus regarding the Roman conquest of Jerusalem. In a Puritanesque reckoning, Franklin surmised that "heaven, justly displeased at our growing wickedness," was "determined to punish this once favored land."

He found historical precedent for this type of divine judgment in Josephus's writings. There, God decided to punish the people of Jerusalem who broke many divine laws, even though they remained scrupulous about observing the Sabbath. Roman general Pompey knew this, so he planned his siege for the Sabbath day. He found little resistance as the Jews rested. For Franklin, the Quaker legislators mimicked those ancient Jews. Their dogged adherence to legalistic religious requirements in the face of immediate menace would prove their undoing.[9]

Even without the support of rigid pacifists, Franklin was still confident that the people of Pennsylvania could defend themselves. He reminded the colonists that they were descendants of Britons and Germans who had fought for their "religion and liberties" throughout history. He harkened back to the Protestant struggle in Ireland to save themselves from the Catholic forces of the "bigoted Popish king" James II (Bonnie Prince Charlie's grandfather) in 1689. If the people of Pennsylvania united, they could expect the blessing of heaven. Franklin closed *Plain Truth* with a rousing prayer:

> May the God of wisdom, strength and power, the Lord of the armies of Israel, inspire us with prudence in this time of danger; take away from us all the seeds of contention and division, and unite the hearts and counsels of all of us, of whatever sect or nation, in one bond of peace, brotherly love, and generous public spirit; may he give us strength and resolution to amend our lives, and remove from among us everything that is displeasing to him; afford us his most gracious protection, confound the designs of our enemies, and give peace in all our borders.

That was the prayer, he wrote, of "A Tradesman of Philadelphia."[10]

Plain Truth worked wonderfully. Soon after it appeared, a packed meeting of supporters assembled at George Whitefield's New Building. The roughly five hundred men accounted for a quarter of Philadelphia's male adults. Soon about half of the city's men had signed on to Franklin's "Defense Association." They agreed to bear arms in a militia to defend Philadelphia. Government official and Anglican minister Richard Peters, the opponent of Franklin and Whitefield, explained the association to England-based Pennsylvania proprietor Thomas Penn. It might seem "odd," Peters noted, to have these people, led by "Franklyn," taking matters into their own hands. Penn found it more than odd: he was outraged. He regarded the association as sheer defiance. But aside from Penn, most Pennsylvania officials viewed the association as a reasonable compromise. The strict Quakers would not have to violate their consciences, but the city could defend itself. (The summoning of popular American militias, outside the bounds of official government authority, would have radical ramifications in the revolutionary crisis three decades later.)[11]

Not wishing to seem utterly passive, the Pennsylvania governor's council proclaimed a general fast at the end of 1747. They recommended that all people take an upcoming Thursday to pray for God's protection from the "calamities of a bloody war." The fast was an unusual step for Pennsylvania, as compared to the New England colonies. Where did they get the idea? Franklin said that he suggested it. "Calling in the aid of religion, I proposed to them the proclaiming a fast, to promote reformation, and implore the blessing of Heaven on our undertaking. They embraced the motion, but as it was the first fast ever thought of in the province, the Secretary had no precedent from which to draw the proclamation." Franklin had some experience in these matters. "My education in New England, where a fast is proclaimed every year, was here of some advantage. I drew it in the accustomed style." Virginia's Patrick Henry and Thomas Jefferson would draw on Puritan proclamations too, when they needed language for a Continental fast day in 1774. Pennsylvania's fast declaration "was translated into German, printed in both languages and divulged through the province. This gave the clergy of the different sects an opportunity of influencing their congregations to join in the Association," Franklin recalled. The pastors complied. Gilbert Tennent commended the association in a sermon delivered in the New Building. Tennent also called *Plain Truth* an "ingenious excellent performance."[12]

In an anonymous *Gazette* piece, building off of Tennent, Franklin once more displayed his skills at making biblical arguments to advance his cause. He said that Tennent's "masterly" sermon had already addressed most of the essential biblical points buttressing the association. He wished to elaborate, however, on several New Testament passages that radical pacifists often cited. Franklin contended that the earliest Christians, some of whom were soldiers when they suffered martyrdom, approved of certain kinds of war and military service. In a move that illuminated his own view of Christianity as of 1747, Franklin emphasized that during the time of the apostles, "the streams flowed pure from the fountain, before the Apostasy had crept in, or the holy doctrines of Jesus and his apostles, were exchanged for the corrupt traditions of men." The truth of Christianity inhered in its earliest, pristine forms, Franklin believed.[13]

Franklin assessed the Gospels' accounts of Peter cutting off the ear of the high priest's servant, for which Christ rebuked him and healed the servant's ear. "They that take the sword, shall perish with the sword," Jesus chided Peter. Did Jesus mean that no one should ever take up arms, Franklin asked? Franklin argued that this verse did not prohibit civil government from taking up arms. The ear-slashing story said nothing about whether Christ permitted using the sword in nonreligious matters. On that topic, Franklin reminded readers of Luke 22:36, in which Jesus had told the disciples, "he that hath no sword, let him sell his garment, and buy one." There must be a place for swords in some circumstances. What more appropriate cause was there for taking up arms than to protect the "helpless and innocent"?[14]

Franklin knew that to mobilize the people of Philadelphia to support a military cause, he must cite the Bible. (This conflation of the religious and the martial would become a longstanding American tradition.) In doing so, he touched a nerve. By the end of 1747, much of the city's white male population was participating in association drills. During the spring of 1748, they held a grand procession before the Provincial Council, flying silk regimental colors sewn by female supporters. These banners, decorated with Latin mottoes, often referenced the Bible. One of them represented a "Glory, in the middle of which is wrote *Jehovah Nissi*," or "The Lord our Banner" [a reference to Exodus 17:15]. Another showed David as he slung the stone that killed the giant warrior Goliath.[15]

Another associational banner—intriguingly—bore the motto "In God We Trust." Although this may seem unexceptional now, this is one of the only extant references to that motto in colonial America. This saying began appearing on American coins only during the Civil War. Before that, perhaps the most famous reference to it came in the fourth verse of Francis Scott Key's "Star-Spangled Banner" (a verse little sung today), where Key rendered it "In God is our trust." The appearance of "In God We Trust" on that regimental design, and its mention in the *Pennsylvania Gazette*'s list of the banners, may suggest that the phrase was fairly common in Franklin's world. But for unknown reasons, the saying rarely found its way into print in early America.[16]

By any measure, Franklin's promotion of the militia succeeded. Not only did he enlist a sizeable portion of the city, but Franklin and association leaders coordinated lotteries to finance the construction of Delaware River forts. Franklin also started discussions with other colonies' governors about purchasing artillery. But then the association's reason for existence disappeared. In 1748, European negotiators achieved a tenuous peace between the warring powers, slowing the activities of privateers. Similar to George Whitefield, however, Franklin had demonstrated the untapped potential in organizing people outside of official agencies, whether churches or governments. The traditional deferential culture of England and America was deteriorating, thanks in no small part to Whitefield and Franklin. Thomas Penn, among the defenders of that hierarchical tradition, worried about Franklin's influence on the "wild unthinking multitude." Penn told Richard Peters that they needed to keep an eye on Franklin. Peters had once accused Whitefield and Franklin of catering to the lower classes. Now Penn echoed a similar concern. Franklin was a "dangerous man and I should be very glad [if] he inhabited any other country, as I believe him of a very uneasy spirit. However he is a sort of Tribune of the People, he must be treated with regard," Penn cautioned.[17]

Imperial conflict did not entirely distract Franklin from his musings on virtue. In spite of George Whitefield's admonitions about his need for Jesus, Franklin was convinced that he could live an ethical life without a conversion experience. In the early 1730s, he had begun tinkering with what he wryly called the "bold and arduous project of arriving at moral perfection." Compiling a master list of thirteen virtues, such as temperance, frugality, industry, and humility, he monitored his daily practice of them. In his annotation for "humility," Franklin reminded himself to "imitate Jesus and Socrates."[18]

Franklin's record book of virtues featured several mottoes to help keep him on track—one from Addison's *Cato*, one from Cicero, and one from Proverbs 3. Proverbs reminded him of wisdom's value: "Length of days is in her right hand; and in her left hand riches and honor. Her ways are ways of pleasantness, and all her paths are peace." Franklin reckoned that a failure to practice virtue sprung from a lack of wisdom. Knowing that God was the source of wisdom, Franklin composed a prayer for God's help. "O powerful Goodness! bountiful Father! merciful Guide! Increase in me that wisdom which discovers my truest interests; strengthen my resolutions to perform what that wisdom dictates. Accept my kind offices to thy other children, as the only return in my power for thy continual favors to me." Sometimes he also used a prayer taken from a book of poetry by the Scottish writer James Thomson:

> Father of Light and Life, thou good supreme,
> O teach me what is good, teach me thy self!
> Save me from folly, vanity and vice,
> From every low pursuit, and fill my soul
> With knowledge, conscious peace, and virtue pure,
> Sacred, substantial, never-fading bliss!

Reflecting on his moral perfection plan in the *Autobiography*, Franklin admitted that he fell far short of his goals but he was better off for having tried to sanctify himself.[19]

His prayers notwithstanding, Franklin's ethical strategy was heavy on self-improvement and light on God's intervention. One scholar has described his experiment as a species of "secular pietism." Another historian, comparing Franklin's and Cotton Mather's views, wrote that for the Puritan Mather, "the self is that which is to be governed, whereas for Franklin the self is that which is to govern." As much as Franklin's project mimicked the Puritans' earnest pursuit of holiness, it also subverted the Puritan concept of God-driven sanctification. He emphasized that although the "scheme was not wholly without religion," he designed it as a nonsectarian plan. He had thought of publishing the scheme as *The Art of Virtue*. This never happened in his lifetime, but he described the plan in the *Autobiography*. He hoped such a work would prove "serviceable to people in all religions." Perhaps this could even include non-Christians. After all, Franklin knew that small numbers of Jews lived in Philadelphia and had begun to meet in organized services as early as the 1740s. (Franklin himself would give a small donation to a Philadelphia synagogue during the revolutionary era.)[20]

The checklist of thirteen virtues exemplified Franklin's doctrineless, moralized Christianity. Some traditional Christians have found the system suspiciously godless, of course. Others have regarded it as a useless relic of the moralistic Puritan code. In one of the most pointed critiques of Franklin ever composed, the English writer D. H. Lawrence in 1924 reviled the list of virtues as the "barbed wire moral enclosure that Poor Richard rigged up." For Lawrence, Franklin's system reflected the worst of both worlds: a moribund system of religious restrictions without Christian transcendence. Franklin's self-invented God was the god of big business, production, and capitalism, Lawrence said. Franklin really had no concern "with the immortal soul." Lawrence insisted that he would never allow himself "to be turned into a virtuous little automaton as Benjamin would have me." Lawrence preferred to be the servant of his "own Holy Ghost."[21]

Nevertheless, Franklin thought that his project could demonstrate the potential of rigorous moral discipline. If Whitefield preached transformation by God, Franklin advocated gradual reformation by daily effort, with biblical precepts as a guide. No internal change or divine regeneration was needed. Whatever the lingering influence of his Puritan heritage, this was a point on which Franklin clearly departed from the Puritans, and from their evangelical successors like Whitefield and Jonathan Edwards. In this focus on harnessing daily habits, Franklin was setting foundational precedents for that distinctively American, quasi-religious genre, the self-help movement. Franklin's "The Way to Wealth" and his *Autobiography* were ur-texts of that movement.[22]

"Imitate Socrates and Jesus." This maxim suggests that the ethical sources of Franklin's self-improvement came from classical antiquity and the Christian tradition. But the advice for which he became best known dealt with hard work and financial management, especially for the middle-class artisans of colonial America. Upwardly mobile working men stood to benefit the most from these precepts. As Max Weber's "Protestant Work Ethic" suggested, Franklin was fashioning a kind of secularized, doctrinally minimal Puritanism. Applying prudence and diligence in one's calling would lead to prosperity. "He that hath a calling hath an office of profit and honor," Franklin wrote. He made explicit reference to the "Way to Wealth" in his 1748 essay "Advice to a Young Tradesman." The way to wealth, he advised, depended on two principles, "Industry and Frugality." If you waste neither time nor money, you will advance in the world. Those who do this will "certainly become rich." Even Poor Richard's occasional mentions of great religious figures such as Luther and Calvin emphasized their hard work and moderation. Calvin, he noted, was "a man of equal temperance and sobriety with Luther, and perhaps yet greater industry." Recalling his lingering belief in God's providential control, Franklin stipulated that some might not succeed, even with hard work and savings. God could still frustrate their efforts, if he chose to do so. The most obvious reason why God might foil a person's hard work was if a person cut ethical corners in the quest for wealth.[23]

Franklin's advice assumed that tradesmen could truly aspire to social mobility in colonial America. Few would travel the path from indentured servant to independent gentlemen like Franklin did. Still, there was some justification for seeing America as a place where free white men had a chance to get ahead. Franklin did not dwell on the fact that one of the main reasons he moved so far up the social ladder was his genius and uncanny sense of timing. Admitting to his innate brilliance would not only violate the principle of humility, it would also obscure the "everyman" quality of his advice. Anyone can become rich, he suggested, if they just commit to the virtuous habits that undergirded wealth-making.

The great summation of Franklin's advice on frugality was "Father Abraham's Speech." It came in the last edition of *Poor Richard*, in 1758. This discourse extracted many maxims from the almanacs and became Franklin's most-often reprinted publication, even more than the *Autobiography*. By the conclusion of the eighteenth century, the speech (often titled "The Way to Wealth") was republished 145 times in seven different languages. In it, Father Abraham addresses a crowd of colonists griping about their financial straits and heavy taxes. (High taxes were a longstanding complaint in the English-speaking world.) Father Abraham tells them that they should take responsibility for the taxes they laid on themselves, in the form of idleness, pride, and folly. "God helps them that help themselves," he reminds them, quoting Poor Richard. Maximize each day's opportunities. Father Abraham's speech echoed the classic Franklin saying, "Early to bed, and early to rise, makes a man healthy, wealthy, and wise."[24]

Some of Franklin's advice almost out-puritaned the Puritans. Pride and conspicuous consumption, in Father Abraham's assessment, were an addictive combination: *Pride is as loud a beggar as want, and a great deal more saucy. When you have bought one fine thing you must buy ten more, that your appearance may be all of a piece; but Poor Dick says, Tis easier to suppress the first desire, than to satisfy all that follow it.*" In a letter to George Whitefield, Franklin commended the evangelist for warning elites about fashions. "There are numbers," he told Whitefield, "that perhaps fear less the being in Hell, than out of fashion." Some of Franklin's advice echoed biblical injunctions on frugality and modesty. Poor Richard's saying that "The Borrower is a Slave to the Lender" quoted Proverbs 22:7 almost verbatim. Indeed, Franklin described Father Abraham's speech as "proverbs," which he "assembled and formed into a connected discourse."[25]

Similar to "Advice to a Young Tradesman," Father Abraham's speech concludes with a reminder that God in his Providence sometimes foils an individual's route to wealth. Frugality does not automatically beget prosperity, because God's power could "blast" your fortune in a moment. "Remember Job suffered, and was afterwards prosperous," the author cautioned. Pray humbly for God's blessings on your work, and do not presume that those who lack material success do so because of indolence.[26]

As Franklin told the story, when Father Abraham stopped speaking, the audience applauded his maxims. Then they "immediately practiced the contrary, just as if it had been a common sermon." They bought unnecessary extravagances without remembering his cautions or their own fear of taxes. Poor Richard, however, came forward to say that he was heartened that Father Abraham had studied his almanacs so closely. Most of the wisdom Father Abraham took from Poor Richard was not original, but "rather the gleanings I had made of the sense of all ages and nations," Richard confessed. The biblical tradition, particularly Proverbs, was front and center. But other wisdom traditions, including the pagan philosophers of ancient Greece and Rome, played a role.[27]

Franklin's moral advice was tethered to scripture but also cast a wider net. He wanted to fashion a nonsectarian moral code that was rooted in his parents' faith, but that was open to all people of good will. Could Franklin craft an ethical system that worked for more than just doctrinaire Christians? A person who could inculcate lasting moral reform, he told Whitefield, would deserve more laurels than the "inventor of the longitude." The cheeky note at the end of Father Abraham's address, with the foolish crowd hearing the word and then ignoring it, spoke to Franklin's own doubts. Could most people reform themselves by moral effort? Perhaps not. Bad habits (as he knew from personal experience) could exercise a deep hold on people. Poor Richard, though, was chastened by Father Abraham. He had thought of purchasing a new coat, Richard said. But Father Abraham convinced him to wear his old one a little longer.[28]

Franklin's hyperactive mind was always planning new ways to do good. By the early 1740s, he had begun to toy with the concept of an academy for Philadelphia. In 1743, he sent a proposal to Anglican minister Richard Peters, who had feuded with Franklin and Whitefield over the Great Awakening. In spite of their differences, Franklin thought Peters would make a good superintendent, but he declined the offer. So Franklin shelved the school idea, as electrical experiments and fear of war with France and Spain stole most of his attention. But he could not get the academy off his mind, and in 1749, he began pushing it again with Junto associates and city leaders. That summer he published a note in the *Gazette* explaining the need for a school where the colony's youths could receive a "polite and learned education." Always eager to draw on ancient sources of wisdom, Franklin included a letter from Pliny the Younger in his appeal. This Roman magistrate explained that with a local academy, children could "receive their education where they receive their birth, and be accustomed, from their infancy, to inhabit and affect their native soil." A local school would mean that the bright sons (formal education was largely an all-male affair in Franklin's time) of Philadelphia would no longer have to go to Boston or England for schooling. Evangelical Presbyterians, allies of Whitefield, had founded the College of New Jersey in 1746, but it was originally located some eighty miles from Philadelphia. Franklin hardly envisioned the academy as a sectarian seminary anyway.[29]

Drawing on John Locke's *Some Thoughts Concerning Education* (1693), Franklin's *Proposals Relating to the Education of Youth in Pennsylvania* (1749) laid out plans for the academy, with educational goals of virtue and practical service. Theology and ancient languages (Greek, Hebrew, and Latin) were deemphasized. English grammar was a primary emphasis, because it was more useful than "foreign and dead languages," Locke had written. Franklin proposed a new canon of English "classicks," including such favorites as Joseph Addison, *Cato's Letters*, and the broadminded archbishop John Tillotson. "Classics" had usually meant the great texts of Greek and Roman antiquity, but Franklin's students would learn to express themselves best in their everyday language. He did concede that students on a ministerial track would need to learn Latin and Greek.[30]

Historical studies, however, remained at the center of the curriculum. History, unlike Greek and Latin, inculcated practical values. Students could read English translations of the ancient Greek and Roman histories. Among history's chief benefits were its lessons in morality and the value of religion. Quoting John Milton's *Of Education* (1644), Franklin noted that students would find the historical basis of law "delivered first and with best warrant by Moses" in the Pentateuch. Reading about moral exemplars in the past would remind students of the "advantages of temperance, order, frugality, industry, perseverance" and other virtues. It would also reveal the "necessity of a public religion," he argued. Franklin even noted that pupils would learn of the "excellency of the Christian Religion above all others ancient or modern." But on that subject, Franklin was terse.[31]

For explanation of Christianity's value, he footnoted Scottish moral philosopher and Anglican minister George Turnbull's *Observations upon Liberal Education* (1742). Saying it was "too long to be transcribed here," he did not quote Turnbull. By contrast, Locke was apparently not too long to quote, as passages from the English philosopher took up great portions of the tract. Franklin restated the essence of Turnbull's view regarding the "excellence of true Christianity above all other religions." Turnbull had contended that Christianity was the best known source of virtue: "That the persuasion of a divine providence, and a future state of rewards and punishments, is one of the strongest incitements to virtue, and one of the most forcible restraints from vice, can hardly be doubted." Turnbull's view of Christianity's practical benefits tracked closely with Franklin's own convictions.[32]

What, then, was the aim of the academy? What was the proper goal of education? For Franklin, it was to impress upon the students the desire "to serve mankind, one's country, friends, and family." Franklin knew that some potential supporters would balk at such a human-centered vision. Thus, in an extended footnote, he insisted that the aim of service to mankind was another way of saying the "glory and service of God." Here Franklin was restating his notion of true religion: "Doing good to men is the only service of God in our power; and to imitate his beneficence is to glorify him." Franklin quoted Milton to bolster his point, even though Milton seems to have shared the older Christian view of education, that students should first learn about and glorify God. Milton wrote that the "end of learning is to repair the ruins of our first parents, by regaining to know God aright." Knowing God aright would lead us to love God and imitate him. This would produce virtue, in Milton's formula. Locke and Turnbull were closer to Franklin's view on this matter. For them, virtue was learning's primary aim, not a secondary result.[33]

Franklin arranged for the underutilized New Building, the preaching venue for George Whitefield, to become the academy's home. He knew that using the building required Whitefield's support. So he sent the itinerant a copy of his plan. Whitefield loved the idea of the school. He did not love the absence of Jesus in the *Proposals*, however. The school "is certainly calculated to promote polite literature," Whitefield told Franklin, "but I think there wants *aliquid Christi* [something of Christ] in it." The itinerant appreciated the proposals' recognition of Christianity's superior merit, but Franklin mentioned the topic too late, and moved on from it too quickly. Virtue in this life was not the main point of education, according to Whitefield. In the context of eternity, this life would pass in a blink. Thus, the great focus of Christian education was not this world but the next. Every Christian school should seek to convince students "of their natural depravity, of the means of recovering out of it, and of the necessity of preparing for the enjoyment of the Supreme Being in a future state. These are the grand points in which Christianity centers. Arts and sciences may be built on this, and serve to embellish and set off this superstructure, but without this, I think there cannot be any good foundation." In case Franklin had not gotten the point, Whitefield circled back at the end of a long letter, saying that he would pray for God to show Franklin how "to promote the best end; I mean, the glory of GOD, and the welfare of your fellow-creatures." Unsurprisingly, the preacher also suggested that each student practice oratory for a couple of hours each day.[34]

For academy president, Franklin attempted to recruit prominent Connecticut Anglican minister and educator Samuel Johnson. He was one of the "Yale apostates," Congregationalist teachers and ministers at the college who had converted to Anglicanism in 1722. Young Franklin, writing as Silence Dogood, had once denigrated these apostates' misguided zeal. Johnson had served as the lead tutor at Yale, a fledgling institution founded in 1701. After returning to Connecticut as an Anglican missionary, he continued to shape Yale students with a moral philosophy textbook he developed in collaboration with the school's rector. He was also conversant with the new scientific learning that had so influenced Franklin. For Johnson, discovering the work of the great English scientist Francis Bacon, as well as that of Locke and Newton, was like "emerging out of the glimmer of twilight into the full sunshine of open day." The University of Oxford awarded Johnson an honorary doctor of divinity degree in 1743. His broadmindedness, Anglican credentials, New England Congregationalist background, and prominence in American and English letters made him an ideal candidate to lead the academy.[35]

But Franklin could not convince Johnson. Some reasons for his reluctance were mundane. For instance, the sickly Johnson had never had smallpox and worried about catching it in Philadelphia. He was unwilling to try inoculation. Franklin tried to assuage some of his fears about the city by advising Johnson in the use of medicinal bark (quinine) as a way to keep a nagging "fever and ague" at bay. He suggested mixing the ground bark with a teacup of milk, a concoction that Franklin said tasted like chocolate. "An ounce of prevention is worth a pound of cure," Franklin told Johnson. Johnson was also concerned that his presence could divide Philadelphia Anglicans, because he would likely want to form a new Anglican congregation as part of his duties in the city.[36]

Despite these concerns, Franklin and Johnson exchanged letters about the curriculum for the academy, with Johnson making practical suggestions that Franklin integrated into his "Idea of the English School." That essay sketched what the individual classes at the academy would study. Aside from reading Milton, Tillotson, and Johnson's own work on moral philosophy, however, Franklin's "Idea" seemed to confirm that overtly Christian content in the curriculum was vanishingly slim.[37]

Over the course of 1751, Johnson's view of the school's presidency soured. Apparently Johnson shared some of Whitefield's concerns that the school's curriculum was not Christian enough. At the end of the year, Franklin wrote a letter apologizing for the lack of Christian content in the "Idea of the English School." It was an unfortunate "omission," he said. "The sacred classics are read in the English school, though I forgot to mention them." Franklin assured Johnson that he would have the English master read scripture or from Christian classics daily, in addition to saying prayers. But it was not enough. A few weeks later Johnson wrote to Franklin, declining the appointment due to poor health. A year later, however, Johnson did accept the presidency at the (more firmly Anglican) King's College in New York City, the forerunner to Columbia University. Over the next couple of years, Franklin's plans switched from focusing on the academy to developing a college. The newly minted Anglican minister William Smith was chosen as provost of the institution, which received a revamped charter in 1755. (Smith would eventually edge Franklin out of the school's governance and take it in a more denominationally Anglican direction.) The school became the "College, Academy and Charitable Schools of Philadelphia," the precursor to the University of Pennsylvania.[38]

Having devoted his fertile mind to so many improving projects, Franklin began to attract suitors to obtain his strategic assistance. Dr. Thomas Bond came to him in 1751 with the idea of a charity hospital. Bond had heard that "there was no such thing as carrying a public spirited project through, without my being concerned in it," Franklin recalled. Franklin loved Bond's idea. A charity hospital represented the epitome of Christian benevolence in Franklin's view. Not only would it assist "poor sick persons" individually, but the city would benefit by establishing a public health option for the indigent. This would help contain the effects of disease and enable those treated to remain productive.[39]

Franklin's "Appeal for the Hospital" was one of the most overtly Christian essays he ever wrote. Serving the "least of these" was the best way to honor God, he said. The piece was headed by Christ's commendation in Matthew 25:36, "I was sick and ye visited me." Noting several examples from the Gospels, Franklin showed that caring for those who were ill was a preeminent Christian obligation. He focused on Jesus's discourse in Matthew 25, always a difficult passage for Christians who believed in salvation by faith alone. In that chapter, Christ anticipated the future division of the sheep from the goats. The sheep (the saved) are distinguished by their works of charity, including their care for the sick. Taking care of suffering people was "essential to the true spirit of Christianity," Franklin contended, "and should be extended to all in general, whether deserving or undeserving." Visiting those who are ill, Franklin noted, "is one of the terms of admission into bliss, and the contrary, a cause of exclusion." (Reformed commentators would argue that good works do mark true believers but that Christians are not saved by them.) Franklin was taking a risk by including this comment about the "terms of admission" into heaven. But it reflected his belief in charity as a condition of being welcomed into God's sheepfold. As Poor Richard commented in 1757, godliness surpassed all earthly goods, for "our good or bad works shall remain forever, recorded in the archives of eternity."[40]

Drawing on lessons learned from Cotton Mather and Daniel Defoe, Franklin insisted that individual charity for the sick was not enough. Collective Christian action was more effective. So he proposed funding the Philadelphia hospital by subscription. Franklin noted with satisfaction that all developed Christian societies had invested in hospitals. He claimed that pagans had never built them. This was an instance where "natural reason" was not sufficient to activate charity. "Christian doctrine," he wrote, "hath a real effect on the conduct of mankind." If the people of Philadelphia had sincere faith, it would steer them toward concerted benevolent projects. Charity hospitals were popping up in many British towns, Franklin observed, and the Providence of God was so favoring these "pious institutions" that none of them lacked for adequate funding. This was a golden opportunity for Philadelphians to establish the seriousness of their faith, as well as to secure the city's reputation as a leading center of British culture in the empire. Franklin successfully petitioned the Pennsylvania legislature for assistance, and his fundraising campaign garnered widespread support. Functioning in temporary quarters, the city hospital began taking patients in 1752. Bond performed the hospital's first operation, a leg amputation, that same year, and the hospital moved into a permanent building in 1756.[41]

In spite of his victories with the academy and the hospital, even Franklin had limits with regard to raising money. He drew a line, for example, at helping Reverend Gilbert Tennent procure funds for a new Presbyterian church building. Many of Tennent's followers had converted under Whitefield's preaching, but Whitefield's New Building had become less convenient for the congregation once the academy started meeting there. Tennent asked Franklin for help, but Franklin said that he feared making himself "disagreeable to my fellow citizens, by too frequently soliciting their contributions." Thus he "absolutely refused" to assist Tennent. Then Tennent asked, would Franklin at least give him the names of the most public-spirited and wealthy Philadelphians? Franklin refused again, saying he did not want to reward their generosity by marking them as targets for other "beggars." Tennent finally asked if he would just give him some fund-raising advice. That Franklin could do. He recommended that the pastor first approach those whom he knew would give. Then go ask the more reluctant, showing them a list of those who had already given. Last, ask even those who Tennent thought would probably not give, lest he be mistaken about their inclinations. Tennent promised to take his advice, and he "did so, for he asked of *everybody*," Franklin recalled. Tennent succeeded and raised sufficient funds to construct the city's Arch Street Church in 1752. Although he did give to causes such as funding a new steeple for Christ Church, social experiments in Christian charity inspired Franklin more than building churches did.[42]

Franklin did not support Christ Church's steeple merely to enhance the church's visibility. It would make the church one of the highest structures in the city—and a promising site for more electrical experiments. In spite of distractions, Franklin continued to conduct new electrical tests, and his supporters popularized them. Former Baptist pastor Ebenezer Kinnersley traversed the colonies promoting Franklin's discoveries. Kinnersley's demonstrations were "pleasing to all sorts of people," reported one correspondent who had seen them at Boston's Faneuil Hall in 1751. Franklin had drafted lectures for Kinnersley to use in his travels. In them he posited that storm clouds contained electrical charges, notwithstanding their heavy loads of water. Even though electricity was a fire, he theorized, it was a different kind of fire, one that could coexist with water. Franklin began to develop the concept of a lightning rod, which could protect structures from fire by drawing off the electrical charge from lightning. By 1750, Franklin had started tinkering with miniature "thunder houses" that would demonstrate how lightning rods worked. Applying a shock to the house would ignite gunpowder inside, blowing it up. But when Franklin inserted a grounded lightning rod, the electrified house remained intact. These little houses appeared in Kinnersley's displays by 1751. Customers paid seven shillings and six pence to hear these lectures, which gave participants "exalted ideas of the AUTHOR of Nature."[43]

In the summer of 1752, Franklin decided to test his theory about the equivalence of electricity and lightning. He had thought of getting closer to clouds by standing in a steeple like that of

Christ Church. But instead he decided to fly a kite up into the clouds. One stormy day, Franklin and his son went into action, sending their kite into the heavens. When the kite drew near a dark cloud, the kite string became electrified. Franklin found that when he put his knuckle close to a key that he had attached to the string, he drew off a spark. He did this repeatedly, so that the "Electrical Fire" streamed "plentifully from the key on the approach of your knuckle." It was a stunning confirmation of his theory.[44]

The experiment was reckless, as well. As the fame of the kite experiment spread around the world, a German scientist named Georg Richmann, residing in Russia, attempted to reenact Franklin's kite test a year later. Richmann was struck by lightning and electrocuted. Franklin's friend and publicist, the Unitarian minister Joseph Priestley, idealized the unfortunate German as a martyr for science and learning. "It is not given to every electrician to die in so glorious a manner as the justly envied Richmann," Priestley wrote.[45]

With his electrical triumphs, Franklin started to become a full-blown international celebrity. Word of his discoveries spread with his *Experiments and Observations on Electricity* (1751), which went through five English editions in twenty-three years. It would come out in eleven languages, including Latin, in Europe before the Revolutionary War. In contrast to the domestic popularity of "Father Abraham's Speech," Franklin's electrical writings found no American publisher until the nineteenth century. Not that he was ignored in America: in a delicious moment for the former servant, Harvard and Yale granted him honorary master's degrees in 1752. The University of St. Andrews, Scotland's oldest university, likewise awarded him an honorary doctorate in 1759, after which he was widely known as "Dr. Franklin." But his greatest scientific honor came in 1753, when London's Royal Society gave him the Copley Medal, their highest award. It was the first time that someone outside of the United Kingdom had won it.[46]

In spite of Franklin's renown, there were still whispers about the propriety of harnessing lightning. Lightning strikes were, after all, one of the most obvious ways in which God seemed to inter-

vene in the natural order. With lightning, God could catch people's
attention, burn buildings, and sometimes strike people dead, as
with Georg Richmann. Lightning struck Presbyterian pastor
Gilbert Tennent in 1745, but he survived to give a whole sermon
on the episode. Saints and sinners alike stood exposed to this "awful artillery of heaven," he reminded his audience. Those who casually indulged sin and ignored God's offer of salvation courted
disaster, for their demise could come at any moment. Although
some wags wondered what sin Tennent had committed to deserve
the near-fatal bolt, he attributed the strike to God's sovereign rule
over his life, not divine retribution.[47]

Still, most colonists assumed that God sent lightning strikes
for a purpose. What did it mean if rods began drawing off the
lightning and mitigating its effects? Was this an affront to God's
power? The issue drew comments from Reverend Thomas
Prince of Boston's Old South Church, an ardent supporter of
Whitefield and frequent commentator on natural philosophy
and the Providence of God. As part of a discourse reflecting on a
1755 earthquake that shook New England, Prince spoke of the
"sagacious Mr. Franklin, born and brought up in Boston, but now
living in Philadelphia," who had "greatly surprised and obliged
the world with his discoveries of the electrical substance." For
Prince, the new learning about electricity spoke to the agency of
God behind all of nature. But there was "no getting out of the
mighty hand of God!" he warned. Thus Prince wondered if the
use of lightning rods might backfire by supercharging the earth,
making it more susceptible to earthquakes. Boston had more lightning rods than any place in New England. Was it any coincidence
that "Boston seems to be more dreadfully shaken"? If you take
electricity out of the air, then God might bring judgment out
of the earth. No temporal safety could substitute for eternal security in Christ.[48]

John Winthrop, the great-great grandson of Massachusetts's
founder and the Hollis Professor of Natural Philosophy at
Harvard, scoffed at both Prince's providential view of nature
and his theory about the electrical roots of earthquakes. The
"ingenious Mr. Franklin" had indeed accounted for the electrical
substance of lightning. But that was no justification for seeing

electricity behind earthquakes, or acting as if electricity "does everything." Prince supposed that each lightning strike happened by divine intervention. But "to have recourse to miraculous interpositions of the 'Divine Direction,'" Winthrop warned, "is to put an entire end at once to all reasonings about electricity, or earthquakes, or any other natural phenomena." Lightning strikes and earthquakes were part of God's natural order, not miracles.[49]

Twenty-year-old John Adams, who would become Franklin's longtime diplomatic colleague, thought that Winthrop had gotten the best of Prince. Adams wrote in the margin of his copy of Winthrop's lecture that Prince and his ilk considered thunder, lightning, and earthquakes "only as judgments and warnings, and have no conception of any uses they can have in nature." Suspicion of the lightning rod came from "superstitions, affectations of piety, and jealousy of new inventions," Adams concluded. A meeting of the Junto in 1760 (Franklin was in London at the time) agreed. While the superstitious and ignorant might regard thunder as the voice of God, and lightning strikes as "bolts launched from his right hand," reasonable people saw these phenomena as elements of nature, subject to study and greater understanding. It was not presumptuous to use lightning rods, the Junto determined. It was foolish not to use them.[50]

Franklin, like many colonists, wondered about America's place in the empire in the mid-eighteenth century. In light of the threats of the 1740s, could Britain or the colonies keep Americans safe from the French and Spanish? These concerns were common. But Franklin cultivated a special concern that America should not be left behind in the burgeoning European conversations on scientific learning, or in the transatlantic progress of Christian benevolence. With daring and ingenuity, he helped America take a place at the scientific table, bolstered by his conviction that science stood at the cusp of great new understandings of God's natural world. Scientists should pursue that understanding, no matter where it led, he believed. No less a philosopher than the German Immanuel Kant expressed awe that Franklin had become the "Prometheus der neuern Zeiten," the Prometheus of a new age. Kant already saw the new vistas of learning held within Franklin's discoveries. To European observers, this former indentured servant, the child of Boston Puritans, had become the eighteenth-century Prometheus. Franklin was stealing fire from heaven, and presenting it as a gift to humanity.[51]

CHAPTER EIGHT

Diplomat

FRANKLIN'S INTERNAL TUG-OF-WAR BETWEEN skepticism and traditional faith persisted through the middle years of the eighteenth century. Although Franklin said little about the naturalistic implications of his scientific discoveries, he realized they were there. The more scientists knew about the workings of lightning and electricity, the less mysterious those phenomena appeared. The more one could control lightning's fury, the less vulnerable the world seemed before God's wrath. Once when Franklin was discussing sun spots with his collaborator Cadwallader Colden, he commented that it was good that they did not live during the Catholic Inquisition. If they had, they might have suffered the fate of scientific pathbreakers such as Galileo. (Galileo's 1613 *Sunspot Letters* prompted the Roman Inquisition to demand that he stop teaching heliocentrism.) Franklin mused that his own "whispers against the orthodox doctrine in private letters, would be dangerous." Whatever criticism they received in America, Colden and Franklin were in it together. "One heretic will surely excuse another," Franklin assured his friend.[1]

Although Franklin no longer flaunted his "heretical" views, traditional Christians still worried about his faith, or lack thereof. Joseph Huey, the "zealous religionist" whom Franklin supposedly healed of paralysis by electrical treatments, exhorted Franklin to turn to Christ. Franklin replied by insisting that his faith showed itself in works (such as his scientific experiments), and that Jesus preferred doing of the Word over "outward appearances." Likewise, the great evangelist George Whitefield admonished Franklin about the perils of fame and Franklin's need for Christ. "I find you grow more famous in the learned world," Whitefield wrote. He knew a lot about celebrity's temptations. Fighting those temptations by moral discipline was not enough, the preacher warned. Franklin needed to be born again.[2]

Poking fun at Franklin's scientific achievements, Whitefield said in 1752 that as Franklin had "made a pretty considerable progress in the mysteries of electricity, I would now humbly recommend to your diligent unprejudiced pursuit and study the mystery of the new-birth." Citing the Gospel of John, Whitefield warned Franklin that without the new birth, no one would see the kingdom of heaven. He asked his friend to forgive him for his boldness: "I must have *aliquid Christi* in all my letters." Franklin had become used to these sorts of overtures from the evangelist, and from family members, especially his sister Jane.[3]

Whitefield kept at it as the years rolled by. By 1755, Whitefield had seen a copy of Franklin's epitaph, and the preacher could not resist commenting on it. "Believe on Jesus, and get a feeling possession of God in your heart," he told Franklin, "and you cannot possibly be disappointed of your expected second edition." Whitefield worried that Franklin might gain all earthly wisdom but neglect God. Franklin equivocally told Whitefield in 1764 that he was sure that he would enjoy as much eternal happiness "as is proper for me." Franklin believed that God loved him. How could he doubt that God would continue to care for him in the present life, and in the next? Franklin communicated almost identical sentiments to a more skeptical friend, William Strahan, a leading British printer, a week later. God would continue to show Strahan the same care in the future as he had in the past, Franklin said. Faith in God's provision "might not be necessary," Franklin admitted. "But as matters are, it may be of use."[4]

As Whitefield suggested, Franklin's celebrity was continuing to crest. In 1751, he was elected to the Philadelphia Assembly.

Although Franklin had previously served as clerk of the assembly, and had taken on public projects such as the Pennsylvania militia, this was his first formal role as a politician. He hoped it would open new opportunities for "doing good."[5]

Franklin would find his political calling not as a legislator, however, but as a diplomat. In 1753, he represented Pennsylvania at a conference with Indians meeting at Carlisle, Pennsylvania. These Native Americans wished to receive more tangible support from Pennsylvania, in light of the growing French presence in the Ohio River Valley. Among those accompanying Franklin was his sometime rival, the Anglican leader Richard Peters. Hamstrung by Quaker officials' pacifism, Peters explained to the Indian delegates that all the Pennsylvanians could offer the Indians were diplomatic gifts.[6]

Like many Anglo colonists, Franklin found Indians exotic and menacing. Anglo and Indian leaders both knew that the rum trade was devastating to Native American people. Pennsylvania delegates at Carlisle (as Franklin told the story) insisted that the Indians not drink until the conference was over. They complied, but once the diplomatic formalities were over, the imbibing began. This precipitated a disturbing episode that elicited one of Franklin's longest reflections on Native Americans:

> In the evening, hearing a great noise among them, the commissioners walked out to see what was the matter. We found they had made a great bonfire in the middle of the square. They were all drunk men and women, quarrelling and fighting. Their dark-colored bodies, half naked, seen only by the gloomy light of the bonfire, running after and beating one another with firebrands, accompanied by their horrid yellings, formed a scene the most resembling our ideas of hell that could well be imagined.

Franklin and his compatriots went to bed, but some Indians banged on their door at midnight, demanding more alcohol. The delegates made it safely through the night, and in the morning the Indian diplomats came to apologize. One "Orator acknowledged the fault, but laid it upon the rum; and then endeavored to excuse the rum, by saying, 'The great Spirit who made all things made everything for some use, and whatever use he designed anything for, that use it should always be put to; Now, when he made rum, he said, let this be for Indians to get drunk with. And it must be so.' " Franklin wondered what the abuse of alcohol might portend for Native Americans as a people. "If it be the design of Providence to extirpate these savages in order to make room for cultivators of the earth," he wrote, "it seems not improbable that rum may be the appointed means."[7]

Franklin's pessimism regarding Indians reflected familiar views of race and ethnicity among Britons, who assumed the superiority of "white" people. Those views were common among prominent philosophers. David Hume had already registered his opinion in 1742 that "negroes and in general all the other species of men (for there are four or five different kinds) to be naturally inferior to the whites." Hume, Franklin, and others speculated about the qualities of the separate human "species," and commented on why they thought Britons stood among the most intelligent and industrious.[8]

Such views also influenced Franklin's attitudes toward slavery and African Americans. Like many of America's founders, Franklin owned slaves but professed reservations about the institution of slavery. Franklin's emerging antipathy was based on the ill effects of slavery and slaves on white culture. America would thrive only if Anglo settlers spread across its abundant lands, he believed. He made the case for America's future in *Observations Concerning the Increase of Mankind*, written in 1751 and published in 1755. In words he omitted from later editions, he emphasized how America needed to foster its white population, at the expense of all the "black, tawny, or swarthy" peoples of the world, whether from Africa, Asia, or eastern or southern Europe. Even Germans (except for "Saxons") represented degeneracy. "Why should the Palatine Boors be suffered to swarm into our settlements, and by herding together establish their language and manners to the exclusion of ours?" These "aliens" were as likely to adopt English customs as they were to change their swarthy complexions, Franklin warned.[9]

He did not stop there. Because the "number of purely white people in the world" was tiny, America urgently needed a growing British and Saxon population. As Thomas Jefferson would do in his

Notes on the State of Virginia (1785), Franklin commented that the "red" people were actually healthful and desirable. As Americans moved into the frontier, "clearing America of woods, and so making this side of our globe reflect a brighter light to the eyes of inhabitants in Mars or Venus, why should we in the sight of superior beings, darken its people?" Franklin asked. "Why increase the Sons of Africa, by planting them in America, where we have so fair an opportunity, by excluding all blacks and tawneys, of increasing the lovely white and red?" This was blunt racialist talk, even for the 1750s. Thus Franklin concluded with a self-deprecating note, "Perhaps I am partial to the complexion of my country, for such kind of partiality is natural to mankind." In an era when many Britons earned enormous profits from slave plantations, Franklin envisioned the American future as led by millions of free, industrious whites. If they could intermarry with whites and live at peace, the "red" people could also fit into that destiny.[10]

To secure the growing American frontier, Franklin hoped that the burgeoning colonies would unite to act against common threats from Catholic powers. The most obvious danger was French aggression in the Ohio River Valley region. Franklin's hope for intercolonial union against the French was illustrated by his best-known cartoon, "Join, or Die," printed in May 1754 in the *Pennsylvania Gazette*. If the colonies did not unite, the *Gazette* warned, the French and their Indian allies would "murder and scalp our farmers, with their wives and children, and take an easy possession of such parts of the British territory as they find most convenient for them."[11]

His quest for British colonial unity inspired Franklin's ill-fated Plan of Union, which he presented at a 1754 conference in Albany, New York. The Virginia colony had recently sent a military force led by young George Washington into western Pennsylvania. They hoped to make the French back off their new settlements. But other British colonies were not interested in assisting Virginia. Thus Washington suffered a humiliating defeat at Fort Necessity on July 4, 1754, while the Albany Congress was meeting. The French were emboldened because of the colonists' "disunited state," Franklin wrote. He proposed forming an intercolonial government, working under British authority. This government would

"*Join, or Die,*" Pennsylvania Gazette, *May 9, 1754. Courtesy Library of Congress.*

have a president-general appointed by the king and a grand council of representatives from the colonies. As far-sighted as the proposal was, leaders in the colonies and in London were unenthusiastic. Colonial officials worried about giving up autonomy, while London thought the union might set the stage for American resistance against imperial policy. Some even posited that the continental union could encourage independence. Most Americans at the time, including Franklin, would have regarded that notion as ridiculous. How could British America ever survive on its own?[12]

A year later, in 1755, the frontier situation became more grim. The British commissioned a major expedition into western Pennsylvania, led by General Edward Braddock. Franklin tried to warn the general about the "ambuscades of Indians," but he scoffed, saying that while the "savages" might give the colonists difficulty, they could do nothing against disciplined British troops. He was wrong. Although Franklin worked to supply Braddock's army for the excursion, a French and Indian force decimated Braddock's army in July 1755. Braddock himself took a bullet to a lung and perished. Two-thirds of Braddock's 1,500 men died or were captured.[13]

Franklin's associate James Read, a relative of Deborah Franklin, lamented Braddock's "shameful defeat." He told Ben that he hoped the legislature would do something to provide for the defense of frontier settlers. Braddock and his officers were cocky and dismissive of the Indians and the French, Read believed, and the British Army was "full of reprobates, who never had any serious thought of what they were about." Quoting the prophet Isaiah, Read surmised that the British troops were "mighty to drink wine, men of strength to mingle strong drink." In other words, they were foolish drunks. Now all Pennsylvania had "an open enemy on our borders, and a popish intestine enemy spread through all the land."[14]

How deeply Franklin himself shared these kinds of anti-Catholic sensibilities was not always clear. He had worked to counter the Catholic French and Spanish threats against the British colonies, in episodes from raising the Pennsylvania militia to supporting Braddock's mission. Moreover, the summer of 1755 saw Franklin and other officials of the new College of Philadelphia swearing an oath of fidelity to King George II and repudiating Catholic power and beliefs. For the new college to expect imperial support, it had to show its loyalty to British power, especially in light of the burgeoning Seven Years' War, which Washington's expedition had started. The college leaders' oath repudiated the pope and the Stuart Pretender to the British throne. The most distinctive theological statement the college leaders made was a denial of transubstantiation, the idea that during the Lord's Supper, the bread and wine became the literal body and blood of Christ. Franklin, Richard Peters, provost William Smith, and the rest agreed to these staples of British Protestant belief, they said, "willingly and truly, upon the true faith of a Christian."[15]

Likewise, Franklin advocated religious toleration, at least for Protestants. But what about for Catholics? Franklin would have assumed that authorities could not tolerate adherents of an opposing religion who wished to harm people and overthrow the government. Certainly, the political and military might of European Catholicism represented that kind of religious threat. But sometimes Franklin suggested a broader scope for religious liberty. Around the same time as the outbreak of the Seven Years' War and the founding of the College of Philadelphia, Franklin composed a mock-scriptural piece, the "Parable against Persecution." These verses about an incident in the life of Hebrew patriarch Abraham purported to be from the book of Genesis. Anyone of Whitefield's Bible-reading habits would have realized this story was not scriptural. But over the decades Franklin liked to recite the parable and tell guests that it was from Genesis, to see if they would recognize the joke. The oft-printed and translated piece became one of Franklin's most popular writings on religion.[16]

In the story, Abraham welcomes a stranger into his tent. When they eat bread together, the man does not bless Abraham's God. He tells Abraham that he has his own god, "which abideth away in mine house, and provideth me with all things." Abraham, enraged at this insolence, beats the man and drives him into the wilderness. God appears that night to Abraham, asking where the stranger had gone. Abraham tells God what he had done but God does not approve. God had been willing to nourish and clothe this pagan for years, in spite of his idolatry. But Abraham (a sinner himself) would not provide one night's hospitality. Abraham realizes his error, prays for forgiveness, brings the man back to his tent, and treats him with kindness.[17]

The "Parable against Persecution" exemplified Franklin's playful skepticism about scripture and religious intolerance. It was not his only attempt at such pseudo-biblical writing. Another was "A Parable on Brotherly Love," a tale about Jacob's sons that borrowed phrases from a number of Old Testament books. Eighteenth-century authors commonly wrote histories in a pseudo-biblical style. It was even more common for Anglo-Americans to speak and write in biblical idioms. (President Lincoln's "four score and seven years ago" in the Gettysburg Address illustrates the persistence of this way of speaking.) Few writers made up pieces that they passed off as authentic scripture, though. Doing so might have seemed irreverent. Could Franklin not have found a story within the Bible that would have made his point about generosity toward strangers? The Good Samaritan, perhaps? In any case, Franklin's parable offered a pseudo-biblical example of toleration, plus it could supply a hearthside joke at a moment's notice. This was all to Franklin's liking.[18]

Franklin's lifelong quest for virtuous discipline took a detour in 1755. As he approached his fiftieth year, he made the acquaintance of the twenty-three-year-old Catherine Ray of Rhode Island and began a sometimes steamy correspondence with her. Ray was the first of a series of younger women with whom Franklin carried on affectionate relationships, which may have occasionally turned amorous. Franklin had regretted his youthful "errata" of seducing James Ralph's girlfriend in London. Now he was an international celebrity, one who knew he could impress young women like Ray. Franklin hinted that Ray rebuffed his physical overtures at least once. He reported to Ray in March 1755 that he had returned to Philadelphia to the "arms of my good old wife and children." Still, his thoughts that winter turned to "Katy." Some, he reflected, "complain of the northeast wind as increasing their malady. But since you promised to send me kisses in that wind, and I find you as good as your word, 'tis to me the gayest wind that blows, and gives me the best spirits. . . . Your favors come mixed with the snowy fleeces which are pure as your virgin innocence, white as your lovely bosom,—and as cold."[19]

In spite of her chilly bosom, Franklin kept writing to Katy. He told her about the status of his relationship with Deborah, especially as it related to Ray. Deborah, he reported, "talks of bequeathing me to you as a legacy." But Franklin thought Ray could do better than him, and he said that he was satisfied with Deborah. If Deborah had any faults, he told Ray, he had been with her for so long he no longer noticed them. (Ever since he had retired from printing, Deborah's and Ben's relationship seems to have grown more distant, in any case.) Moreover, "since she is willing I should love you as much as you are willing to be loved by me; let us join in wishing the old lady a long life." In the same letter, he spoke of how he still relished "all the pleasures of life" and that he had all of them "in my power." That "happy situation" would "continue as long as God pleases."[20]

In one of the most peculiar letters in Ray's and Franklin's correspondence, he offered her some "fatherly advice." She should consecrate herself for her future marriage, he told her. "Be a good girl, and don't forget your catechism. Go constantly to meeting—or church—till you get a good husband; then stay at home, and nurse the children, and live like a Christian." This advice may have been sarcastic, as the rest of the letter was filled with flirty puns. But perhaps he was serious. Recall that he once gave similar advice to Jane Mecom about becoming a "good housewife." Likewise, he told Deborah that he hoped his thirteen-year-old daughter Sally "continues to love going to church." Franklin wanted Sally to read the Anglican spiritual classic *The Whole Duty of Man*, a treatise on Christian obedience. (Some evangelicals loved *The Whole Duty of Man*, but George Whitefield had denounced it as promoting works-righteousness.) Franklin also enjoined Sally to observe the rituals of the Book of Common Prayer, preferring the traditional wisdom of the Anglican liturgy over contemporary sermons. But she should not neglect sermons, either, even from preachers she did not like. "The discourse is often much better than the man," he told Sally, "as sweet and clear waters come to us through very dirty earth."[21]

Whatever Franklin meant to convey in his letters to Katy Ray, he told her that as a wife, she would need to master addition (industry and frugality), subtraction (of unnecessary expenses), and multiplication (having children). Regarding the third trait, Franklin said that he would have "gladly taught you that myself, but you thought it was [not?] time enough, and wouldn't learn." Conceding that she would marry another man, he hoped that when they met again he would find her fruitful like a grapevine, "surrounded with clusters, plump, juicy, blushing, pretty little rogues, like their Mama."[22]

Was Ben's and Katy's relationship a full-blown affair? We do not know. At a minimum it was, as historians of Franklin's private life put it, "a romance in the Franklinian manner, somewhat risqué, somewhat avuncular," and probably "a little beyond the platonic but short of the grand passion." However sexually aggressive Franklin became, the doctor derived great pleasure from flirting with young women like Ray. How he reconciled this with his program of moral discipline, he did not explain.[23]

Public affairs distracted Franklin from writing to Ray as much as he wanted. He found composing letters to her a welcome break.

"Begone, business, for an hour," he wrote, "and let me chat a little with my Katy." But the Seven Years' War kept pressing in. During it, Franklin resumed his role as one of Pennsylvania's chief military organizers. In early 1756, he received an appointment as the supervisor of the colony's frontier defenses. He oversaw the erection of several forts. A "zealous Presbyterian minister" named Charles Beatty accompanied the construction crew, and Beatty led prayers both morning and evening. When he complained about the men's lack of devotion, Franklin proposed a tactic to get the men to attend the services. Franklin observed that the men were never late to receive their daily ration of rum. Thus he suggested that Beatty distribute the rum, but only after saying prayers. Beatty agreed to the plan, and "never were prayers more generally and more punctually attended." Franklin regarded this as a better system than punishing the men for absences. Prayer services did the soldiers good, Franklin figured. Sometimes they could be "quarrelsome" and even "mutinous," and prayer reminded the men of their sacred duties.[24]

Franklin envisioned a brighter future for the western frontier. Writing to George Whitefield, Franklin suggested that the two of them might even found a colony together in the Ohio River Valley. "What a glorious thing it would be, to settle in that fine country a large strong body of religious and industrious people," Franklin reflected. "What a security to the other colonies; and advantage to Britain, by increasing her people, territory, strength and commerce. Might it not greatly facilitate the introduction of pure religion among the heathen, if we could, by such a colony, show them a better sample of Christians than they commonly see in our Indian traders, the most vicious and abandoned wretches of our nation?" The colony would help protect the eastern British colonies and open new opportunities for the flourishing of "pure religion" among Indians and Anglos.[25]

Why would Franklin be thinking of such a colony in 1756? Turning fifty had turned his thoughts to his remaining years. "Life, like a dramatic piece, should not only be conducted with regularity, but methinks it should finish handsomely," he told Whitefield. "Being now in the last act, I begin to cast about for something fit to end with. . . . In such an enterprise I could spend the remainder of life with pleasure; and I firmly believe God would bless us with success, if we undertook it with a sincere regard to his honor, the service of our gracious king, and (which is the same thing) the public good." Franklin and Whitefield still did not agree on the nature of true religion, but Franklin believed they had much common ground on the matter of public service.[26]

They also agreed on the primacy of British Protestant power. The immediate occasion for Franklin's letter about the colony was his publication of Whitefield's popular sermon *A Short Address to Persons of All Denominations*. Whitefield had delivered this sermon in England in response to fears of a French invasion. The minister connected that threat to the ongoing turmoil on the American frontier. He recommended that British readers attend to the "shocking accounts of the horrid butcheries, and cruel murders committed on the bodies of many of our fellow-subjects in America, by the hands of savage Indians, instigated thereto by more than savage Popish priests." Britons could expect the same treatment if the French conquered them. Confronting threats to British Protestant supremacy drew Franklin and Whitefield even closer together.[27]

Squabbling between Pennsylvania's proprietors and its legislature precipitated the pivotal transition of Franklin's career. The assembly chose Franklin to serve as an emissary to London to negotiate on their behalf. So Franklin, his son William, and two slaves named Peter and King set out in 1757; Deborah and Sally stayed behind in Philadelphia. King would soon run away from Franklin. He found work in a home where the lady of the house was, as Franklin put it, "fond of the merit of making him a Christian." Franklin reluctantly let King stay there. Perhaps part of the reason he did so was that in these same years, Franklin became involved with Dr. Bray's Associates, an Anglican philanthropic agency that sought to establish schools for "negroes" in the colonies. His doubts about doctrine notwithstanding, Franklin supported "making sincere good Christians" out of African American students. In the early 1760s, Franklin visited the associates' Philadelphia school and was impressed. It gave him a "higher opinion of the natural capacities of the black race."[28]

On its way to London, Franklin's ship dodged French priva-teers, landing in Falmouth, England, in July 1757. A well-placed lighthouse had guided them along the coast at a critical moment, which delighted Franklin. What an example of technology serving the public good! When they came to Falmouth, the passengers on Franklin's ship went to church as soon as bells rang for the next service. "With hearts full of gratitude," Franklin wrote, the ship-mates "returned sincere thanks to God for the mercies we had re-ceived." He mused that if he were a Catholic, he might vow to build a chapel to a patron saint. "But as I am not," he wrote, "if I were to vow at all, it should be to build a lighthouse."[29]

London intoxicated Franklin, even more than it had three de-cades earlier. Many Britons feted him as a hero of science. He met leading experimenters and politicians whom he had admired from across the sea. Receiving equally warm treatment in Scotland in 1759, he conversed with Adam Smith and David Hume, and re-ceived his honorary doctorate at St. Andrews. The business that brought him to London did not go so well, however. John Fothergill, one of Franklin's allies, wrote in 1758 that Franklin's "obstructions are next to insurmountable: Great pains have been taken, and very successfully to render him odious" to the propri-etors. Franklin got so frustrated that he advocated putting Pennsylvania under direct royal governance. This would relieve the colony of the Penn family's negligence. Franklin, and most col-onists during the Seven Years' War, saw major advantages to British power in America. As Franklin put it in 1760, he was not an American colonist alone, but a "Briton" from America. Franklin also derived benefits from his royal connections. They helped him secure the governorship of New Jersey for his son William in 1762. Franklin was still hoping that Pennsylvania and all the American colonies could be organized under a uniform, constitutional mon-archy, but with relatively independent legislatures.[30]

In the midst of his long tenure in London, Franklin wrote less on religion than he had in his Philadelphia years as a printer. But he kept writing to his sister Jane Mecom. She remained his closest sib-ling and longest-standing interlocutor on matters of faith. In England, he had done some genealogical digging and discovered some Franklin relatives, including a cousin named Jane. Their uncle

Benjamin had once composed a religious acrostic on cousin Jane Franklin's name, which Ben transcribed and sent to Jane Mecom in an extraordinary letter of September 16, 1758. He used the acrostic to comment on the value of charity over faith. Uncle Benjamin had exhorted their cousin to "raise faith and hope three stories higher," which Ben took as a reference to I Corinthians 13's great trio of "faith, hope, and charity." Ben regarded charity as the greatest of these three virtues, and exhorted Jane not to linger in the bottom two floors of faith and hope. "For my part," he teased, "I wish the house was turned upside down, 'tis so difficult (when one is fat) to get up stairs." (Portraits from the time showed Franklin's growing girth.) Hope and faith were built on charity. Good works were the foundation of authentic piety, in Franklin's estimation.[31]

For an internationally known scientist and diplomat, Franklin took a remarkable amount of time to exegete this religious acrostic. Raising faith and hope "three stories higher" represented a temptation to vanity, he continued. At those heights a person was more exposed to the storms of life. The foundation of the house of faith might not sustain the higher levels, either, if "you build with such light stuff as straw and stubble." Referencing I Corinthians 3, he reminded Jane that a flammable foundation would not withstand a divine trial by fire. Biblical passages like these gave Jane and Ben a common vocabulary with which to talk about the balance between faith and good works.[32]

Franklin then turned to another of Uncle Benjamin's exhortations, to express "kindness of heart by words." That sentiment did not sit well with Franklin. "Strike out words and put in deeds," he told Jane. "The world is too full of compliments already," Franklin insisted. "They are the rank growth of every soil, and choke the good plants of benevolence and beneficence." Echoing the disappointment he had experienced under the preaching of Presbyterian Jedidiah Andrews, Franklin argued that too many people valued "good words" over "good deeds." That is, they prized "seemingly pious discourses instead of humane benevolent actions." Turning his sights on the Calvinist scruples of his upbringing, he lamented how many Christians disparaged good works, "calling morality *rotten morality*, righteousness *ragged righteousness*, and even *filthy rags*." When you even mentioned the word "virtue" to Calvinist precisionists, he lamented, "they pucker up their noses as if they smelt a stink." If they hear "an empty canting harangue" on theological technicalities, however, they breathe it in as a fragrant aroma.[33]

Franklin summed up his concern to Mecom with the proverb "A man full of words and not of deeds, Is like a garden full of weeds." Puritans inverted the proverb, as it were, to say, "A man of deeds and not of words, Is like a garden full of ——." Franklin told Jane that he couldn't think of the last word in the rhyme. " 'Tis something the very reverse of a perfume," he wrote.[34]

Franklin later admitted that this letter was "a little rude," and Jane seems to have taken exception to his characterization of doctrinaire Calvinists. He tried to soothe the hurt. He meant his September 16 letter only as a "reflection on our sect," he explained. "Our sect," he wrote, meaning the sect of the Franklin family, the one against which his spiritual musings reacted. "We zealous Presbyterians," he cautioned her, are "too apt to think ourselves alone in the right."[35]

His parents' brand of Calvinism gave "to Satan in a lump" all non-Christians, as well as Catholics. But Calvinists went further: "Other sects of Christian Protestants that do not agree with us, will hardly escape perdition." He suggested that she try being more charitable with respect to the eternal destiny of other Christians. Certainly he hoped, but did not say, that she would not regard Franklin himself as hell-bound. But Franklin was also thinking of George Whitefield's interdenominational bent, which led him to work with Presbyterians, Baptists, and other kinds of Christians who supported the revivals. (Whitefield often quarreled with Christians who did not agree with his Calvinism, though.) Franklin insisted that he did not mean to upbraid his sister. But then he proceeded to do so again. Her only "fault," he wrote, was that she was too touchy, especially regarding his comments on religion. Franklin knew that this could offend her even more, so he vacillated for two months before finally sending the letter. He added gifts of a cloak and a piece of fine linen in the package, hoping that Jane would not be mad at him.[36]

His ongoing argument with Jane about morality reflected Franklin's continuing quest to craft a doctrineless Christianity of ethics and self-improvement. Shortly after his exchange with Jane,

Franklin informed Henry Home, Lord Kames, one of the leaders of Scotland's Enlightenment, about his planned volume *The Art of Virtue*. Franklin met Kames in 1759, impressing the philosopher with a recitation of the "Parable against Persecution." (Kames published a version of it, which deprived Franklin "of a good deal of amusement" because its new notoriety spoiled his ability to pass it off as being in the Bible.) Lord Kames and other Scottish intellectuals promoted the idea of an innate moral sense. Noble acts intuitively win people's approval, they contended. A person did not necessarily need revelation from God to distinguish right from wrong, even though Kames and most Scottish Enlightenment writers regarded institutional religion as a positive good. Lord Kames's view of morality was rational, practical, and a "branch of duty to our Maker."[37]

Franklin liked this approach to ethics. He thought Kames would resonate with *The Art of Virtue*. Franklin posited that many people were locked into bad habits they wished to change but could not do so because they did not know how. Evangelicals like Whitefield argued that only God's power could change hearts and habits. Franklin admitted that the Christian injunction to put "faith in Christ" worked for some devout believers. But "all men cannot have faith in Christ," he noted. Some had only a weak faith, the kind that precipitated no transformation. To Franklin, the key to moral change was the "art" of virtue. His plan could help those with no faith, faltering faith, or even those with strong faith. Two decades later, however, Franklin and correspondents such as Joseph Priestley were not so sure about the feasibility of a "moral algebra." Hard science had advanced so much (partly through Priestley's and Franklin's experiments), but Franklin wondered if "moral science" had progressed at all. In the midst of the Revolutionary War, he still speculated about methods to help men stop behaving like "wolves to one another." Franklin tried to do his part to ennoble humanity: the plan for virtue would become one of the most beloved parts of his *Autobiography*.[38]

Franklin also established a correspondence with Scotland's David Hume, Lord Kames's protégé and sometime antagonist. Hume was the most notorious figure of the Scottish Enlightenment. He reviled institutional Christianity and the Bible's supposed miracles. Hume saw Franklin as a kindred spirit and called him America's "first great man of letters." They corresponded in 1762, discussing a theological tempest involving Earl Marischal, the governor of Neuchâtel in Prussia. Marischal was a theological liberal who found himself mediating a clerical dispute over the eternity of torments in hell. (This was a common debate in British circles, one in which George Whitefield had advocated for the doctrine of eternal punishment.) Hume saw the dispute as a farce, telling Marischal that he should abridge "these torments as much as possible." Franklin later ironically praised "that excellent Christian David Hume" as "the good Samaritan," because of Hume's hospitality when Franklin visited Edinburgh.[39]

Franklin had learned to hate heresy-hunting from his Puritan upbringing and from his defense of Presbyterian pastor Samuel Hemphill in the 1730s. So, like Hume, he saw the Marischal controversy as "ridiculous." He compared it to a story about a Puritan town where residents were arguing about erecting a festive maypole. (Nathaniel Hawthorne would immortalize this distinctly Puritan fracas in his 1837 story "The May-Pole of Merry Mount.") The impatient mayor told the disputants to leave each other alone: "You that are for having no maypole shall have no maypole; and you that are for having a maypole shall have a maypole." Franklin believed that Marischal should similarly tell the bickering parties in Prussia, "You that are for no more damnation than is proportioned to your offences, have my consent that it may be so: and you that are for being damned eternally, G-d eternally d—n you all."[40]

Franklin's work in London inaugurated another longstanding relationship with a young woman, the engaging Polly Stevenson, the daughter of Franklin's landlady. Polly was eighteen years old when they first met. Their correspondence was flirty, bookish, and replete with religious topics. Little evidence would suggest that their relationship ever became sexual. As with Katy Ray, there were suggestive notes in their letters, such as when Franklin explained the aphrodisiac qualities of Spanish fly, and suggested that Polly's first-born child looked a lot like him. Much of their correspondence concerned science and ethics, though. Stevenson shared Franklin's zeal for scientific understanding. But they agreed that the study of nature should never detract from one's "essential duties." Franklin even admitted that "no rank in natural knowledge"—even a rank as high as the one he had achieved—could match the importance of being a good parent or child, husband or wife, subject or citizen. Honoring these roles was the essence of what it meant to be a devout "Christian." Deborah and Sally might have thought Franklin needed to take his own advice, as they waited at home in Philadelphia. Franklin seemed to relish quasi-spousal relationships with women (especially younger ones) other than Deborah. Deborah occasionally received what Franklin called "idle reports" of his licentious behavior in England. But Franklin promised her that as long as "God vouchsafes me his protection," he would do "nothing unworthy of the character of an honest man."41

Polly Stevenson agreed with Franklin's view of Christianity as essentially a code of ethics. Citing an anti-deist book by dissenting clergyman Humphrey Ditton, she wrote that "those who have multiplied the duties of Christianity have been its most effective enemies." Ditton mistakenly contended that Christianity required more than the "strict discharge of moral obligation," she said. By adding assent to doctrine to ethical duty, Ditton "wrongs his cause." Christian faith, Stevenson wrote, did motivate honest believers to perform its "moral obligation." But God did not expect any more of Christians than fulfillment of those responsibilities. She presumably meant that God did not even require faith in the basic tenets of Christianity. Franklin agreed, and told her that she should just "continue to be a good girl, and thereby lay a solid foundation for expected future happiness."42

Polly and Ben exchanged views on technical points of Bible interpretation, too. One topic was Christ's fasting and temptation by the devil in the wilderness, recorded in the three synoptic Gospels. Polly concurred with Ben's suggestion that Christ's experiences were "visionary," rather than literal. They may have been responding to a contemporary debate on the wilderness account spurred by the dissenting minister Hugh Farmer's 1761 *Inquiry into the Nature and Design of Christ's Temptation in the Wilderness*. (John Adams would later count Farmer and other dissenting clergymen as intellectual companions in London in the 1780s. Adams said that "Unitarianism and biblical criticism were the great characteristics of them all.") Polly said that she had always wondered what to make of the temptation narrative and its claim that the devil showed Jesus "all the kingdoms of the world in a moment of time." In a physical sense, this could not be true. Moreover, how could the devil perform miracles on the Son of God? Why would an omnipotent Jesus allow the devil to carry him to the top of a mountain to see all earthly kingdoms? She conceded that those who knew Greek would be able to interpret the passage better than she could.[43]

Polly told Ben that she had tried to engage a devout friend of theirs in discussion about the wilderness narrative. It did not go well. "Our dear little friend you know is cautious of inquiring into subjects she holds sacred," she wrote. Their friend's piety was sincere, but Polly wished that "she had not imbibed some superstitions, that are prejudicial to that religion she so warmly professes." Scripture must comport with reason, both Polly and Ben believed. Interpreting Christ's temptation as a vision rather than as a physical experience seemed more rational. Those who defended credulous interpretations of the Bible were harming Christianity, both insisted. Promoting irrational readings of scripture would only feed more skepticism.[44]

Polly declared that in his scientific and religious writings, Franklin was serving the cause of true piety. Franklin and Stevenson believed that they were modifying traditional faith in order to preserve Christianity itself. She told him that her growing scientific knowledge reminded her to "pay a grateful adoration to the Great Creator whose wisdom and goodness are so manifest in the operations of nature." She loathed skeptics who denied the First Cause of all natural phenomena. Understanding nature and theology would lead to purer worship of God, whom she prayed would continue to bless Franklin.[45]

Franklin visited Holland and Flanders (Belgium) in 1761, his first trip to the Continent. The scenes there offered new fodder for discussion with Polly. During their visit, Ben and his son William got an up-close view of Catholic churches and devotional practices. They were impressed. William averred that the lovely Dutch Catholic churches "surpassed anything I had ever seen before or conceived." They also visited Catholic nunneries with some English women in residence. Ben wrote to Polly and told her that, contrary to the awful view of Catholics with which he was raised, the Catholics he had observed were admirably zealous. He thought English Protestants were lukewarm by comparison.[46]

Polly responded by gently chiding Ben for his own lack of Christian practice. She wished that all Protestants shared Ben's strong "piety." If only English Protestants could tout him as one of the pillars of their church! But they could not, because he would not attend Sunday services (at least not enough for her taste). She asked forgiveness for her boldness but added, "I have a little zeal for religion, and I know nothing that would promote the cause of it so much as Dr. Franklin's adding the performance of its rituals to that inward devotion of his heart and his truly virtuous conduct." She had limited regard for particular doctrines, but she believed it incumbent upon all who professed Christ to observe the rituals of the faith.[47]

Seeing the Continent made a lasting impact on Franklin, broadening his view of religion. His brief visit did not afford a deep understanding of Continental Catholic culture. But its contrasts with the Puritan society of his youth prodded him to reconsider some of his anti-Catholic sentiments. In Flanders he observed gross violations of the Sabbath that would have scandalized New Englanders. People of all classes frolicked on Sunday afternoons with much "singing, fiddling and dancing." He cringed, looking around for signs of God's wrath, but found no evidence of impending doom. Instead, cities, markets, and farms were all thriving. It "would almost make one suspect, that the Deity is not so angry at [Sabbath-breaking] as a New England justice" is, Franklin mused. But his suspicion of Catholics did linger. When he learned in the 1780s that John Thayer, a New England pastor, had converted to Catholicism, Franklin scoffed that "to change now from Presbyterianism to Popery, seems to me refining backwards, from white sugar to brown."[48]

Franklin returned to America in 1762 to attend to family and business matters. He continued to advocate for more royal authority in Pennsylvania. But atrocities between frontier settlers and Indians in late 1763 swept him up in a threat posed by an uprising of the so-called Paxton Boys. The Paxton vigilantes targeted Christian

Indians at Conestoga, murdering six. Then they attacked more Conestogas who had sought refuge at a prison in Lancaster, butchering fourteen men, women, and children. The Paxton Boys "shot, scalped, hacked, and cut to pieces" the Conestogas in the jail yard. Paxtonites then threatened to move against Philadelphia, where friendly whites were sheltering hundreds more Christian Indians.[49]

Franklin, appalled by the indiscriminate violence, responded with *A Narrative of the Late Massacres*. It excoriated the Paxton killers, who were ostensibly Christians (many of them Scots-Irish Presbyterians). As a writer, Franklin was often coolly rationalist or wryly satirical. But *A Narrative* was a Christian humanist screed. After introducing some of the Indian victims by name, Franklin described how the Conestogas were "inhumanly murdered." Franklin proclaimed that guilt would burden the land until justice was done. "THE BLOOD OF THE INNOCENT WILL CRY TO HEAVEN FOR VENGEANCE," he thundered. Although Franklin harbored racial prejudices himself, he insisted that the Conestogas had suffered only because of the color of their skin and hair. It was abominable to kill bystander Indians just because other Indians had committed outrages against frontier whites. Target the offending Indians, Franklin said, not an entire race of people.[50]

According to Franklin, some of the Paxton Boys had used scripture to justify their acts, citing the command given to Joshua in the Old Testament to "destroy the heathen." "Horrid perversion of Scripture and of religion!" Franklin scoffed. "To father the worst of crimes on the God of peace and love!" Surveying world history, Franklin showed how everyone from the pagan Greeks to Muslims and Spanish Catholics prohibited murder of defenseless captives. The Conestogas would have been safer among any of those groups than among the "enlightened Protestants" of frontier Pennsylvania. The Paxton killers were nothing but "Christian white savages," Franklin concluded.[51]

Through this pamphlet, and through personal appeals to Paxton leaders, Franklin helped to spare remaining Christian Indians and the city of Philadelphia. But Franklin paid a price for defending the Conestogas. Scots-Irish Presbyterian settlers and leaders of Pennsylvania's "Presbyterian Party" faction lambasted Franklin for not caring about whites living on the frontier. They also saw his overheated rhetoric as a ploy to promote royal government, which many Presbyterians opposed. Adversaries used the Paxton controversy "to stir up against me those religious bigots, who are of all savages the most brutish," Franklin observed. Resentment over his protection of the Conestogas, combined with Franklin's longstanding rivalry with Pennsylvania's proprietors, made him a political target. Governor John Penn told his uncle Thomas that Franklin was a "villain" with a "black heart."[52]

Franklin faced bitter opposition for his assembly seat in 1764. Proprietary forces and their Presbyterian allies lambasted him. Although many of Pennsylvania's political allegiances were framed in confessional terms (Anglican, Presbyterian, and Quaker), Franklin asserted that religion was not really an issue in the 1764 election. "Religion has happily nothing to do with our present differences," he wrote, "though great pains are taken to lug it into the squabble." To him, the ineffective leadership of the proprietary government was the main problem. One of the key leaders of the proprietary faction was his former ally, Reverend William Smith, provost of the College of Pennsylvania. Smith reminded Pennsylvanians how Franklin had denigrated the "savage" Presbyterians as well as German settlers (citing his "Palatine boors" comment from a decade earlier). The famous Dr. Franklin "belongs to no religious society, and regards none, so he is alike detested by all," Smith insisted. In the election, Franklin lost his seat. But he still had many supporters in the assembly. They chose him to return to London, to keep pushing for concessions from the Penn family.[53]

Franklin went back to London just in time to face the emerging furor over the Stamp Act, the first major controversy between Britain and the colonies in the 1760s. Britain had incurred enormous debts during the Seven Years' War, which concluded in 1763 with the Treaty of Paris. The British administration wanted American colonists to shoulder more of the financial burden, so they concocted a new tax plan. Franklin was not necessarily opposed to the idea of additional taxes. Defeating the French and their Indian allies had required sacrifice by all. He suggested taxes that would have fallen primarily on the rich. But Franklin became worried when Parliament passed the Stamp Act. This tax on printed goods affected all Americans, and it threatened the livelihood of printers more than most professions. Whatever his concerns, Franklin took far too long to realize how angry Pennsylvanians and other Americans had become over this new tax. Franklin even appointed a political ally as Pennsylvania's stamp agent. The controversy over the Stamp Act nearly destroyed Franklin's career. Writing to Jane, Franklin reviled the "unthinking undiscerning multitude" who had turned against him. Those kinds of people were "apt to cry hosanna today, and tomorrow, crucify him."[54]

Jane was equally indignant about the abuse Franklin received. To her, it was another demonstration of the world's wickedness. But Ben disagreed with her universal assessment. "The world is not to be condemned in a lump because some bad people live in it," he cautioned her. "Their number is not great, [and] the hurt they do is but small." He reminded her of some advice that their "friend good Mr. Whitefield" had given him. Whitefield said that he read some attacks on Franklin but was not in a position immediately to evaluate the facts. So he assumed that the controversy just meant that Franklin was being "useful to the public." He compared it to seeing children in the distance pelting a tree with rocks. Even though he could not discern what kind of tree it was, Whitefield concluded that it must have fruit on it. Fruitfulness drew out rock-throwers, the itinerant advised.[55]

Franklin found redemption in Americans' eyes when he testified against the Stamp Act before Parliament in early 1766. George Whitefield attended the testimony to support his old friend.[56] Franklin controlled the interrogation from the first question. "What is your name, and place of abode?" the legislators asked him. "Franklin, of Philadelphia," he replied. The clumsy act had destabilized British rule in the colonies, he explained. Parliament had no right to impose "internal" taxes on the colonists, who had no representatives in the British legislature. Franklin arranged for a letter in the *Pennsylvania Gazette* from "an eminent clergyman in London" (likely Whitefield) to commend his performance. Franklin's testimony helped to secure the repeal of the Stamp Act—and to save his public career. The repeal would "make thousands of hearts leap for joy," Whitefield wrote.[57]

Franklin and Whitefield's friendship had proven useful to Franklin again. But Franklin's time in London also exposed him to more of

England's leading skeptics and deists. His range of religious influences prompted increased reflection on what doctrinally minimal Christianity might look like. His continuing desire for an action-oriented, up-to-date version of Christianity helps explain Franklin's composition of modern-language versions of the Lord's Prayer, other parts of scripture, and the Book of Common Prayer.

Franklin probably drew up his new version of the Lord's Prayer in 1768. In the King James Bible, the prayer had opened "Our Father, which art in heaven." In Franklin's rendering, it became

> Heavenly Father, May all revere thee,
> And become thy dutiful Children and faithful Subjects.
> May thy Laws be obeyed on Earth as perfectly as they are in heaven.
> Provide for us this Day as thou has hitherto daily done.
> Forgive us our Trespasses, and enable us likewise to forgive those that offend us.
> Keep us out of Temptation, and deliver us from Evil.

We do not know much about the circumstances under which Franklin composed this prayer, but he believed that the new version was "more concise, equally expressive, and better modern English." He also regarded it as "less exceptionable" than the King James wording. Not that he considered his version a more accurate translation. That was beside the point. He regarded his rendering as an improvement, as some of the prayer's old Jewish theology needed updating. For instance, "keep us out of temptation" was better than "lead us not into temptation." Unlike the ancient Jews, he wrote, "we now suppose that temptation, so far as it is supernatural, comes from the devil only."[58]

Fourteen years later, in 1782, Franklin was still tinkering with an updated English text of scripture. The style of the King James was "obsolete," he said, decreasing the readership for this "excellent book." He reckoned "it would be well to procure a new version, in which, preserving the sense, the turn of phrase and manner of expression should be modern." He did not possess the requisite skills to produce such a volume (presumably because he would need more familiarity with Greek and Hebrew). But he updated a few verses from the book of Job, chapter 1, to give an idea of what he had in mind for prospective publishers. In that passage, God and the devil debate the reasons for Job's faithfulness. The devil proposes that if God withdraws his blessings from Job, Job would turn against him. In the King James, the devil says, "Put forth thine hand now, and touch all that he hath, and he will curse thee to thy face." Franklin's verse reads, "Try him; only withdraw your favor, turn him out of his places, and withhold his pensions; and you will soon find him in the opposition." For Americans nearing the end of the Revolutionary War, Franklin's account sounded much like a political controversy in London's royal courts. Updated language would strengthen the usefulness of the holy text, Franklin professed. He did not bother with the question of whether a modernized, nonliteral paraphrase could blunt the divine power that traditional believers considered inherent in the text.[59]

We know more about the occasion for Franklin's shortening of the Book of Common Prayer. This 1773 effort was the most remarkable product of Franklin's affiliation with English deists. The Anglican Church's Book of Common Prayer was so central to Anglo-American religious life that abridging it was almost like shortening the Bible. (Fellow skeptic Thomas Jefferson would later do just that to the Gospels in his "Jefferson Bible.") Franklin produced the new prayer book in partnership with his friend Sir Francis Dashwood, known as "Hell Fire Francis." As a younger man, Dashwood had reportedly engaged in mock-religious rituals and orgies. These were "rites of a nature so subversive of all decency, and calculated, by an imitation of the ceremonies and mysteries of the Roman Catholic Church, to render religion itself an object of contumely." While there is no evidence that Franklin himself participated in these lewd festivities, associating with a man like Dashwood sent quite a different message than associating with George Whitefield.[60]

In light of Dashwood's exotic background, his abridged Book of Common Prayer with Franklin was fairly benign. It spoke respectfully of "social worship" but called for truncating Anglican services in order to appeal to both infirm older folks and busy young people. The new version took out swaths of the traditional liturgy. It deleted half of the Apostles' Creed, including virtually all of its doctrinal assertions about the person of Jesus Christ, his virgin birth, and his resurrection. Franklin and Dashwood removed many of the Psalms, contending that they were often repetitive and of more interest to the "ancestors of the Jews" than to "us." Finally, they excised the imprecatory prayers of the Commination (including "Cursed is he that lieth with his neighbor's wife"). "All cursing of mankind," Franklin opined, was "best omitted in this abridgment." He later explained that he did not think the imprecatory prayers reflected the "Christian doctrine of forgiveness of injuries." Dashwood and Franklin insisted that their updated version promoted true Christianity and would encourage more turnout at Anglican services. (It got little circulation, so it likely had no impact on church attendance.)[61]

The critical implications of Franklin's approach to scripture and the prayer book are unmistakable. There was a fine line between updating the language of the Bible and adjusting the fundamental meaning of the text. Franklin believed in the Bible as a moral guide, but he showed little interest in the scripture as divine in origin. He was certainly more respectful of the Bible than radical skeptics such as Tom Paine. But Franklin knew the work of early biblical critics such as Thomas Hobbes and Benedict Spinoza, whom he had cited in his 1730 piece "Letter of the Drum." Franklin himself wondered whether Moses had written all of the Pentateuch (the Hebrew Bible's first five books). His library also contained a copy of Spinoza's *Theologico-Political Treatise*, which had argued against Mosaic authorship in the 1670s.[62]

Franklin was too rooted in traditional Christianity to sanction overt antagonism toward it, especially after his youthful dalliances with radical deism. In a 1757 letter, Franklin advised a skeptical author not to publish an inflammatory manuscript Franklin had read for him. (Some have dated the letter much later and argued that the author in question was Tom Paine.) Franklin expressed dismay that the deist writer had questioned the doctrine of particular Providence. Without that belief, Franklin cautioned, there was no motive to worship God, to fear his displeasure, or to pray for his protection. What good would it do to air such skeptical views anyway? Educated people might have sufficient motives to live virtuous lives without religion, Franklin acknowledged. But most people required faith to inculcate moral discipline. "Think how great a proportion of mankind consists of weak and ignorant men and women, and of inexperienced and inconsiderate youth of both sexes, who have need of the motives of religion to restrain them from vice, to support their virtue, and retain them in the practice of it till it becomes habitual, which is the great point for its security." Even enlightened speculators like Franklin's correspondent were often indebted to their early "religious education, for the habits of virtue upon which you now justly value yourself." (Franklin could have said the same about his own Puritan upbringing.) The doctor advised his correspondent against "unchaining the Tyger." Consider the costs of rampant unbelief, he said. "If men are so wicked as we now see them *with religion*, what would they be if *without it?*"[63]

In October 1770, Deborah Franklin wrote in rough script to her long-absent husband. She had melancholy news. "Yisterday came the a Counte of the Death of our verey kind Friend Mr. White Feld it hurte me indeaid." The news of George Whitefield's passing hurt Ben as well. As soon as he heard it, he wrote with condolences to Jane Mecom "on the death of my dear old friend Mr. Whitefield." Franklin's and Whitefield's friendship, and friendly banter over faith, had lasted for thirty years.[64]

One of Franklin's and Whitefield's ongoing debates was over the role of Providence in human affairs. The question weighed on Franklin as he watched the crisis between Britain and the colonies unfold during the decade after the Stamp Act. Whitefield and Franklin had agreed that British authorities had mismanaged the taxes. But unlike Whitefield, Franklin was unsure that God was overseeing these worldly affairs. While he believed that "the general government of the universe" was well administered, he did not necessarily think that God noticed the smaller details of history. Perhaps God left those contingencies up to chance or human determination. He knew that Whitefield would disagree with this "uncomfortable thought," so he did not insist on it. Disagree Whitefield did, writing in a letter's margin that the idea that God was not in control was "uncomfortable" and "unscriptural."[65]

To the end, Whitefield kept telling Franklin to embrace Jesus. The ailing preacher had reminded Franklin that this world would be consumed in apocalypse in the last days, and "we shall see eternity rising out of its ashes." He prayed that he and Franklin would both be in the heavenly throng who would cry "Hallelujah" at the earth's conflagration. But as Franklin noted in his autobiography, Whitefield apparently went to his grave (during his last visit to Massachusetts in 1770) without confidence that God had answered his prayers for Franklin's conversion. After the minister's death, Franklin still spoke affectionately about Whitefield: "His integrity, disinterestedness, and indefatigable zeal in prosecuting every good work, I have never seen equaled."[66]

CHAPTER NINE

The Pillar of Fire

A MONTH AFTER THEY partnered on the Declaration of Independence, Benjamin Franklin and Thomas Jefferson teamed with John Adams to draft a Great Seal for the United States. Franklin, who had stopped believing that reconciliation with Britain was possible, left his diplomatic post in England in March 1775. He spent some of his last moments there with the great orator Edmund Burke, who would warn Parliament about the perils of conflict with America just days after Franklin's ship sailed for America. On his very last day in London, though, Franklin bade a tearful farewell to his Unitarian friend and fellow scientist Joseph Priestley.

Franklin spent much of the second half of his life in Britain and France. His 1775 return to America would be brief but monumentally significant. Pennsylvania elected him as a delegate to the Second Continental Congress, where he worked on the committee that produced the Declaration. Franklin received Jefferson's rough draft of the Declaration the third week of June 1776. While he proposed only a few changes, one of his edits now rings through American history. Where Jefferson originally wrote, "We hold these truths to be sacred and undeniable," it seems to have been Franklin who inserted the sparse, rationalist phrase, "We hold these truths to be self-evident." God did still appear nearby as the one who created us equal. But with self-evident truths, Franklin nudged Jefferson's phrasing away from the divine and toward the human.[1]

On the Great Seal, however, Jefferson and Franklin associated the nation's birth with a symbol from the Bible. The deistic pair advocated a more overtly biblical seal than the nation would ultimately adopt. (Adams, who was drifting toward Unitarianism, proposed a scene from the myth of Hercules.) In his draft of the seal, virtually identical to Jefferson's, Franklin suggested an image from the book of Exodus: "Moses standing on the shore, and extending his hand over the sea, thereby causing the same to overwhelm Pharaoh" and his army. From above, he would show "rays from a pillar of fire in the clouds reaching to Moses to express that he acts by command of the Deity." As God blessed Moses, so God would bless the Patriots' undertakings. Over the design, a banner would proclaim, "Rebellion to Tyrants Is Obedience to God," an expression coined by Franklin in 1775. The skeptical child of the Puritans still wanted to remind America of how God shepherded human events.[2]

The Stamp Act's repeal in 1766 hardly settled matters between Britain and the colonies, but Franklin remained hopeful that Parliament would back off. He still was quite fond of King George III, telling Polly Stevenson that the king was "the very best in the world and the most amiable." The Townshend Duties, customs duties on imported goods including paper and tea, agitated the colonies once again in 1767, however. Franklin was sympathetic toward the duties because he regarded them as "external" taxes relevant to the empire as a whole. Many colonists disagreed. They tried to enact programs of nonimportation and nonconsumption, hitting British merchants and politicians in their wallets.[3]

Franklin's ostensible purpose for being in London was becoming less and less relevant. There seemed to be no chance that Pennsylvania would ever become a royal colony instead of a proprietary one. Yet other colonies made him their agent, too. His selection as Massachusetts's agent in London was the most controversial, because of escalating Patriot resistance in the province. So Franklin stayed in London, year after year, in spite of repeated notes telling

Deborah that he hoped to come home soon. He missed Sally's wedding, even as he enjoyed the company of Stevenson and her mother. Deborah suffered a stroke in 1769 ("a partial palsy in the tongue and a sudden loss of memory"). The Franklins' family doctor told Franklin that, even though she had recovered some functions, the stroke would likely shorten her life. Still, Franklin lingered. Finally, Deborah passed away in late 1774. Their son William attended the funeral, and told Franklin that he wished he had come back before she died: "Her disappointment in that respect preyed a good deal on her spirits." One month after hearing of Deborah's death, Franklin boarded the ship to return to Pennsylvania.[4]

Franklin's presence in London had put him in an awkward position. His indignation tended to lag behind that of radical Patriots in America, perhaps because he was more aware of reconciliation's fragile prospects. But because he represented several colonies, he became a target for British anger over American resistance. Franklin's role in the crisis took a decisive turn in 1772, when he arranged for the private distribution of incriminating letters written by royal executives in Massachusetts. These officials had informed London that only harsh measures could bring unruly colonists under control. Franklin thought that the circulation of the letters might cool the Patriots' anger toward London. Perhaps the letters would show colonists that native sons of Massachusetts, like Governor Thomas Hutchinson, were to blame as much as London politicians and the king. Citing the book of Leviticus, Franklin imagined that, "like the scape goats of old," the disgraced Hutchinson "might have carried away into the wilderness all the offenses which had arisen between the two countries." The Massachusetts officials' letters (inevitably) were published in 1773, and Massachusetts called for Hutchinson's dismissal. Boston Patriots exulted that God had "wonderfully interposed to bring to light the plot that has been laid for us by our malicious and invidious enemies." The Patriots hardly limited their fury to Hutchinson, though. Anger over the letters, plus the Tea Act of 1773, precipitated Boston's Tea Party. In that episode, Patriots dumped hundreds of chests of East India Company tea into Boston Harbor.[5]

London officials blamed Franklin for inciting Massachusetts with the secret letters. Shortly after word of the Tea Party arrived,

London's solicitor general humiliated a speechless Franklin at a Whitehall venue called the Cockpit. Soon thereafter, Francis Dashwood, Franklin's old friend with whom he had coauthored the shortened Book of Common Prayer, advised Franklin that he was being dismissed as America's postmaster. He had held that position since 1753. Like many American supporters, Jane Mecom was outraged at the way British officials were treating Ben. She compared his experience to Jesus's, who gave up all for the good of others. She encouraged her brother to imitate Christ in holiness and "in that way trust in Him for eternal happiness." Millions of American prayers were going up daily for him, she said, and for the Patriot cause.[6]

When Parliament rejected a reconciliation measure in early 1775, Franklin vowed to return home at last. "Corruption, venality, and schemes of arbitrary power continue to overflow the land," he lamented. (Jane had advised him that "our God has told us that all our suing for a reconciliation will prove abortive without a regeneration of morals.") On March 19, 1775, he visited the scientist and dissenting minister Joseph Priestley, who had been in the audience for Franklin's scolding at the Cockpit. The two had met in London a decade earlier, and Franklin had helped his protégé publish *The History and Present State of Electricity* (1767), which offered the most detailed account of Franklin's kite experiment. In his memoirs, Priestley offered worried reflections about Franklin's faith. These echoed Whitefield's concerns, in spite of Priestley's non-evangelical, rationalist beliefs. Priestley regretted that such a fine man as Franklin "should have been an unbeliever in Christianity, and also have done so much as he did to make others unbelievers." Franklin's friend, the London dissenting minister Richard Price, similarly wished that Franklin's talents "had been aided by a faith in Christianity and the animating hopes of a resurrection to an endless life with which it inspires." Priestley's comment about Franklin's recruiting others to unbelief does not quite match up with what we know about his proselytizing, or lack thereof. Instead of trying to undermine the beliefs of traditional Christians, Franklin tended to confirm the tendencies of friends who were already skeptics.[7]

Franklin admired Priestley's willingness to publicize his non-traditional views. Long after the Revolution concluded, the doctor hailed him as the "honest heretic Dr. Priestley." Franklin reflected that

> all the heretics I have known have been virtuous men. They have the virtue of fortitude or they would not venture to own their heresy; and they cannot afford to be deficient in any of the other virtues, as that would give advantage to their many enemies; and they have not like orthodox sinners, such a number of friends to excuse or justify them. Do not, however mistake me. It is not to my good friend's heresy that I impute his honesty. On the contrary, 'tis his honesty that has brought upon him the character of heretic.

Denying orthodox doctrine made people like Priestley a target for critics. Nothing was to be gained by questioning beliefs like the Trinity, Franklin figured. Nothing was to be gained but the truth.[8]

Franklin left the door open to Priestley's brand of rationalist faith, admitting (with dubious self-deprecation) that "he had not given so much attention as he ought to have done to the evidences of Christianity." Before leaving London for Philadelphia, Franklin asked Priestley for good books on the subject, promising he would read them and share his reactions. Priestley suggested David Hartley's Universalist text *Observations on Man* (1749), which Priestley regarded as the best book he had ever read, second only to the Bible. Priestley also recommended his own *Institutes of Natural and Revealed Religion* (1772–1774), which posited that authentic revelation always comported with natural religion. Like many rationalists, Priestley argued for a return to "primitive Christianity," which was Unitarian, non-dogmatic, and ethics-centered. Priestley was not a traditional Christian, to be sure, but even he exercised a tethering effect on the lengths of Franklin's radical skepticism. Because of the outbreak of the Revolutionary War, however, Priestley's discussions with Franklin on religion faltered.[9]

The first battles of the Revolutionary War, at Lexington and Concord, transpired as Franklin was sailing across the Atlantic. The Anglo-American empire had begun to collapse. Franklin was not often "sufficiently at leisure," as Priestley put it, in these years to give sustained attention to what he believed about Jesus. Upon his return from London, Pennsylvania elected Franklin, now almost seventy years old, as a delegate to the Second Continental Congress, which began meeting in Philadelphia within a week of his landing. It put Franklin in company with other colonies' Patriot leaders, including George Washington, Thomas Jefferson, Patrick Henry, and John Adams. Adams, who would have a long, contentious partnership with Franklin, observed that Franklin said little at the Congress. The doctor often slept in his chair. Some wondered if (when he was awake) Franklin would continue pushing for reconciliation with Britain. By mid-summer 1775, however, Adams regarded Franklin as "the firmest spokesman for separation." Franklin assured Parliament member David Hartley (a son of the Universalist philosopher) that an independent America would enjoy the burgeoning strength which England had squandered. "God will protect and prosper it: You will only exclude yourselves from any share in it," he concluded. Franklin's passion for the revolutionary cause led to permanent estrangement from his son William. As royal governor of New Jersey, William chose to remain faithful to the empire.[10]

Although the fighting in the Revolutionary War had already begun, it took some time for the Patriot movement to unify behind independence from Britain. By mid-1775, Franklin had concluded that independence was inevitable. But separating from Britain was risky to discuss publicly. Independence found its great champion in Franklin's protégé Tom Paine. Franklin had met this promising writer in London. When Paine decided to move to America in 1774, Franklin provided him a letter of introduction, describing him as an "ingenious, worthy young man." When Paine anonymously published *Common Sense* in January 1776, it shifted the public discussion from resistance against Britain to revolution. He indicted monarchy by reference to the Israelites' foolish request for a king in I Samuel 8. Although Paine would later become the most notorious skeptic in America, he knew that the case for independence required biblical grounding. The debate raged for six more months, but the Continental Congress finally embraced independence in July 1776. As the story goes, when they signed the Declaration, Franklin told delegate John Hancock that they must "all hang together, or most assuredly we shall all hang separately."[11]

That revolutionary summer found Franklin busy working in Congress, framing the Declaration of Independence, and helping to develop a constitution for independent Pennsylvania. Like all the states, Pennsylvania grappled with church-state relations as it framed its new governing document. William Penn's colony had a deep tradition of religious liberty, but Christian assumptions and ethics remained woven into its laws. Franklin worked behind the scenes to secure full religious freedom. The commonwealth of Pennsylvania did affirm liberty of conscience, promising that no theist would lose civil privileges on account of his beliefs. Pennsylvania adopted a rigorous religious oath for assembly members, however. Officials had to affirm that they believed in "one God, the creator and governor of the universe, the rewarder of the good and the punisher of the wicked." Moreover, they had to affirm that the whole Bible was inspired by God.[12]

Franklin explained his opposition to these kinds of tests— and to state-supported churches—in a 1780 letter about Massachusetts's new constitution. Religion became corrupt when its clergy looked to the state for assistance. "If Christian preachers had continued to teach as Christ & his Apostles did, without salaries, and as the Quakers now do, I imagine tests would never have existed: For I think they were invented not so much to secure religion itself, as the emoluments of it," he suggested. "When a religion is good, I conceive that it will support itself; and when it cannot support itself, and God does not take care to support, so that its professors are obliged to call for the help of the civil power, 'tis a sign, I apprehend, of its being a bad one." Many Americans from across the religious spectrum agreed with Franklin. Deists and many evangelicals—especially Baptists—asserted that state involvement corrupted religion.[13]

Franklin believed that religious pluralism and toleration would invigorate American culture. He even concluded his 1784 promotional Paris imprint *Information to Those Who Would Remove to America* with assurances that religious commitment was widespread and respected in the former British colonies. The lack of established churches in places such as Pennsylvania had not fueled unbelief. Atheism was unknown in America, he wrote. Religious "infidelity [was] rare and secret, so that persons may live to a great age in that country without having their piety shocked by meeting with either an atheist or an infidel." Moreover, God approved of the kindness with which the differing sects treated one another. (Here Franklin strained credulity: he knew as well as anyone how much religiously based conflict there was in America.) In reward for its benevolence and toleration, God showered the country with prosperity. Europeans seeking religious refuge would find safe harbor in America.[14]

In spite of the heady work of independence, Franklin was eager to get back to Europe. He jumped at the chance to join the American delegation to Paris, which would try to persuade the French to enter the war on America's side. The irony of allying with British America's longtime Catholic enemy did not escape the notice of Loyalist critics in America. But Patriots argued that French support for American liberty might signal that Catholicism was crumbling in France anyway. So the septuagenarian Franklin set sail for Europe in October 1776. He arrived in Paris on December 21, four days before George Washington's Continental Army crossed a sleety Delaware River prior to the Battle of Trenton. Upon his departure, Franklin assured Boston pastor Samuel Cooper (Jane Mecom's and John Adams's minister) that, in spite of incessant bad news on the war front, the Patriots would succeed "by the blessing of God. . . . 'Tis a glorious task assigned to us by Providence." Cooper wrote back and told him that Providence was certainly intervening on their behalf. Later in the war, Franklin told a correspondent that "the Almighty has favoured the just cause." He prayed God would establish America as a refuge for all who sought freedom.[15]

The French, knowing well his scientific and political reputation, embraced Franklin as the representative American. John Adams thought that everyone from kings to chambermaids knew Franklin's name and considered him a "friend to human kind." Franklin told Polly Stevenson (now Polly Hewson) to imagine him, "an old man with grey hair appearing under a marten fur cap among the powdered heads of Paris." French authorities assumed that Franklin wore his simple garb because he was a Quaker. Crowds gathered to catch glimpses of him, and Franklin's image

Benjamin Franklin—peint d'après nature pour la famille—exposé au Salon
de 1779, *lithograph by Antoine Maurin, [between 1824 and 1860] (detail).
After a painting by Joseph-Siffrède Duplessis. Courtesy Library of Congress.*

appeared on innumerable gewgaws, from vases and medallions to
snuffboxes and handkerchiefs. Franklin told Jane Mecom that his
face was "almost as well known as that of the moon." King Louis
XVI reportedly grew so tired of seeing images of Franklin that he
had a chamber pot made with the American's visage at the bottom.
Adams, who joined Franklin in Paris in 1778, grumbled that "all
the atheists, deists and libertines, as well as the philosophers and
ladies are in his train—another Voltaire and Hume." Adams always
thought Franklin got too much credit for the Revolution, as if it
transpired by a mere wave of his "electric wand."[16]

Paris was an assault on the eyes, ears, and nose, even for a man
used to London. Rustics from America "set down in the tourbillion
[whirlwind] of such a great city as Paris," Franklin said, "must necessarily be for some days half out of his senses." (Paris had about
600,000 residents, twenty times those of Philadelphia.) But Franklin
made friends easily. He became a member and grand master of the
Neuf Soeurs, Paris's most prestigious Masonic Lodge, which was a

hotbed of pro-American sentiment. The elderly philosopher Voltaire, France's most notorious opponent of church power, joined the lodge around the same time. Voltaire died shortly thereafter. French church authorities were determined that their great antagonist should not have a Christian funeral, so the Neuf Soeurs held a memorial for him instead. Franklin and other Masons laid crowns at the foot of a painting of Voltaire's apotheosis. French officials were disgusted by the provocative service, and contemplated shutting down the lodge, but Franklin's role in the episode gave the Masons political cover. The priests and police backed off.[17]

In spite of his popularity, Franklin and other American delegates struggled to foster French enthusiasm for an alliance. The French government had long viewed Americans as part of a menacing British Protestant empire. Franklin also had little of practical value that he could offer the French in exchange for military support. Befitting the mission's dim hopes, a New York Loyalist newspaper erroneously reported in early 1778 that Franklin had died. "It was supposed," the report crowed, "the late ill success of the Americans had hastened his end." Jane Mecom told him that hearing the news had made her heart tremble.[18]

Not dissuaded by the obstacles, the ever-charming Franklin exploited French concerns that British and American reconciliation could threaten French power in the Western hemisphere. Many French observers believed that the Patriots had little chance of defeating the British, however, even if the French helped them. The devastating British loss at Saratoga, New York, in October 1777 gave Franklin tangible evidence that the Americans could win. Thus, in February 1778, France signed a military treaty with the United States. A key diplomat in England told Franklin that the French alliance would be the greatest barrier to peace between Britain and America. Franklin indignantly replied that King George III, whom he had once admired, "hates Whigs and Presbyterians [and] thirsts for our blood." So America would align with their old Catholic enemy instead. Because of the weakness of the American military, French help was essential to America's success in the conflict.[19]

Franklin's tenure in France would keep him away from much of his family for eight and a half more years. But his sixteen-year-old grandson William Temple Franklin (born to an unmarried William Franklin in London) and seven-year-old grandson Benjamin Franklin (Benny) Bache (Sally's son) did accompany him to Paris. The family thought that living in Europe would benefit the boys. Franklin was not sure about how French learning would affect Benny, however. Seeking "a Presbyterian as well as a republican" education, Franklin shipped Benny off to school in Geneva, Switzerland, a key center of John Calvin's Reformed Christianity. Franklin explained to eleven-year-old John Quincy Adams, who knew the doctor's grandson, that since Benny would eventually live in a "Protestant country and a republic," he should finish his education "where the proper principles prevail." Sally also kept Franklin updated about how Willy, a younger grandson, was getting along in Philadelphia. Once, Willy had a nightmare, jumped out of bed, and began praying. He prayed not to Jesus, though, but to the Greek hero Hercules. With a giggle, Sally asked if it was best to let him keep doing this? Or should she "instruct him in a little religion"? Franklin replied drily that she should show him how to "direct his worship more properly, for the deity of Hercules is now quite out of fashion."[20]

More seriously, Franklin still advised young people—as he had once advised Sally—to attend to religious duties. He told Samuel Cooper Johonnot, a grandson of Reverend Samuel Cooper and a classmate of Benny's, that our future happiness depended on wise behavior. Hard work at school and diligence in "religion and virtue" would benefit Johonnot in this life and the next. "You will possess wisdom," he encouraged the boy, "which is nearly allied to happiness." The doctor cited Proverbs 3:16–17, "Length of Days are in her right hand, and in her left hand Riches and Honours; all her Ways are Ways of Pleasantness, and all her Paths are Peace!"[21]

Franklin realized that the best sources of wisdom and virtue remained a disputed matter between rationalists and traditional Christians. In 1782, for example, Franklin read and commended as a "great pleasure" the evangelical writer William Cowper's *Poems*. But in the poem "Charity," Cowper insisted that at the last judgment, God would accept no good works that did not square "truly with the Scripture plan, nor spring from love to God, or love to man." Cowper, following Whitefield, believed that true virtue required inner transformation by God.[22]

Paris offered the widowed doctor some distracting new friendships. One was with Madame Anne-Louise Brillon de Jouy, a wealthy neighbor half Franklin's age. She called him "Mon Cher Papa." Following the pattern of relationships with Katy Ray and Polly Stevenson (with whom he also reunited in Paris), Franklin's dalliance with Madame Brillon was romantically charged. But their conversations were also suffused with religious topics. Madame Brillon habitually sat on his lap, and they stayed up late together. At one point Brillon's husband accused Franklin of kissing his wife. In another remarkable scene, Franklin played chess in her bathroom while she relaxed in the sudsy water of the tub. Their relationship was likely never consummated, however. As historian Claude-Anne Lopez put it, they hovered in a "rare atmosphere which is more than close friendship and less than love of the flesh—what the French call *amitié amoureuse*."[23]

Anton Hohenstein, Franklin's Reception at the Court of France, 1778, *Philadelphia, [1860s] (detail). Courtesy Library of Congress.*

Franklin liked discussing the path to salvation with his lady friends. This was a way to foster intimacy with his younger romantic interests. By early 1778, Franklin had entrusted Madame Brillon with his "conversion." The Catholic Brillon teased him, knowing his doubts about the things of the spirit. "As long as [Franklin] loves God, America, and me above all things, I absolve him of all his sins, present, past and future; and I promise him paradise where I shall lead him along a path strewn with roses," she assured him. Continuing the theme, she walked through a list of six of the seven deadly sins, from pride to sloth, and absolved him of each. On lust, however, she paused. Nobody was perfect. All great men were tainted with inappropriate desires. What was wrong with loving, she asked, and being loved in return? "Go on doing great things and loving pretty women; provided that, pretty and lovable though they may be, you never lose sight of my principle." Love God, America, and Madame Brillon above all.[24]

Her letter was catnip to Franklin. He drooled over his "spiritual guide" who promised to lead him "to heaven in a road so delicious" that he would endure any troubles as long as she was with him. "I am in raptures," he exclaimed, delighted with her absolution. He pivoted from the seven deadly sins to the Ten Commandments, which he said he had long regarded as twelve in total. The eleventh law, for Franklin, was "increase and multiply" (Genesis 1:28). The twelfth was "love one another," from John 13:34. (Franklin conspicuously left out Christ's "first commandment" of Mark 12:30, "Love the Lord thy God.") He actually preferred the "increase" and "love" commandments to any in the Decalogue. He obeyed them at every opportunity, he said. Would his obedience to those two commandments substitute for breaking one of the ten (namely, coveting his neighbor's wife)? He broke that one all the time, especially when he saw Madame Brillon. He could never repent of it, even if he won the "full possession of her." Musing fancifully, he asked whether the best way to be done with a temptation was to indulge it as often as necessary? He had once read a church father teaching this principle, but he was not sure the sentiment was orthodox.[25]

After receiving this slobbery letter, Brillon teasingly pranced away. Men may have desires and yield to them, she chided. Women should never yield. And while she pardoned his lustful advances, she insisted that she would need to consult with the "neighbor whose wife you covet" (i.e., Monsieur Jacques Brillon) before deciding the final outcome. Admitting that she too wanted Franklin's affection, she noted that all their "desires will eventually lead us to paradise." Keeping him at a flirtatious arm's length, she assured him that he had taken the place of her father in her heart. He replied that he was infinitely pleased to become her adoptive father. Still, he pushed for more. Since she was as rich as an archbishop in Christian virtues, he contended, she could afford to sacrifice a little of them for his sake. No one would notice. But she would not budge. "Such is your charity toward an unfortunate who used to enjoy plenty and is now reduced to begging your alms," he lamented.[26]

Madame Brillon had her own sources of frustration, especially after she discovered that her husband was having an affair. Unfulfilled desire turned Franklin's and Brillon's thoughts to the afterlife, when all would be set right. When they had both passed away, Brillon imagined, they would be reunited and enter a relationship that would never end. They would eat roasted apples, play Scottish tunes (Franklin's favorites), and all their chess games would end in ties. Franklin's gout, from which he suffered terribly, would vanish, as would all their earthly struggles with sin. Franklin found her idea of paradise charming, if not altogether plausible. He suspected that he might arrive in heaven four decades before her (he was close on death's date—she would pass away thirty-four years after him). In the intervening years she might forget about him. The doctor considered asking her not to renew her vows to Monsieur Brillon in the next life. And she did promise herself to Franklin when she got there, on the condition that he not "ogle the virgins too much while waiting for me." Whatever the case, Franklin pledged that he would love her "for all eternity." However, if she rejected him, he speculated that he might take up heavenly housekeeping with Madame Brillon's mother.[27]

In spite of these amorous overtures, his gout and kidney stones rendered Franklin almost immobile during his last years in Paris. His sickness fueled in him a "growing curiosity" about the afterlife. He became convinced that people continued in both matter and consciousness after death. In 1785, he reasoned that God never

destroyed created matter; the things of this world only took different forms over time. God exercised "great frugality as well as wisdom in his works." That led Franklin to doubt the notion of the
"annihilation of souls." Instead, he figured that he would "in some
shape or other always exist. And with all the inconveniences human
life is liable to, I shall not object to a new edition of mine; hoping
however that the errata of the last may be corrected." The "errata"
presumably included the gout, stones, and (as suggested in the
Autobiography) foolishness of his youth.[28]

Brillon's and Franklin's running dialogue about heaven helped
inspire the doctor's "Conte" (1778), a popular anecdote he published on religious toleration. In it, St. Peter invited Christians of
all kinds—even Catholics—to pass through the pearly gates. To a
French officer who had no faith, Peter said, "Too bad. I don't know
where to place you; but come in anyway, you will take a place
wherever you can." In response to this "bagatelle," Madame Brillon
wrote that if Peter asked her what religion she was, she would tell
him she believed that the "Eternal Being is perfectly good and in-
dulgent; of the religion whereby people love all those who resem-
ble Him. I have loved and idolized Doctor Franklin." She expected
that Peter would usher her in to sit next to Franklin, who would be
standing next to God in a place of honor.[29]

Franklin's dream of marrying Madame Brillon remained elusive, so he set his sights on pairing his grandson Temple with the
Brillons' daughter Cunégonde. Monsieur Brillon refused, citing
the Franklins' Protestantism. Drawing on the themes of "Conte,"
Franklin insisted that this denominational difference should present no problem. Good Christians all believed the same things, he
asserted. Among these tenets were five basic propositions, ones that
Franklin would repeat almost verbatim on later occasions, including in the *Autobiography*. These were the closest Franklin ever got
to offering a formal statement of his beliefs as an older man:

1. That there is one God who created the universe, and
   who governs it by his Providence.
2. That He ought to be worshipped and served.
3. That the best service to God is doing good to men.
4. That the soul of man is immortal, and

5. That in a future life, if not in the present one, vice will
   be punished and virtue rewarded.

Other doctrines were nonessential. Denominations, he wrote, were like loaves of sugar that came wrapped in different paper and tied with assorted kinds of string. The sugar, however, always remained the point of the package. The Brillons agreed with his religious sentiments. But when marrying off their daughter, they needed to observe the customs of the country. Cunégonde went on to wed a Catholic.[30]

There was no chance of Franklin formalizing his relationship with Madame Brillon. But he did try to marry Anne-Catherine de Ligniville, Madame Helvétius, the widow of a prominent philosopher and Freemason. Madame Helvétius presided over an influential salon that attracted numerous "statesmen, philosophers, historians, poets, and men of learning," such as a broadminded priest, the Abbé Morellet. The loose social scenes at the salon were too much for the staid New Englander John Adams, especially with Catholic priests in the mix. Madame Helvétius's ministers, Adams supposed, had "as much power to pardon a sin as they have to commit one. . . . What absurdities, inconsistencies, distractions and horrors would these manners introduce into our republican governments in America." John's wife, Abigail, who had joined him in Paris in 1784, regarded Madame Helvétius as a virtual bawd, with her loud voice and "fangled" hair. After one dinner, Helvétius flopped on a couch where she flashed "more than her feet," sniffed Abigail. Franklin loved Madame Helvétius's wit and style, however. He proposed to her on multiple occasions, but she repeatedly refused. The game of romance was better when it never concluded.[31]

Lest we forget, Franklin was in France on American business. He performed his job well, under difficult circumstances. The French alliance did not solve all problems for George Washington's army or for the diplomats in Paris. America always needed fresh infusions of cash. Franklin told John Adams—another son of traditional Congregationalists from Massachusetts—that he still had "two of the Christian graces, faith and hope: But my faith is only that of which the Apostle speaks, the evidence of things not seen

[Hebrews 11:1]." Those "things not seen" were additional French livres. Although the French loaned America tens of millions, it never seemed like enough. Franklin, referencing Joshua 9, complained to Adams that he was "quite sick of my Gibeonite office, that of drawing water for the whole congregation of Israel."[32]

Adams was a brilliant political mind, but he was also a true American rustic and an inexperienced diplomat. (It was his first time in Europe.) The doctor's incessant joking grated on Adams, who thought that the Americans needed to take a tough line in Paris. "The old conjurer," Adams scoffed, was "too old, too infirm, too indolent and dissipated, to be sufficient for the discharge of all the important duties" pressing on the delegation in Paris. Adams was impolite to French foreign ministers, so they preferred dealing only with Franklin. The doctor appreciated Adams's fierce patriotism but regarded him as reckless. Franklin told the president of the American Congress that he hoped Americans would ignore the "ravings of a certain mischievous madman here against France." He reminded Adams that peacemakers were blessed by God, but that in this world they were "more frequently cursed." Sometimes even their fellow diplomats cursed them, he silently mused.[33]

Feuding between American representatives in Paris, and rampant deception by America's supposed friends, tested Franklin's nerves. Sometimes his anger sent him grasping for the Christian vocabulary of damnation and judgment. He directed some of his most venomous barbs at Thomas Digges, a Marylander to whom Franklin had sent funds to provide relief for American prisoners in England. Digges absconded with the money. When Franklin found out, he thundered that "We have no name in our language for such atrocious wickedness. If such a fellow is not damned, 'tis not worthwhile to keep a Devil." Digges assured Franklin that he would come to Paris to justify himself. The doctor replied that "I have not half as much faith in Digges's coming here as I have in his going to Hell." Franklin probably had little faith in either scenario.[34]

The war had darkened Franklin's view of human nature. He was bitter over what he saw as British pride and recalcitrance, and over their ruthlessness in prosecuting the war against Americans. He said that Loyalist opponents of the Revolution were America's "Judases ready to betray their country for a few paltry pieces of silver." His struggles in Paris, including his advancing age and illness, cast a pall over his typically cheery disposition. Even by early 1777, he told Joseph Priestley that the war had convinced him that "Mankind are wicked enough to continue slaughtering one another as long as they can find money to pay the butchers." The War for Independence struck him as an especially ugly conflict. "Of all the wars in my time, this on the part of England appears to me the wickedest; having no cause but malice against liberty, and the jealousy of commerce." But he thought the crime would turn back against the British, who would lose their own liberty and destroy their economy.[35]

Five years later, as he tried to restart their prewar conversations on research and religion, Franklin told Priestley in 1782 that he longed for the leisure to resume his scientific pursuits. But he was worn out with the moral nature of man, which "disgusted" him:

Men I find to be a sort of beings very badly constructed, as they are generally more easily provoked than reconciled, more disposed to do mischief to each other than to make reparation, much more easily deceived than undeceived, and having more pride & even pleasure in killing than in begetting one another, for without a blush they assemble in great armies at noon day to destroy, and when they have killed as many as they can, they exaggerate the number to augment the fancied glory. . . . A virtuous action it would be, and a vicious one the killing of them, if the species were really worth producing or preserving; but of this I begin to doubt.[36]

This conversation about preserving humanity led Franklin into some dark joking. Franklin knew that as a pastor, Priestley wished to bring people to redemption. But Priestley did not show the same care for animals, Franklin noted. Priestley had sacrificed the lives of many "honest harmless mice" in his scientific experiments. Did Priestley ever privately wish, Franklin wondered, that he could use boys and girls in his experiments instead of mice, to prevent more human sin? After all, more people meant more viciousness.[37]

To illustrate the brutal state of the world, the doctor shared a tale of a young angel who was paired with an older one on a mission to the Caribbean. They landed in the midst of a naval battle, where they saw a maelstrom of smoke and mangled bodies. "You blundering blockhead," the younger angel exclaimed, "you undertook to conduct me to the Earth, and you have brought me into Hell!" No, said the older one, devils would "never treat one another in this cruel manner." The Calvinist views of Franklin's parents had proven to be all too true during the Revolutionary War. But he still hoped that a few enlightened individuals—including himself—could transcend humankind's viciousness. Indeed, on the eve of his seventy-eighth birthday he told New York leader John Jay that, by God's grace, no person existed "who can justly say, Ben Franklin has wronged me." How this comported with the "errata" he confessed in his *Autobiography*, he did not say.[38]

The Revolutionary War did not just entail violence between whites. Franklin also grieved over the massacre of ninety-six Christian Indians—men, women, and children—at Gnadenhutten, in the Ohio Territory, in early 1782. Pennsylvania militiamen accused these Indians, living at a Moravian mission, of participating in frontier raids. The vigilantes bludgeoned the unarmed Lenapes to death, then scalped them and burned their bodies. The episode brought back memories of the Paxton Boys' atrocities two decades earlier, and it gave Franklin "infinite pain and vexation." He learned of it from the Moravian leader James Hutton, a longtime correspondent who had once served as George Whitefield's publicist. "The dispensations of Providence in this world puzzle my weak reason," Franklin told Hutton. Why are cruel men permitted to murder the innocent? Why does such violence so often fall on children? Franklin saw Gnadenhutten as emblematic of the massive loss of life during the war. For these needless deaths, he mostly blamed King George III. He called the king that "single man in England, who happens to love blood, and to hate Americans." In order to kill Americans, the king had hired German mercenaries and Indian "savages." Doing so generated a vicious backlash, especially among frontier settlers. The king lived in comfort while thousands died cruel deaths at his bidding.[39]

Surely God would address these injustices—eventually. "I wonder at this, but I cannot therefore part with the comfortable belief of a divine Providence," Franklin confessed to Hutton. "The more I see the impossibility, from the number & extent of his crimes of giving equivalent punishment to a wicked man in this life, the more I am convinced of a future state, in which all that here appears to be wrong shall be set right, all that is crooked made straight. . . . It is the only comfort in the present dark scene of things." For King George, Thomas Digges, and the Gnadenhutten killers, a future reckoning was in order. (Still, we might wonder about the depth of Franklin's indignation about the massacre of Indians. Only months before he had faked a newspaper article about Senecas scalping whites, in order to generate sympathy for the American cause.)[40]

Still, there were hopeful signs that the violence would end soon. After six grinding years of war and stalemate, George Washington scored the decisive victory over the British at Yorktown in 1781. An eccentric correspondent named Peter Labilliere, writing to Franklin from his "Temple of Liberty" in London, hailed Yorktown as "the late very complete & providentially timed victory, in favor of your oppressed nation, and . . . the opening of the gates of freedom to the whole world." Labilliere believed that Yorktown augured the time when "the cup of iniquity is filled and that Pharaoh [King George III] has gone out with all his host against the children of Israel and is overthrown." Jane Mecom was a bit more circumspect, celebrating the "glorious news" from Virginia and hoping it would mean that her brother could come home soon. She had blunted her queries about Franklin's spiritual state since the Revolution began. On Independence Day 1784, she prayed, "God grant I may see you again here, but if not that we may spend a happy eternity together in His presence." Franklin had a bit more work to do in this life, however. He told Madame Brillon that he would guard against presumption, even if the war appeared to be over. "In bad fortune I hope for good, and in good I fear bad," he wrote.[41]

The outcome of Yorktown, and shifting tides in the London government, made the British ready to recognize American independence. Following preliminary peace terms in late 1782, Franklin demanded that the British concede the autonomy of the United States, ratify clear boundaries (south of the Great Lakes and east of the Mississippi), and evacuate British troops from

America. He won all these points, in exchange for recognition of debts owed to the British and equitable treatment of Loyalists. The Treaty of Paris of 1783, which codified the agreement, was arguably the greatest diplomatic achievement in American history. A friendly British politician declared that Franklin was "chosen by Providence to be a principal instrument of this great Revolution, a Revolution that has stronger masks of divine interposition superseding the ordinary course of human affairs, than any other event which this world hath experienced. Even where God is supposed to work miracles, He uses human means; and it hath pleased him to make you the means of this blessing to America."[42]

The war had also made Franklin more amenable to this kind of providential reading of human events. In 1784, he told his skeptical friend the printer William Strahan that "if it had not been for the justice of our cause, and the consequent interposition of Providence in which we had faith," the Americans surely would have lost the war. "If I had ever before been an atheist I should now have been convinced of the being and government of a deity," he assured Strahan. (This was an intriguing phrasing: had he ever been a full-blown "atheist"?) Franklin was sure that God "abases the proud and favors the humble! May we never forget his goodness to us, and may our future conduct manifest our gratitude." In an effusive passage he wrote on the tenth anniversary of the Declaration of Independence, Franklin told Jane Mecom that he was thankful that God put an end to the Revolutionary War "much sooner than we had reason to expect. His Name be praised." Whatever God was doing, Franklin was glad that the war was over. He told his longtime friend and correspondent Jonathan Shipley, the Anglican bishop of St. Asaph, that he thought there never was such a thing as "a good war, or a bad peace."[43]

The early 1780s, then, saw Franklin gravitating back toward Calvinist views of human depravity and of providential interpretations of history. But we must not confuse these trajectories with renewed sympathy for the particulars of orthodox Christianity. For instance, he still doubted the divine origins of some parts of the Bible. When explaining his opposition to a religious test oath in the Pennsylvania constitution, he noted that he regarded "several things in the Old Testament impossible to be given by divine inspi-

ration." He singled out the "abominably wicked and detestable action of Jael," the woman who executed the military leader Sisera in
Judges 4 by using a hammer to drive a tent peg through his skull.
Franklin found Jael's act revolting. Yet the Bible praised Jael as
"blessed above women." Franklin thought that "if the rest of the
Book were like that, I should rather suppose it given by inspiration
from another quarter, and renounce the whole." Sometimes the
Bible could be hellish, he thought. Americans certainly should not
require officeholders to affirm everything in it.[44]

In 1785, Thomas Jefferson arrived in Paris as the new American
minister to France, and Franklin reluctantly returned to
Philadelphia. Although he had come under furious criticism from
Patriot critics during his tenure in France, Franklin was welcomed
home in Pennsylvania as a returning hero due "immortal honor."
He had been gone for so long, and won such notoriety, that power-
brokers seized on him as the one man who could unite
Philadelphia's ever-feuding factions. Before he had settled back
into town, Franklin had become president of the Pennsylvania
Executive Council. Because he was a member of the council and
not the assembly, Franklin did not have to take the oath affirming
the divine inspiration of the whole Bible. As Pennsylvania's chief
executive, he successfully worked to have that religious test repealed anyway.[45]

In early 1787, the Pennsylvania Assembly selected Franklin for
a convention meeting in Philadelphia at which delegates were to
propose revisions to the Articles of Confederation. The state-based
Articles were America's first constitution, but many believed that
they were not adequate to meet the new nation's challenges. As it
assembled, the eighty-one-year-old Franklin struck one participant
at the convention as "a short, fat, trunched old man, in a plain
Quaker dress, bald pate, and short white locks." Providence had yet
one more role for the elderly Doctor Franklin to play.[46]

Conclusion

Franklin's work at the Constitutional Convention was the culmination of his spectacular career. He and George Washington, twenty-six years his junior, were not the architects of the Constitution. That role fell to James Madison, Alexander Hamilton, and others. But Franklin and Washington were the two most famous Americans, and delegates looked on the returning octogenarian Franklin with respect and awe. There seemed little doubt that Washington, the imposing Virginia general, would become president of the convention. If there was any competitor for chair, it was the venerable Franklin. ("The very heavens obey him," a dazzled Georgia delegate noted.) But Franklin was ambivalent about continuing in political life at all. He had planned to nominate Washington as chair himself, if a storm had not kept him home for the opening day of the meeting.[1]

This son of Boston Puritans had come a long way to get to that Philadelphia meeting hall. In the late spring of 1787, he exchanged letters with Jane Mecom, reminiscing about their humble beginnings (a modest status in which Mecom had remained). He told her that the course of his life struck him "with wonder; and fills me with humble thankfulness to that divine Being who has graciously conducted my steps, and prospered me in this strange land to a degree that I could not rationally have expected, and can by no means conceive myself to have merited. I beg the continuance of his favor."[2]

Like Washington, Franklin did not say much at the convention. Although his chronic ailments made it difficult for him to stand and speak, he did offer occasional comments, seeking to steer the delegates toward a successful conclusion. But early on he also made a substantive speech, arguing against paying a salary to the president or other members of the executive branch. He based this argument on his dim view of human nature and of politicians' temptations to personal aggrandizement. "There are two passions which have a powerful influence in the affairs of men," he declared. "These are ambition and avarice; the love of power, and the love of money. . . . Place before the eyes of such men a [post] of honor that shall at the same time be a place of profit, and they will move heaven and earth to obtain it." Such corruption had ruined British politics, and he wished to uncouple America's government from the profit motive. Citing Exodus 18:21, Franklin reminded delegates that the best rulers were "men hating covetousness."[3]

Howard Chandler Christy, Scene at the Signing of the Constitution of the United States, *1940. Courtesy Wikimedia Commons.*

If you turned politics into an avenue for personal gain, only the most "bold and violent" men would want to enter. Lest delegates dismiss his pay proposal as utopian, he cited examples of offices in which people served for little or no money. The arbiters of Quaker meetings heard disputes that would have otherwise gone to secular courts. These duties were tedious, yet Quaker leaders performed them for no compensation. Once again, he presented the Quakers' simplicity as illustrative of pristine Christianity. Christians had turned away from the apostolic model when ministers began to accept salaries. This declension culminated, Franklin argued, in the "establishment of the papal system." He also pointed to the virtuous Washington, who took no salary as general of the Continental Army (though, to be fair, he did submit expenses). The convention declined to adopt Franklin's proposal. But Franklin was participating in a bigger conversation that ran through all of the constitutional debates. What kind of government could best account for the dangers inherent in human nature? Although Americans disagreed on the answer, they did not dispute the premise. Humans were not angels, as Madison wrote in *Federalist* no. 51. They could not be trusted with unchecked power.[4]

Franklin joined a more controversial debate at the convention with his proposal for prayer on June 28. The convention was struggling to resolve the tension between large and small states, which possessed equal power under the Articles of Confederation. To large states, that system was unfair. And so the state delegations feuded as the warm summer days dragged on. The impasse prompted Franklin's request. He had lived a long time, he reminded delegates, and he had become ever more certain that God oversaw human affairs. Franklin was convinced that Providence had shepherded Americans through the revolutionary crisis. It was foolish not to call on God again.

He reminded them of the early days of the war, when the Patriots prayed, often in that same room, for God's help. At its best, faith inculcated public-spiritedness and suffocated selfishness. God had led them to the point where they could now frame the best possible government. "And have we now forgotten that powerful Friend?" he asked. Citing Psalm 127, Franklin said that "except the Lord build the house, they labor in vain that build it."

Furthermore, he declared, "I firmly believe this; and I also believe that without his concurring aid, we shall succeed in this political building no better than the builders of Babel." Prideful strife would confound their work and turn their proceedings into a farce.[5]

This was the most remarkable religious episode of Franklin's life. It was stunning, and not just because of the stage on which he was proposing prayer. Franklin was nearly alone among the delegates in wishing to bring prayer into the convention's proceedings. Connecticut's Roger Sherman, one of the most devout Christians in attendance, seconded Franklin's motion. And Virginia's Edmund Randolph proposed that they hire a pastor to preach on Independence Day, less than a week later. That minister could then open subsequent meetings with prayer. Beyond these three men, delegates seemed uninterested in arranging for prayers. Someone pointed out that they had not budgeted funds for a chaplain. Alexander Hamilton worried that calling in a pastor might signal that the convention was becoming desperate. So the motion fizzled. Franklin was exasperated, jotting a note at the bottom of his speech that *"The Convention except three or four persons, thought prayers* unnecessary!!"[6]

Franklin and the convention moved on. Perhaps his speech did remind delegates of the need for compromise, even if it prompted no formal recourse to God. In a speech two days after proposing prayer, Franklin explained the root of the tension between the large and small states. If representation was proportioned according to population, "the small states contend that their liberties will be in danger. If an equality of votes is to be put in its place, the large states say their money is in danger." Both sides were going to have to give up some demands to ensure a successful outcome. Drawing on earlier discussions regarding a two-house legislature, Franklin suggested that the convention create a House of Representatives with proportional representation and a Senate with equal representation between the states. This became the "Great [or Connecticut] Compromise" (because of Roger Sherman's influence on the idea), arguably the key settlement of the whole Convention.[7]

In his final speech before the assembly, Franklin warned against dogmatism, which might derail the Constitution. He saw this species of moralistic perfectionism both in religion and in politics. "Most men indeed as well as most sects in religion, think themselves in possession of all truth, and that wherever others differ from them it is so far error." He recalled an English wag who explained the difference in doctrine between the Roman Catholic Church and the Church of England by saying that "the Romish Church is infallible, and the Church of England is never in the wrong." Delegates should be willing to support the Constitution, even if they did not regard it as perfect. No better frame of government would emerge from additional meetings. Franklin was "not sure that it is not the best" that they could do, as it currently stood. The framers' enemies were longing to hear that their councils had been confounded, "like those of the builders of Babel." The convention needed to present a unified front as the Constitution went out for ratification. Multiple forms of government could work well when administered by virtuous people anyway. According to an oft-repeated story, when someone asked Franklin after the convention whether they had created a monarchy or a republic, he replied, "A republic, if you can keep it."[8]

The Constitution went to the states for ratification in fall 1787. Writing to Franklin, Jane Mecom noted that there were "some quarilsome spirits against the constetution but it does not apear to be those of superior judgment. My greatest comfort is God reigns we are in His hands." As at the convention, the frail Franklin did not participate much in the ratification debates. But in one April 1788 editorial, he compared the Constitution's opponents to the Israelites who resisted Moses after God gave him the law. God himself had framed the Mosaic "Constitution," but still people grumbled about it. Some called for Moses to be stoned, just as some Jews called for Jesus to be crucified. From these precedents, Franklin inferred that "popular opposition to a public measure is no proof of its impropriety." The doctor admitted that he did not believe that the Constitution was "divinely inspired." Nevertheless, he had "so much faith in the general government of the world by Providence, that I can hardly conceive a transaction of such momentous importance ... should be suffered to pass without being in some degree influenced, guided and governed by that

omnipotent, omnipresent and beneficent Ruler, in whom all inferior spirits live and move and have their being [Acts 17:28]." He
and the Constitution's backers won enough states to secure ratification by mid-1788.⁹

Franklin knew that the Constitution had imperfections, but he
resolved to remain silent about them in public. Presumably one of
the imperfections was the Constitution's acceptance of slavery.
English antislavery activist Granville Sharp told Franklin that the
Constitution's provisions countenancing slavery were "null and
void by their iniquity." The slave South gained political advantages
under the three-fifths compromise. That agreement gave the white
South partial representation for its slaves, meaning more power for
slaveholders in the House of Representatives and in the Electoral
College, which chose the president. In spite of antislavery activists
who implored him to speak out, Franklin chose not to agitate for
antislavery provisions in the Constitution. Doing so would have
jeopardized its successful framing and ratification, especially
among proslavery advocates.¹⁰

Franklin's personal views on slavery had undergone a slow
transformation. His slave owning had concluded in 1781, with the
death of his last household slave, a man named George. In Britain
and France, he made friends with a number of antislavery activists.
In 1773, Franklin told Patriot leader Benjamin Rush that he hoped
"that the friends to liberty and humanity will get the better of
[slavery,] a practice that has so long disgraced our nation and religion." Still, Franklin's opposition to slavery did not really become
evident until after the Constitutional Convention, at the very end
of his life. Franklin joined Pennsylvania's Society for Promoting
the Abolition of Slavery in 1787, and became its president. (The
society realized the publicity value of Franklin's name.) In late
1789, the society declared that slavery is "an atrocious debasement
of human nature."¹¹

The society petitioned Congress in 1790. Drawing on the "political creed of Americans," the petition argued that "the Christian
religion teaches us to believe" that God had created all people and
equally designed them for happiness. Congressional policy should
reflect these truths. Southern members were angry at the petitioners, including Franklin. South Carolina senator Ralph Izard railed

against the "fanatics" of the Pennsylvania society. His fellow
South Carolina senator Pierce Butler attacked Franklin personally,
accusing him of trying to break up the union. "The doctor, when
member of the Convention," Butler said, "has consented to the
federal compact. Here was he acting in direct violation of it."
Representative James Jackson of Georgia insisted that, contrary to
the "Quaker" petitioners, "Christianity is not repugnant to slavery."
The society's members actually opposed the "commands of their
divine master, Jesus Christ," Jackson charged, "who allowed it in
his day, and his apostles after him." Jackson reviewed New
Testament verses that seemed to accept slavery. Those verses enjoined masters and slaves to accept their social status and obey God
in their respective stations.[12]

Jackson's speech prompted Franklin's last great satire, the
speech of an Algerian leader named Sidi Mehemet Ibrahim.
Franklin claimed that Ibrahim had given the speech a hundred
years earlier, but the doctor was really using a Muslim African's
voice to ridicule Jackson's proslavery argument. In response to
Muslims who wished to abolish the slave trade, Ibrahim argued
that without enslaving Christians, their economy would collapse.
Moreover, the Christian slaves "are brought into a land where the
sun of Islamism gives forth its light, and shines in full splendor, and
they have an opportunity of making themselves acquainted with
the true doctrine, and thereby saving their immortal souls."
Ibrahim insisted that the Qur'an endorsed slavery, requiring that
slaves obey their masters, and that masters treat slaves with kindness. Associating white southerners with the proslavery position of
an African Muslim was a classic Franklin move. Americans in the
revolutionary era often pointed to Muslim countries as exemplars
of religious and political despotism. The fact that the doctor published this piece less than a month before his death concluded his
career on a high note, even if it has given him a greater posthumous reputation for antislavery sentiments than he deserved.[13]

Franklin knew that he was dying. Opium was his only relief from
the gout and kidney stones. Jane Mecom was praying for him.
Reports of his dire condition distressed her, "but alas I can do
nothing to alleviate it. All I can do is to wish and pray for your

returning health and that you may at all times have the Spirit of
God comforting and sustaining you, that will be support when
flesh and heart fails." Franklin had been thinking about this moment since before he left France. He wrote in 1782 that he would
be "happy to sing with Old Simeon, *Now lettest thou thy Servant
Depart in Peace, for mine Eyes have seen thy Salvation.*" This harkened
to the words of the "just and devout" Simeon of the Gospel of
Luke, upon seeing the Christ child at the Jerusalem temple.[14]

Old acquaintances were passing away, too. One of the most revealing letters Franklin wrote in his last years reflected on the
death of Benjamin Kent, a longtime friend from Boston who had
called him "Brother Ben." Two years Franklin's junior, Kent had
graduated from Harvard and was ordained to the ministry, but in
1735, a clerical council removed him from his pastorate because of
heterodox beliefs (he was reportedly an Arian, believing that Jesus
was created by the Father). Franklin wrote to a Boston relative
about Kent, saying that he hoped Kent had gone to "the regions of
the blessed; or at [least?] to some place where souls are prepared
for those regions!" Here he was musing on the possibility of
Purgatory, the penal state before heaven taught by Catholics. More
strikingly, Franklin told his correspondent that "I found my hope
on this, that though not so orthodox as you and I, he was an honest
man, and had his virtues." Franklin here classed *himself* among the
"orthodox," at least as compared to Benjamin Kent. In Franklin's
formulation, the key to Kent's or anyone's salvation was not orthodoxy but virtue. Morality was preeminent, not doctrine. The doctor closed with a cautionary note about precisionists who damned
people of other denominations. "With regard to future blessings I
cannot help imagining, that multitudes of the zealously orthodox
of different sects, who at the last day may flock together, in hopes
of seeing [. . .] damned, will be disappointed, and obliged to rest
content with their [own] salvation." Franklin always thought the
precisionists would be surprised by who ends up in heaven.[15]

For some time, Jane Mecom had stopped asking Ben about the
nature of his faith. On his eighty-fourth birthday, she commended
him for his good works and thankfulness to God. "Grat Increece of
Glory and Happines I hope Await you," she told him. George
Whitefield and Jane Mecom had been the most persistent inquirers

about the state of his soul. From the 1740s onward, those two did the most to tether Franklin to traditional faith.[16]

One last inquirer now came on the stage. Franklin had known Yale College president Ezra Stiles since Yale granted Franklin an honorary master's degree in 1753. Stiles, a Congregationalist minister and broadminded Calvinist, realized that Franklin was near death. "You have merited and received all the honors of the Republic of Letters; and are going to a world, where all sublunary glories will be lost in the glories of immortality," Stiles wrote him. But Stiles paused. Would it be impertinent of him to ask about his belief in Christ? "As much as I know of Dr. Franklin," Stiles confessed, "I have not an idea of his religious sentiments. I wish to know the opinion of my venerable friend concerning JESUS of Nazareth." Stiles adored Franklin, but still he wished Franklin would have clear title to "that happy immortality which I believe Jesus alone has purchased for the virtuous and truly good of every religious denomination." London Unitarian minister Richard Price also registered concern in 1790 about Franklin's continuing unbelief but personally assured Franklin of the "equal happiness hereafter of all equally virtuous men and honest inquirers," whatever the nature of their faith.[17]

Franklin respected Stiles, so five weeks before his death he penned a response, which he asked Stiles to keep confidential. "You desire to know something of my religion. *It is the first time I have been questioned upon it*," Franklin wrote. (This was of course untrue. His parents, Jane Mecom, George Whitefield, and others had been asking him about it all his life.) "But I do not take your curiosity amiss, and shall endeavor in a few words to gratify it," he wrote. "Here is my creed: I believe in one God, Creator of the universe. That he governs it by his Providence. That he ought to be worshipped. That the most acceptable service we can render to him, is doing good to his other children. That the soul of man is immortal, and will be treated with justice in another life respecting its conduct in this."[18]

Lutheran pastor Nicholas Collin, who conversed with Franklin in his last weeks, confirmed that the doctor believed all moral crimes would be punished in this life or the next, and good actions would be likewise rewarded. According to Collin, Franklin anticipated "beholding the Glorious Father of spirits, whose essence is incomprehensible to the wisest of mortals." How much of this musing about the afterlife was Franklin's, and how much Collin's, is unclear. In any case, at the end of his life Franklin was a providentialist, a believer in the duties of worship and benevolence, and he expected God would rule in a final judgment.[19]

"As to Jesus of Nazareth, my opinion of whom you particularly desire, I think the system of morals and his religion as he left them to us, the best the world ever saw, or is likely to see," Franklin wrote to Stiles. But he still had doubts. "I apprehend [Christ's teachings have] received various corrupting changes, and I have with most of the present dissenters in England, some doubts as to his divinity: though it is a question I do not dogmatize upon, having never studied it." Franklin never doubted how admirable Christ's moral teachings were. He just did not know if he could accept the New Testament's doctrinal claims about Jesus. Franklin's (supposed) failure to study Jesus's divinity probably harkened back to his conversations with Joseph Priestley, the ones that the Revolutionary War had short-circuited. Franklin thought "it needless to busy myself with it now, when I expect soon an opportunity of knowing the Truth with less trouble." In this life, he was not sure he could know the truth about Christ and salvation. But he would find out soon.[20]

In spite of his qualms about traditional Christianity, he saw "no harm however in its being believed, if that belief has the good consequence as probably it has, of making his doctrines more respected and better observed." For Franklin, the point was never just belief but virtuous action. "I shall only add respecting myself," he concluded his letter to Stiles, "that having experienced the goodness of that Being, in conducting me prosperously through a long life, I have no doubt of its continuance in the next, though without the smallest conceit of meriting such goodness." God had always been good to him, and Franklin saw no reason to think that God's kindness would stop when he died. And die he did, on April 17, 1790. In his will he bequeathed a "new quarto Bible, Oxford edition," which he hoped would become the family scriptures for his godson, William Hewson, the child of Polly Stevenson Hewson.[21]

Polly Hewson, who had moved to Philadelphia in the mid-1780s, was actually with Franklin when he died. According to an anecdote from the time of his passing, Polly noticed an old picture at the foot of Franklin's deathbed. It was a painting of the Day of Judgment, "where the awful Judge was enthroned in glory, and giving sentence." In an image from Matthew 25, some souls were going off to the right, into the heavenly kingdom, and some to the left, into "everlasting fire." Hewson asked the nurse where the picture had come from. The nurse said that Franklin had owned it for years but had kept it in his attic. As his health failed, he asked the nurse to bring it out and put it where he could see it.[22]

Let's assume this story is true. (There are other versions of it. Parson Weems's biography has him looking at a picture of Jesus dying on the cross.) What was going on in Franklin's mind, as he gazed at God separating the saved and the damned? To the end, Franklin's faith was enigmatic. It was clear that by the end of his life, he affirmed God's Providence, and God's future rewards and punishments. But after a lifetime of questions by his parents, his sister Jane, and friends like Whitefield and Stiles, doubts still lingered. He had sought to live by a code of Christian ethics. But had he fully lived up to them? The doctor believed that those who enter heaven must do so by their virtue. But he knew that the Calvinist questioners saw this as false hope. No one merited salvation by their goodness, they said. They thought Franklin was wrong. He thought they were wrong. And so Franklin waited, with ragged breathing, eyes fixed on the painting.[23]

Notes

Introduction

1. Franklin, "Convention Speech Proposing Prayers," June 28, 1787, franklinpapers.org.
2. John Adams, Extract from the *Boston Patriot*, May 15, 1811, in Charles Francis Adams, ed., *The Works of John Adams* (Boston, 1856), 1:661.
3. M. L. Weems, *The Life of Benjamin Franklin* (Philadelphia, 1873), 221; John Foster, "From the *Eclectic Review*, 1818," in J. A. Leo Lemay and P. M. Zall, eds., *Benjamin Franklin's Autobiography* (New York, 1986), 255–256; Carla Mulford, "Franklin, Women, and American Cultural Myths," in Larry E. Tise, ed., *Benjamin Franklin and Women* (University Park, Penn., 2000), 109.
4. Max Weber, *The Protestant Ethic and the Spirit of Capitalism*, trans. Stephen Kalberg, 4th edn. (1905; New York, 2009), 70–74.
5. Jerry Weinberger, "Benjamin Franklin Unmasked," in Paul E. Kerry and Matthew S. Holland, eds., *Benjamin Franklin's Intellectual World* (Lanham, Md., 2012), 20; Ralph Frasca, *Benjamin Franklin's Printing Network: Disseminating Virtue in Early America* (Columbia, Mo., 2006), 40, 206; Michael J. McClymond and Gerald R. McDermott, *The Theology of Jonathan Edwards* (New York, 2012), 52. For an excellent overview of scholarly perspectives on Franklin's religion, see John Fea, "Benjamin Franklin and Religion," in David Waldstreicher, ed., *A Companion to Benjamin Franklin* (Malden, Mass., 2011), 129–145.
6. Ralph Lerner, "Dr. Janus," in J. A. Leo Lemay, ed., *Reappraising Benjamin Franklin: A Bicentennial Perspective* (Cranbury, N.J., 1993), 415; Alfred Owen Aldridge, *Benjamin Franklin and Nature's God* (Durham, N.C., 1967), 8, 11.
7. Kerry S. Walters, *Benjamin Franklin and His Gods* (Urbana, Ill., 1999), 10, 77.

8. Allen C. Guelzo, *Abraham Lincoln as a Man of Ideas* (Carbondale, Ill., 2009), 35.

9. Franklin to Samuel Cooper, May 15, 1781, franklinpapers.org.

10. Robert Bellah, *Habits of the Heart: Individualism and Commitment in American Life*, rev. edn. (1985; Berkeley, Calif., 2008), 221; Thomas Paine, *The Theological Works of Thomas Paine* (London, 1822), 4.

11. Teresa Jordan, *Year of Living Virtuously (Weekends Off)* (Berkeley, Calif., 2014), xviii, 134.

12. Christian Smith with Melinda Lundquist Denton, *Soul Searching: The Religious and Spiritual Lives of American Teenagers* (New York, 2005), 162–163; Jennifer Leclaire, "Oprah Winfrey: I Am a Christian," *Charisma News*, Apr. 26, 2012, http://www.charismanews.com/us/33290-oprah-winfrey-i-am-a-christian.

13. Thomas Jefferson to Benjamin Rush, Apr. 21, 1803, in Isaac Kramnick, ed., *The Portable Enlightenment Reader* (New York, 1995), 163–165.

14. J. A. Leo Lemay, *The Life of Benjamin Franklin*, vol. 1, *Journalist, 1706–1730* (Philadelphia, 2006), 8.

Chapter 1. Child of the Puritans

1. Franklin, "Silence Dogood No. 14," *New-England Courant*, Oct. 8, 1722, in Leonard W. Labaree et al., eds., *Papers of Benjamin Franklin*, 41 vols. to date (New Haven, Conn., 1959–), 1:43–44 (hereafter PBF).

2. Acrostic from Benjamin Franklin (the Elder), Commonplace Book of Benjamin Franklin (the Elder), July 15, 1710, PBF, 1:4–5.

3. *The Autobiography of Benjamin Franklin*, eds. Leonard W. Labaree, Ralph L. Ketcham, Helen C. Boatfield, and Helene H. Fineman, 2nd edn., with a new foreword by Edmund S. Morgan (New Haven, Conn., 2003), 50 (hereafter Franklin, *Autobiography*).

4. Franklin, *Autobiography*, 50.

5. Nian-Sheng Huang, "Franklin's Father Josiah: Life of a Colonial Boston Tallow Chandler, 1657–1745," *Transactions of the American Philosophical Society* 90, pt. 3 (2000): 3; Carla J. Mulford, *Benjamin Franklin and the Ends of Empire* (New York, 2015), 32.

6. Mulford, *Ends of Empire*, 33.

7. David J. Appleby, "From Ejectment to Toleration in England, 1662–89," in Alan P. F. Sell, ed., *The Great Ejectment of 1662: Its Antecedents, Aftermath, and Ecumenical Significance* (Eugene, Ore., 2012), 111–113.

8. Franklin, *Autobiography*, 51; Mulford, *Ends of Empire*, 19, 27.

9. Walter Isaacson, *Benjamin Franklin: An American Life* (New York, 2003), 9–10.

10. Increase Mather, *An Earnest Exhortation to the Inhabitants of New-England* (Boston, 1676), 2.

11. Huang, "Franklin's Father Josiah," 51; J. A. Leo Lemay, *The Life of Benjamin Franklin*, vol. 1, *Journalist, 1706–1730* (Philadelphia, 2006), 44.

12. Robert H. Bremner, ed., *Children and Youth in America: A Documentary History*, vol. 1, *1600–1865* (Cambridge, Mass., 1970), 42; Franklin, *Autobiography*, 55.

13. Huang, "Franklin's Father Josiah," 15.

14. Huang, "Franklin's Father Josiah," 33–34.

15. Franklin, *Autobiography*, 53; Franklin, "Proposal re. Daylight Saving," [Apr. 26, 1784], franklinpapers.org.

16. Franklin, *Autobiography*, 57, 72; Gerald Stourzh, "Reason and Power in Benjamin Franklin's Political Thought," in Peter S. Onuf, ed., *The New American Nation, 1775–1820*, vol. 1, *The Revolution in American Thought* (New York, 1991), 298n10.

17. Robert Burton, *The Kingdom of Darkness* (London, 1728), iv; Lemay, *Life of Franklin*, 1:45.

18. Franklin, *Autobiography*, 58; Mulford, *Ends of Empire*, 41–43.

19. Franklin, *Autobiography*, 58; Lemay, *Life of Franklin*, 1:44–45.

20. Lemay, *Life of Franklin*, 1:45, 47.

21. Cotton Mather, *Bonifacius: An Essay upon the Good* (Boston, 1710), 19–20, 23; Lemay, *Life of Franklin*, 1:47; Rick Kennedy, *Cotton Mather: The First American Evangelical* (Grand Rapids, Mich., 2015), 64; Daniel Defoe, *Essays upon Several Projects* (London, 1702), 1. On scholarly comparisons of Mather and Franklin, see Mitchell Robert Breitwieser, *Cotton Mather and Benjamin Franklin: The Price of Representative Personality* (New York, 1984), 13–14.

22. Franklin to Samuel Mather, May 12, 1784, franklinpapers.org.

23. David Waldstreicher, *Runaway America: Benjamin Franklin, Slavery, and the American Revolution* (New York, 2004), 41.

24. Lemay, *Life of Franklin*, 1:116; Franklin, *Autobiography*, 170.

25. Franklin to Samuel Mather, July 7, 1773, PBF, 20:287.

26. Franklin, *Autobiography*, 53; Isaacson, *An American Life*, 18–19, 25–27.

27. Lemay, *Life of Franklin*, 1:55; Gordon S. Wood, *The Americanization of Benjamin Franklin* (New York, 2004), 19.

28. Franklin, *Autobiography*, 59–60.

29. Joseph Addison, *The Spectator*, no. 185 (Oct. 2, 1711): 369; Wood, *Americanization*, 19–20.

30. Franklin, *Autobiography*, 63; Addison quoted in Kerry S. Walters, *Benjamin Franklin and His Gods* (Urbana, Ill., 1999), 29; Franklin, *Poor Richard Improved* (Philadelphia, 1748), PBF, 3:254.

31. Thomas Tryon, *The Way to Health* (London, 1683), 65, 79; Franklin, *Autobiography*, 63.

32. Franklin, *Autobiography*, 87.

33. Franklin, *Autobiography*, 63, 88; Franklin, *Poor Richard*, *1742* (Philadelphia, [1741]), PBF, 2:340–341; Nancy Glazener, "Benjamin Franklin and the Limits of Secular Civil Society," *American Literature* 80, no. 2 (June 2008): 221.

34. John Locke, *An Essay Concerning Humane Understanding* (London, 1706), 585–586, 592; Gerald R. Cragg, *Reason and Authority in the Eighteenth Century* (Cambridge, Eng., 1964), 5–12.

35. Locke, *Essay*, 588, 592; Cragg, *Reason and Authority*, 30–31.

36. Franklin, *Poor Richard Improved*, PBF, 3:259.

37. Anthony Ashley Cooper, Earl of Shaftesbury, *Characteristicks of Men, Manners, Opinions, Times* (London, 1732), 22; Anthony Collins, *A Discourse of Free-Thinking* (London, 1713), 27; James Green, *Poor Richard's Books* (Philadelphia, 1990), 18; Walters, *Franklin and His Gods*, 32–34; Michael J. McClymond and Gerald R. McDermott, *The Theology of Jonathan Edwards* (New York, 2012), 53.

38. Franklin, *Autobiography*, 64, 113.

39. Franklin, *Autobiography*, 64, 113–114; Elizabeth E. Dunn, "From a Bold Youth to a Reflective Sage: A Reevaluation of Benjamin Franklin's Religion," *Pennsylvania Magazine of History and Biography* 111, no. 4 (Oct. 1987): 517.

40. Ezra Stiles, "Memoir and Conjecture," May 1, 1769, PBF, 16:123.

41. *Boston News-Letter*, Aug. 28, 1721.

42. Franklin, *Autobiography*, 67–68.

43. Lemay, *Life of Franklin*, 1:144.

44. Franklin, "Silence Dogood No. 4," *New-England Courant*, May 14, 1722, PBF, 1:15–16.

45. Franklin, "Silence Dogood No. 4," PBF, 1:17; Thomas S. Kidd, *George Whitefield: America's Spiritual Founding Father* (New Haven, Conn., 2014), 54–55; Elizabeth Christine Cook, *Literary Influences in Colonial Newspapers, 1704–1750* (New York, 1912), 25.

46. Franklin, "Silence Dogood No. 9," *New-England Courant*, July 23, 1722, PBF, 1:30–31; Lemay, *Life of Franklin*, 1:164.

47. Todd N. Thompson, "Representative Nobodies: The Politics of Benjamin Franklin's Satiric Personae, 1722–1757," *Early American Literature* 46, no. 3 (Nov. 2011): 455.

48. Franklin, *Autobiography*, 68–70.

49. *New-England Courant*, Jan. 28, 1723; Franklin, *Autobiography*, 71.

50. Franklin, *Autobiography*, 71.

Chapter 2. Exodus to Philadelphia, Sojourn in London

1. Franklin, *Autobiography*, 76.

2. Franklin, *Autobiography*, 43; Rosalind J. Beiler, *Immigrant and Entrepreneur: The Atlantic World of Caspar Wistar, 1650–1750* (University Park, Penn., 2008), 90.

3. Gary B. Nash, *The Urban Crucible: The Northern Seaports and the Origins of the American Revolution*, abridged edn. (1979; Cambridge, Mass., 1986), 74–75.

4. Nash, *Urban Crucible*, 76; Jane T. Merritt, "Tea Trade, Consumption, and the Republican Paradox in Prerevolutionary Philadelphia," *Pennsylvania Magazine of History and Biography* 128, no. 2 (Apr. 2004): 127.

5. Simon P. Newman, "Benjamin Franklin and the Leather-Apron Men: The Politics of Class in Eighteenth-Century Philadelphia," *Journal of American Studies* 43, no. 2 (Aug. 2009): 162–163. Franklin used the term "leather-apron man" in his first Silence Dogood essay. See Allan Kulikoff, "Silence Dogood and the Leather-Apron Men," *Pennsylvania History* 81, no. 3 (Summer 2014): 366 and *passim*, for the origins of Franklin's usage.

6. David Waldstreicher, *Runaway America: Benjamin Franklin, Slavery, and the American Revolution* (New York, 2004), 24.

7. Franklin, *Autobiography*, 74; J. A. Leo Lemay, *The Life of Benjamin Franklin*, vol. 1, *Journalist, 1706–1730* (Philadelphia, 2006), 223.

8. Waldstreicher, *Runaway America*, 61.

9. Franklin, *Autobiography*, 79–80; Waldstreicher, *Runaway America*, 63.

10. Franklin, *Autobiography*, 81–82.

11. Franklin, *Autobiography*, 82–83.

12. Franklin, *Autobiography*, 83–84. On similarities between *Pilgrim's Progress* and the *Autobiography*, see Douglas Anderson, *The Unfinished Life of Benjamin Franklin* (Baltimore, 2012), 19–26, 53–57.

13. Franklin, *Autobiography*, 84.

14. Franklin, *Autobiography*, 85; Gilbert Burnet, *A Sermon Preached at the Coronation of William III and Mary II* (London, 1689), 28.

15. Franklin, *Autobiography*, 88.

16. Franklin, *Autobiography*, 88.

17. Franklin, *Autobiography*, 88–89.

18. Franklin, *Autobiography*, 89–90.

19. James Boswell, *The Life of Samuel Johnson* (London, 1791), 2:160; London *Daily Post*, Dec. 25, 1724.

20. Leo Damrosch, *Jonathan Swift: His Life and His World* (New Haven, Conn., 2013), 113–120; Franklin, *Autobiography*, 94–95.

21. Franklin, *Autobiography*, 89, 96.

22. Lemay, *Life of Franklin*, 1:262; William Wollaston, *The Religion of Nature Delineated* (London, 1724), 26.

23. Norman Fiering, *Jonathan Edwards's Moral Thought and Its British Context* (Chapel Hill, N.C., 1981), 132–136; Franklin, *Autobiography*, 96.

24. Franklin, *A Dissertation on Liberty and Necessity, Pleasure and Pain* (London, 1725), PBF, 1:58; Lemay, *Life of Franklin*, 1:271; Kerry S. Walters, *Benjamin Franklin and His Gods* (Urbana, Ill., 1999), 46; Kevin Slack, "Benjamin Franklin's Metaphysical Essays and the Virtue of Humility," *American Political Thought* 2, no. 1 (Spring 2013): 36–37; Elizabeth E. Dunn, "From a Bold Youth to a Reflective Sage: A Reevaluation of Benjamin Franklin's Religion," *Pennsylvania Magazine of History and Biography* 111, no. 4 (Oct. 1987): 512.

25. Walters, *Franklin and His Gods*, 45; Franklin to Benjamin Vaughan, Nov. 9, 1779, PBF, 31:59; Dunn, "Reevaluation of Benjamin Franklin's Religion," 507; Daniel Walker Howe, *Making the American Self: Jonathan*

Edwards to Abraham Lincoln (New York, 1997), 30; David L. Parker, "From Sound Believer to Practical Preparationist: Some Puritan Harmonics in Franklin's *Autobiography*," in J. A. Leo Lemay, ed., *The Oldest Revolutionary: Essays on Benjamin Franklin* (Philadelphia, 1976), 74.

26. Franklin, *Dissertation on Liberty and Necessity*, PBF, 1:59.
27. Franklin, *Dissertation on Liberty and Necessity*, PBF, 1:61.
28. Franklin, *Dissertation on Liberty and Necessity*, PBF, 1:63, 65, 71.
29. Franklin, *Autobiography*, 96; Franklin to Benjamin Vaughan, Nov. 9, 1779, PBF, 31:59; Lemay, *Life of Franklin*, 1:271; Joseph Priestley to Franklin, May 8, 1779, PBF, 29:454.
30. William Lyons, *The Infallibility of Human Judgment*, 5th edn. (1719; London, 1725), 102–103.
31. Bernard Mandeville, *The Fable of the Bees*, 3rd edn. (1714; London, 1724), 3, 5; Slack, "Franklin's Metaphysical Essays," 37; Waldstreicher, *Runaway America*, 70; Franklin, *Autobiography*, 97.
32. Franklin to Jane Mecom, Dec. 30, 1770, PBF, 17:315; James A. Herrick, "Jacob Ilive," *Oxford Dictionary of National Biography*, http://www.oxforddnb.com/view/article/14361; Lemay, *Life of Franklin*, 1:288.
33. Franklin to Jane Mecom, Dec. 30, 1770, PBF, 17:315.
34. Franklin, *Autobiography*, 98–99; Walters, *Franklin and His Gods*, 65.
35. Franklin, *Autobiography*, 99, 115; William Breitenbach, "Religious Affections and Religious Affectations: Antinomianism and Hypocrisy in the Writings of Edwards and Franklin," in Barbara B. Oberg and Harry S. Stout, eds., *Benjamin Franklin, Jonathan Edwards, and the Representation of American Culture* (New York, 1993), 18–19; Melvin H. Buxbaum, *Benjamin Franklin and the Zealous Presbyterians* (University Park, Penn., 1975), 10; Ralph Frasca, *Benjamin Franklin's Printing Network: Disseminating Virtue in Early America* (Columbia, Mo., 2006), 11–12, 36–37.
36. Franklin, *Autobiography*, 99–101.
37. Franklin, *Autobiography*, 101–103.
38. Franklin, *Autobiography*, 103.
39. Franklin, *Autobiography*, 103.
40. Franklin, *Autobiography*, 103–104.
41. Franklin, *Autobiography*, 105.
42. Franklin, "Plan of Conduct," [1726], PBF, 1:99–100; Alan Craig Houston, *Benjamin Franklin and the Politics of Improvement* (New Haven, Conn., 2008), 33.
43. Franklin, *Autobiography*, 106; Franklin, "Plan of Conduct," PBF, 1:100.

Chapter 3. Philadelphia Printer

1. Franklin, *Autobiography*, 147–148.
2. Franklin, "Journal of a Voyage, 1726," PBF, 1:91, 99.
3. J. A. Leo Lemay, *The Life of Benjamin Franklin*, vol. 1, *Journalist, 1706–1730* (Philadelphia, 2006), 319.

4. Franklin to Jane Franklin, Jan. 6, 1727, PBF, 1:100–101; Jill Lepore, *The Whites of Their Eyes: The Tea Party's Revolution and the Battle over American History* (Princeton, N.J., 2010), 49. On Jane Franklin's life, see Lepore, *Book of Ages: The Life and Opinions of Jane Franklin* (New York, 2014).

5. Lemay, *Life of Franklin*, 1:318; Franklin, *Autobiography*, 107.

6. Franklin, *Autobiography*, 107.

7. Franklin, "Epitaph," [1728], PBF, 1:109–111. There are three known autograph texts of the epitaph, and the Franklin Papers edition combines features of all three in their rendering.

8. Robert Zaretsky, *Boswell's Enlightenment* (Cambridge, Mass., 2015), 15–16; James A. Herrick, *The Radical Rhetoric of the English Deists: The Discourse of Skepticism, 1680–1750* (Columbia, S.C., 1997), 182; Lewis P. Simpson, "The Printer as a Man of Letters: Franklin and the Symbolism of the Third Realm," in J. A. Leo Lemay, ed., *The Oldest Revolutionary: Essays on Benjamin Franklin* (Philadelphia, 1976), 4. The epitaph date of 1728 comes from a Franklin note written around 1784. Lemay, *Life of Franklin*, 1:320.

9. Franklin, *Autobiography*, 107–108.

10. Franklin, *Autobiography*, 108–109.

11. Franklin, *Autobiography*, 112–113.

12. Franklin, *Autobiography*, 110–111.

13. Franklin, *Autobiography*, 118; Leo Damrosch, *Jonathan Swift: His Life and His World* (New Haven, Conn., 2013), 157; Samuel Butler, *Hudibras* (London, 1793), 2:561; Robert Creighton, *The Vanity of the Dissenters' Plea* (London, 1682), 18; Lemay, *Life of Franklin*, 1:332.

14. Cotton Mather, *Bonifacius: An Essay upon the Good* (Boston, 1710), 84, 87.

15. Franklin, *Autobiography*, 116–117; David S. Shields, "Franklin in the Republic of Letters," in Carla Mulford, ed., *The Cambridge Companion to Benjamin Franklin* (New York, 2008), 54.

16. Franklin, *Autobiography*, 118.

17. John Locke, "Rules of a Society," in *The Works of John Locke*, 5th edn. (London, 1751), 3:756; Benjamin Franklin, *Political, Miscellaneous, and Philosophical Pieces* (London, 1779), 536; Lemay, *Life of Franklin*, 1:339.

18. Mather, *Bonifacius*, 173; Franklin, *Philosophical Pieces*, 534; Lemay, *Life of Franklin*, 1:341.

19. Franklin, *Philosophical Pieces*, 534; William Pencack, "Benjamin Franklin's *Autobiography*, Cotton Mather, and a Puritan God," *Pennsylvania History* 53, no. 1 (Jan. 1986): 2–3.

20. Franklin, *Philosophical Pieces*, 535; Gordon Wood, *The Americanization of Benjamin Franklin* (New York, 2004), 42; Alan Craig Houston, *Benjamin Franklin and the Politics of Improvement* (New Haven, Conn., 2008), 80–81.

21. Franklin, *Philosophical Pieces*, 535.

22. Franklin, "On Conversation," *Pennsylvania Gazette*, Oct. 15, 1730, PBF, 1:178.

23. Franklin, "On Conversation," PBF, 1:178–179.
24. Franklin, *Autobiography*, 114.
25. Franklin, "On the Providence of God in the Government of the World," 1732, PBF, 1:264.
26. Franklin, "On the Providence of God," PBF, 1:264–265.
27. Franklin, "On the Providence of God," PBF, 1:265–266.
28. Franklin, "On the Providence of God," PBF, 1:266–267.
29. Franklin, "On the Providence of God," PBF, 1:267–268.
30. Franklin, "On the Providence of God," PBF, 1:267.
31. Franklin, "On the Providence of God," PBF, 1:267–268.
32. Allan Arkush, *Moses Mendelssohn and the Enlightenment* (Albany, N.Y., 1994), 8–9.
33. Franklin, "On the Providence of God," PBF, 1:269.
34. E. Brooks Holifield, *Theology in America: Christian Thought from the Age of the Puritans to the Civil War* (New Haven, Conn., 2003), 8–10.
35. Franklin, *Autobiography*, 119.
36. Kerry S. Walters, *Benjamin Franklin and His Gods* (Urbana, Ill., 1999), 94.
37. Franklin, "Articles of Belief and Acts of Religion," Nov. 20, 1728, PBF, 1:101.
38. Franklin, "Articles of Belief," PBF, 1:102. Alfred Owen Aldridge interpreted the "Articles of Belief" as an affirmation of polytheism, in Aldridge, *Benjamin Franklin and Nature's God* (Durham, N.C., 1967), 29. Elizabeth E. Dunn sees "cleverly disguised irreverence" in the production, in Dunn, "From a Bold Youth to a Reflective Sage: A Reevaluation of Benjamin Franklin's Religion," *Pennsylvania Magazine of History and Biography* 111, no. 4 (Oct. 1987): 512. See also Walters, *Franklin and His Gods*, 78–82, and Ralph Lerner, "The Gospel According to the Apostle Ben," *American Political Thought* 1, no. 1 (Spring 2012): 132–135.
39. Franklin, "Articles of Belief," PBF, 1:102.
40. Franklin, "Articles of Belief," PBF, 1:102.
41. Franklin, "Articles of Belief," PBF, 1:102–103; Daniel Walker Howe, "Franklin, Edwards, and the Problem of Human Nature," in Barbara B. Oberg and Harry S. Stout, eds., *Benjamin Franklin, Jonathan Edwards, and the Representation of American Culture* (New York, 1993), 78.
42. Traditional commentators have conventionally understood the Bible's "gods" as angels or human rulers.
43. Franklin, "Articles of Belief," PBF, 1:103–104; Aldridge, *Franklin and Nature's God*, 29–30.
44. Franklin, "The Busy-Body, No. 3," *American Weekly Mercury*, Feb. 18, 1729, PBF, 1:119–120; Lemay, *Life of Franklin*, 1:383.
45. Franklin, "Articles of Belief," PBF, 1:104–105.
46. John Ray, *The Wisdom of God Manifested in the Works of the Creation*, 6th edn. (1691; London, 1714), preface; Douglas Anderson, *The Radical Enlightenments of Benjamin Franklin* (Baltimore, 1997), 124–129; Peter J. Thuesen, ed., *Jonathan Edwards: Catalogues of Books* (New Haven, Conn., 2008), 70.

47. The other greatest poet besides Milton was the Scottish poet James Thomson. Franklin, "Reply to a Piece of Advice," *Pennsylvania Gazette*, Mar. 4, 1735, PBF, 2:21–26; Bruce Hindmarsh, "The Inner Life of Doctrine: An Interdisciplinary Perspective on the Calvinist-Arminian Debate among Methodists," *Church History* 83, no. 2 (June 2014): 391.

48. Franklin, "Articles of Belief," PBF, 1:106.

49. Franklin, "Articles of Belief," PBF, 1:106–107; Franklin, "Busy-Body, No. 3," PBF, 1:121; Anderson, *Radical Enlightenments*, 65.

50. Franklin, "Articles of Belief," PBF, 1:107.

51. Franklin, "Articles of Belief," PBF, 1:107–108; Jerry Weinberger, "Benjamin Franklin Unmasked," in Paul E. Kerry and Matthew S. Holland, eds., *Benjamin Franklin's Intellectual World* (Lanham, Md., 2012), 20; Paul Putz, " 'The Fool Hath Said in His Heart, There Is No God': Atheism in American Public Discourse, 1693–1783," Baylor University seminar paper, 2013, 3; Philipp Blom, *A Wicked Company: The Forgotten Radicalism of the European Enlightenment* (New York, 2010), 89; John Adams, diary, June 23, 1779, in C. James Taylor et al., eds., *The Adams Papers Digital Edition* (Charlottesville, Va., 2008–2016), http://rotunda. upress.virginia.edu/founders/default.xqy?keys=ADMS-search-1- 3&expandNote=on#match1. For a judicious review of the nature of Franklin's beliefs and his growing openness to God's active Providence, see Lorraine Smith Pangle, *The Political Philosophy of Benjamin Franklin* (Baltimore, 2007), 185–214. On the Puritans, set forms, and hypocrisy, see, among others, Abram Van Engen, *Sympathetic Puritans: Calvinist Fellow Feeling in Early New England* (New York, 2015), 14.

52. Franklin, "Articles of Belief," PBF, 1:108.

53. Franklin, "Articles of Belief," PBF, 1:108; Franklin, *Autobiography*, 145; David Waldstreicher, *Runaway America: Benjamin Franklin, Slavery, and the American Revolution* (New York, 2004), 26; Konstantin Dierks, "Benjamin Franklin and Colonial Society," in David Waldstreicher, ed., *A Companion to Benjamin Franklin* (Malden, Mass., 2011), 89–90, 100.

54. Franklin, "Articles of Belief," PBF, 1:109.

55. John Wise, *A Vindication of the Government of New England Churches*, in Alan Heimert and Andrew Delbanco, eds., *The Puritans in America: A Narrative Anthology* (Cambridge, Mass., 1985), 362; Van Engen, *Sympathetic Puritans*, 9, 41.

56. *The Constitutions of the Free-Masons* (Philadelphia, 1734), 48; Steven C. Bullock, *Revolutionary Brotherhood: Freemasonry and the Transformation of the American Social Order, 1730–1840* (Chapel Hill, N.C., 1996), 33; Margaret C. Jacob, *Living the Enlightenment: Freemasonry and Politics in Eighteenth-Century Europe* (New York, 1991), 31.

57. *Pennsylvania Gazette*, Dec. 15, 1730; J. A. Leo Lemay, *The Life of Benjamin Franklin*, vol. 2, *Printer and Publisher, 1730–1747* (Philadelphia, 2006), 83–86.

58. *Pennsylvania Gazette*, May 20, 1731; Wood, *Americanization*, 43–44.
59. *The Constitutions of the Free-Masons*, 7.
60. Lemay, *Life of Franklin*, 2:92.
61. Franklin, "Observations on Reading History," May 9, 1731, PBF, 1:193.
62. Franklin, *Autobiography*, 162–163; Lemay, *Life of Franklin*, 2:59–60. Franklin composed the creed by memory decades later in the autobiography, but a 1731 document he titled "Docts. to be prea[che]d" gave more details about virtue and God's attributes. For example, it noted that God was "infinitely good, Powerful and wise," and that he was "omnipresent." Franklin, "Doctrine to Be Preached," 1731, PBF, 1:213; Ralph Lerner, "Franklin, Spectator," in *The Thinking Revolutionary: Principle and Practice in the New Republic* (Ithaca, N.Y., 1987), 46–47.
63. Zaretsky, *Boswell's Enlightenment*, 56.

Chapter 4. Poor Richard

1. Gordon S. Wood, *The Americanization of Benjamin Franklin* (New York, 2004), 53.
2. Franklin, *Poor Richard, 1733* (Philadelphia, [1732]), PBF, 1:293–294; Todd N. Thompson, "Representative Nobodies: The Politics of Benjamin Franklin's Satiric Personae, 1722–1757," *Early American Literature*, 46, no. 3 (Nov. 2011): 463.
3. Franklin, *Poor Richard, 1733*, PBF, 1:303.
4. Franklin, *Poor Richard, 1733*, PBF, 1:300.
5. Franklin, *Autobiography*, 122–123; "From Hugh Meredith: Dissolution of Partnership," July 14, 1730, PBF, 1:175.
6. Franklin, *Autobiography*, 128; Franklin, "Silence Dogood, No. 13," *New-England Courant*, Oct. 8, 1722, PBF, 1:42; J. A. Leo Lemay, *The Life of Benjamin Franklin*, vol. 2, *Printer and Publisher, 1730–1747* (Philadelphia, 2006), 6.
7. Robert Zaretsky, *Boswell's Enlightenment* (Cambridge, Mass. 2015), 223–225.
8. Lemay, *Life of Franklin*, 2:6–7.
9. Franklin, *Autobiography*, 96; J. A. Leo Lemay, *The Life of Benjamin Franklin*, vol. 1, *Journalist, 1706–1730* (Philadelphia, 2006), 265–266.
10. Franklin, *Autobiography*, 107, 129.
11. Franklin, *Autobiography*, 129.
12. Lemay, *Life of Franklin*, 2:5, 9; David Waldstreicher, *Runaway America: Benjamin Franklin, Slavery, and the American Revolution* (New York, 2004), 91, 107–108.
13. Franklin, "Rules and Maxims for Promoting Matrimonial Happiness," 1730, in J. A. Leo Lemay, ed., *Benjamin Franklin: Writings* (New York, 1987), 152.
14. Franklin, "Rules and Maxims," in Lemay, ed., *Franklin: Writings*, 153–154.

15. John Meredith, *A Short Discourse, Proving that the Jewish or Seventh-Day Sabbath is Abrogated and Repealed* (Philadelphia, 1729); Isaac Watts, *The Psalms of David, Imitated in the Language of the New Testament, and Apply'd to the Christian State and Worship*, 7th edn. (Philadelphia, 1729); Nathan R. Kozuskanich, *Benjamin Franklin: American Founder, Atlantic Citizen* (New York, 2015), 45.

16. Franklin, "The Busy-Body, No. 5," *American Weekly Mercury*, Mar. 4, 1729, PBF, 1:127–129.

17. *The Tatler*, no. 14, in *The Tatler and the Guardian. Complete in One Volume* (Edinburgh, 1880), 34; Lemay, *Life of Franklin*, 1:387; Christopher Krentz, "Duncan Campbell and the Discourses of Deafness," in Brenda Jo Brueggemann and Marian Lupo, eds., *Disability and/in Prose* (New York, 2007), 29–30; Katie Trumpener, *Bardic Nationalism: The Romantic Novel and the British Empire* (Princeton, N.J., 1997), 98–100.

18. Arthur Conan Doyle, *Micah Clarke, His Statement* (New York, 1894), 465; Emerson W. Baker, *The Devil of Great Island: Witchcraft and Conflict in Early New England* (New York, 2007), 22–24.

19. [Franklin], "Letter of the Drum," *Pennsylvania Gazette*, Apr. 23, 1730, in Lemay, ed., *Franklin: Writings*, 145; on Franklin's authorship, see J. A. Leo Lemay, *The Canon of Benjamin Franklin, 1722–1776: New Attributions and Reconsiderations* (Cranbury, N.J., 1986), 42–43; "bogeyman" in Jonathan Israel, *Radical Enlightenment: Philosophy and the Making of Modernity, 1650–1750* (New York, 2001), 159.

20. [Franklin], "Letter of the Drum," in Lemay, ed., *Franklin: Writings*, 145–147.

21. David Hume, "Of Miracles," in Stephen Buckle, ed., *An Enquiry Concerning Human Understanding and Other Writings* (New York, 2007), 101.

22. [Franklin], "On that Odd Letter of the Drum," *Pennsylvania Gazette*, May 7, 1730, in Lemay, ed., *Franklin: Writings*, 148; on Franklin's authorship, see Lemay, *Canon*, 43–46.

23. [Franklin], "On that Odd Letter of the Drum," in Lemay, ed., *Franklin: Writings*, 149. On revelation, see Franklin, *Autobiography*, 114–115.

24. [Franklin], "On that Odd Letter of the Drum," in Lemay, ed., *Franklin: Writings*, 149; Lemay, *Life of Franklin*, 1:438–439.

25. [Franklin], "On that Odd Letter of the Drum," in Lemay, ed., *Franklin: Writings*, 150–151.

26. Emerson W. Baker, *A Storm of Witchcraft: The Salem Trials and the American Experience* (New York, 2015), 4, 209, 262–263.

27. Susan E. Klepp and Billy G. Smith, eds., *The Infortunate: The Voyage and Adventures of William Moraley, an Indentured Servant*, 2nd edn. (University Park, Penn., 2005), 141–145. Lemay considered Moraley's account a "feeble imitation of Franklin's hoax." Lemay, *Life of Franklin*, 1:444.

28. Franklin, "A Witch Trial at Mount Holly," *Pennsylvania Gazette*, Oct. 22, 1730, PBF, 1:182.

29. Franklin, "A Witch Trial at Mount Holly," PBF, 1:182–183.

30. Franklin, "A Witch Trial at Mount Holly," PBF, 1:183.

31. Owen Davies, *America Bewitched: Witchcraft after Salem* (New York, 2013), 101; Christina Hole, *Witchcraft in England* (New York, 1947), 67; Paul E. Kerry, "Franklin's Satiric Vein," in Carla Mulford, ed., *The Cambridge Companion to Benjamin Franklin* (New York, 2008), 41–42.

32. Franklin, "Apology for Printers," *Pennsylvania Gazette*, June 10, 1731, PBF, 1:197; Lemay, *Life of Franklin*, 2:11, 376–377.

33. Franklin, "Apology for Printers," PBF, 1:194–195.

34. Franklin, "Apology for Printers," PBF, 1:195–196; James N. Green, "English Books and Printing in the Age of Franklin," in Hugh Amory and David D. Hall, eds., *A History of the Book in America*, vol. 1, *The Colonial Book in the Atlantic World* (New York, 2000), 267.

35. Franklin, "Apology for Printers," PBF, 1:196.

36. Franklin, "Apology for Printers," PBF, 1:197.

37. Franklin, "Apology for Printers," PBF, 1:197–199.

38. Franklin, *Autobiography*, 125–126.

39. *Pennsylvania Gazette*, Nov. 27, 1731, June 22, 1738. J. A. Leo Lemay argues that Franklin was not actually selling the slaves but merely serving as a source of further information about the sales. Lemay, *Life of Franklin*, 2:280. Others contend that Franklin sold slaves; see David Waldstreicher, "Benjamin Franklin, Capitalism, and Slavery," in David Waldstreicher, ed., *A Companion to Benjamin Franklin* (Malden, Mass., 2011), 217. On selling the slave couple, see Franklin to Abiah Franklin, Apr. 12, 1750, PBF, 3:474, and Gary B. Nash and Jean R. Soderlund, *Freedom by Degrees: Emancipation in Pennsylvania and Its Aftermath* (New York, 1991), ix–x.

40. Lemay, *Life of Franklin*, 2:17–18; Jeff Bach, *Voices of the Turtledoves: The Sacred World of Ephrata* (University Park, Penn., 2003), 3–5.

41. Franklin, *A Catalogue of Choice and Valuable Books* (Philadelphia, 1744), A2, 6, and *passim*.

42. Franklin, *Autobiography*, 130.

43. Franklin, *Autobiography*, 130n5, 142–143; Carl Van Doren, *Benjamin Franklin* (New York, 1938), 104–105.

44. Franklin, *Autobiography*, 130; Franklin, *A Catalogue of Books Belonging to the Library Company of Philadelphia* (Philadelphia, 1741), 6, 8, 21; Lemay, *Life of Franklin*, 1:335.

45. Franklin, *Library Company*, 21, 26, 29, 39, 56; Thomas S. Kidd, *American Christians and Islam: Evangelical Culture and Muslims from the Colonial Period to the Age of Terrorism* (Princeton, N.J., 2008), 9–10.

46. Franklin to Sarah Davenport, [June? 1730], PBF, 1:171; Franklin to Jane Mecom, June 19, 1731, PBF, 1:200.

47. Lemay, *Life of Franklin*, 2:23–24; *Pennsylvania Gazette*, June 30, 1737, Aug. 6, 13, 1741, PBF, 2:188, 328–329; Van Doren, *Franklin*, 125–127; Jennifer Reed Fry, " 'Extraordinary Freedom and Great Humility': A Reinterpretation of Deborah Franklin," *Pennsylvania Magazine of History and Biography* 127, no. 2 (Apr. 2003): 177–178.

48. Franklin, *Autobiography*, 170; Lemay, *Life of Franklin*, 2:24.

49. Franklin, *Autobiography*, 144; *Pennsylvania Gazette*, Dec. 28, 1732, PBF, 1:280; Max Weber, *The Protestant Ethic and the Spirit of Capitalism*, trans. Stephen Kalberg, 4th edn. (New York, 2009), 73; Cotton Mather, *The Boston Ephemeris* (Boston, 1683), n.p.; Lemay, *Life of Franklin*, 2:172.

50. Franklin, *Poor Richard, 1733*, PBF, 1:287; Titan Leeds, *The American Almanack* (Philadelphia, 1733), 1; Mather, *Boston Ephemeris; Poor Robin, 1680* (London, 1680), A3; Lemay, *Life of Franklin*, 2:172.

51. Franklin, *Poor Richard, 1733*, PBF, 1:288.

52. Franklin, *Poor Richard, 1733*, PBF, 1:288; Titan Leeds, *Leeds 1734* (Philadelphia, 1734), 2; Lemay, *Life of Franklin*, 2:173–175; Leo Damrosch, *Jonathan Swift: His Life and His World* (New Haven, Conn., 2013), 188–189.

53. Franklin, *Poor Richard, 1734* (Philadelphia, [1733]), PBF, 1:349–350.

54. Franklin, *Poor Richard, 1734*, PBF, 1:350.

55. Franklin, *Poor Richard, 1740* (Philadelphia, 1739), PBF 2:245–246.

56. Franklin, *Poor Richard, 1740*, PBF, 2:245–246.

Chapter 5. Ben Franklin's Closest Evangelical Friend

1. *Pennsylvania Gazette*, July 26, 1739; Frank Lambert, *"Pedlar in Divinity": George Whitefield and the Transatlantic Revivals* (Princeton, N.J., 1994), 103.

2. Franklin, *Autobiography*, 177.

3. Franklin, *Autobiography*, 178; Lisa Smith, *The First Great Awakening in Colonial American Newspapers* (Lanham, Md., 2012), 4–5; Nathan R. Kozuskanich, *Benjamin Franklin: American Founder, Atlantic Citizen* (New York, 2015), 45.

4. J. A. Leo Lemay, *The Canon of Benjamin Franklin, 1722–1776: New Attributions and Reconsiderations* (Cranbury, N.J., 1986), 78.

5. Gregory Lynall, *Swift and Science: The Satire, Politics, and Theology of Natural Knowledge, 1690–1730* (New York, 2012), 18–20; Catherine A. Brekus, *Sarah Osborn's World: The Rise of Evangelical Christianity in Early America* (New Haven, Conn., 2013), 225–226; Leo Damrosch, *Jonathan Swift: His Life and His World* (New Haven, Conn., 2013), 106–107; J. A. Leo Lemay, *The Life of Benjamin Franklin*, vol. 2, *Printer and Publisher, 1730–1747* (Philadelphia, 2006), 72.

6. [Franklin], "A Meditation on a Quart Mugg," *Pennsylvania Gazette*, July 19, 1733, in J. A. Leo Lemay, ed., *Benjamin Franklin: Writings* (New York, 1987), 216–217.

7. [Joshua Smith], "Meditation on the Vanity and Brevity of Human Life," *Pennsylvania Gazette*, Aug. 8, 1734. On the case for Franklin's authorship of the parody, see Alfred Owen Aldridge, "A Religious Hoax by Benjamin Franklin," *American Literature* 36, no. 2 (May 1964): 204–209.

8. [Franklin], "Parody and Reply to a Religious Meditation," *Pennsylvania Gazette*, Aug. 8, 1734, in Lemay, ed., *Franklin: Writings*, 230–232; Franklin to Jane Mecom, July 10, 1764, PBF, 11:253.

9. [Franklin], "Parody and Reply to a Religious Meditation," in Lemay, ed., *Franklin: Writings*, 231–232.

10. [Franklin], "Parody and Reply to a Religious Meditation," in Lemay, ed., *Franklin: Writings*, 232–233. On "sleep of death," see Aldridge, "A Religious Hoax," 207.

11. [Franklin], "The Death of Infants," *Pennsylvania Gazette*, June 20, 1734, in Lemay, ed., *Franklin: Writings*, 228; Jill Lepore, *The Whites of Their Eyes: The Tea Party's Revolution and the Battle over American History* (Princeton, N.J., 2010), 49. On Franklin's authorship, see Lemay, *Canon*, 84–86.

12. [Franklin], "Death of Infants," in Lemay, ed., *Franklin: Writings*, 228–229.

13. [Franklin], "Death of Infants," in Lemay, ed., *Franklin: Writings*, 229–230.

14. Merton A. Christensen, "Franklin on the Hemphill Trial: Deism versus Presbyterian Orthodoxy," *William and Mary Quarterly*, 3rd ser., 10, no. 3 (July 1953): 424–425; [Franklin], *Some Observations on the Proceedings against the Rev. Mr. Hemphill*, 2nd edn. (Philadelphia, 1735), PBF, 2:40.

15. Christensen, "Franklin on the Hemphill Trial," 424–427.

16. Franklin, *Autobiography*, 167. On the Hemphill controversy, see Melvin H. Buxbaum, *Benjamin Franklin and the Zealous Presbyterians* (University Park, Penn., 1975), 93–115.

17. Franklin, "Dialogue between Two Presbyterians," *Pennsylvania Gazette*, Apr. 10, 1735, PBF, 2:28–33; Edwin S. Gaustad, "The Nature of True— and Useful—Virtue: From Edwards to Franklin," in Barbara B. Oberg and Harry S. Stout, eds., *Benjamin Franklin, Jonathan Edwards, and the Representation of American Culture* (New York, 1993), 51.

18. *An Extract of the Minutes of the Commission of the Synod* (Philadelphia, 1735), 11, 17; [Franklin], *Some Observations on the Proceedings against the Rev. Mr. Hemphill*, 2nd edn. (Philadelphia, 1735), PBF, 2:37–38.

19. [Franklin], *Observations on the Proceedings against Mr. Hemphill*, PBF, 2:56–57. On Franklin and the antinomian theme, see William Breitenbach, "Religious Affections and Religious Affectations: Antinomianism and Hypocrisy in the Writings of Edwards and Franklin," in Oberg and Stout, eds., *Franklin and Edwards*, 13–26.

20. [Franklin], *A Letter to a Friend in the Country* (Philadelphia, 1735), PBF, 2:66–67.

21. [Franklin], *A Letter to a Friend*, PBF, 2:84–85.

22. [Franklin], *A Letter to a Friend*, PBF, 2:84–85.

23. Obadiah Jenkins, *Remarks upon the Defence of the Reverend Mr. Hemphill's Observations* (Philadelphia, 1735), 18; Franklin, *Autobiography*, 167–168; Gerald R. Cragg, *Reason and Authority in the Eighteenth Century* (Cambridge, Eng., 1964), 34–36; Peter J. Thuesen, ed., *Jonathan Edwards: Catalogues of Books* (New Haven, Conn., 2008), 73–75.

24. [Franklin], ed., *A Defence of the Rev. Mr. Hemphill's Observations* (Philadelphia, 1735), 96–97; Alfred Owen Aldridge, *Benjamin Franklin and Nature's God* (Durham, N.C., 1967), 96; Judith C. Mueller, "*A Tale of a Tub* and Early Prose," in Christopher Fox, ed., *The Cambridge Companion to Jonathan Swift* (New York, 2003), 205.

25. [Franklin], *Defence*, 103–105.

26. [Franklin], *Defence*, 103–110; *A Vindication of the Reverend Commission of the Synod* (Philadelphia, 1735), 46; Daniel Walker Howe, *Making the American Self: Jonathan Edwards to Abraham Lincoln* (New York, 1997), 35.

27. [Franklin], *Defence*, 118–120.

28. E. Brooks Holifield, *Theology in America: Christian Thought from the Age of the Puritans to the Civil War* (New Haven, Conn., 2003), 166–167; Gerald R. McDermott, *Jonathan Edwards Confronts the Gods: Christian Theology, Enlightenment Religion, and Non-Christian Faiths* (New York, 2000), 18.

29. [Franklin], *Defence*, 113.

30. Howe, *Making the American Self*, 22–23.

31. Lemay, *Life of Franklin*, 2:288–289; H. W. Brands, *The First American: The Life and Times of Benjamin Franklin* (New York, 2000), 150–151; Steven C. Bullock, *Revolutionary Brotherhood: Freemasonry and the Transformation of the American Social Order, 1730–1840* (Chapel Hill, N.C., 1996), 65–66.

32. Franklin, "A Defense of Conduct," *Pennsylvania Gazette*, Feb. 15, 1738, PBF, 2:199; *American Weekly Mercury*, Feb. 14, 1738, PBF, 2:199.

33. *Pennsylvania Gazette*, June 23, 1737.

34. Franklin, "A Defense of Conduct," PBF, 2:199–201.

35. Franklin to Josiah and Abiah Franklin, Apr. 13, 1738, PBF, 2:204.

36. Franklin to Josiah and Abiah Franklin, Apr. 13, 1738, PBF, 2:202–203; Sarah Rivett, *The Science of the Soul in Colonial New England* (Chapel Hill, N.C., 2011), 342; Kerry S. Walters, *Benjamin Franklin and His Gods* (Urbana, Ill., 1999), 134–135.

37. Franklin to Josiah and Abiah Franklin, Apr. 13, 1738, PBF, 2:203.

38. Franklin mistakenly wrote chapter 26, suggesting that he did not have his Bible open in front of him when recalling this passage.

39. Franklin to Josiah and Abiah Franklin, Apr. 13, 1738, PBF, 2:202–203.

40. Sylvanus Urban, *Gentleman's Magazine for 1734* (London, n.d.), 4 (Oct. 1734): 562; Franklin, *Poor Richard, 1739* (Philadelphia, [1738]), PBF, 2:223–224.

41. Howe, *Making the American Self*, 25. Franklin's promised amount of support is not known. "Subscription to Christ Church," May 7, 1739, PBF, 2:227–228.

42. *New-York Weekly Journal*, June 13, 1737; *Pennsylvania Gazette*, July 7, 1737, July 26, 1739.

43. *Pennsylvania Gazette*, Nov. 8, 1739.

44. *American Weekly Mercury*, Nov. 22, 1739; George Whitefield, *George Whitefield's Journals* (Carlisle, Penn., 1960), 360; *Pennsylvania Gazette*, Nov. 15, 1739.

45. Lambert, *"Pedlar in Divinity,"* 113–114; Lemay, *Life of Franklin*, 2:424.

46. George Whitefield, *The Works of the Reverend George Whitefield* (London, 1772), 5:240; Lambert, *"Pedlar in Divinity,"* 115–116.

47. Lambert, *"Pedlar in Divinity,"* 118.

48. Thomas S. Kidd, *George Whitefield: America's Spiritual Founding Father* (New Haven, Conn., 2014), 122.

49. Franklin, *Autobiography*, 179.

50. Franklin, *Autobiography*, 179; Kidd, *George Whitefield*, 76–77; Buxbaum, *Franklin and the Zealous Presbyterians*, 139.

51. Franklin, *Autobiography*, 178.

Chapter 6. Electrical Man

1. Franklin to Joseph Huey, June 6, 1753, PBF, 4:504–505.

2. Edmund S. Morgan, *Benjamin Franklin* (New Haven, Conn., 2002), 24; Franklin to Joseph Huey, June 6, 1753, PBF, 4:505–506. John C. Van Horne says that for Franklin, "benevolence toward humanity" was "a kind of religion." Van Horne, "Collective Benevolence and the Common Good in Franklin's Philanthropy," in J. A. Leo Lemay, ed., *Reappraising Benjamin Franklin: A Bicentennial Perspective* (Cranbury, N.J., 1993), 425.

3. J. A. Leo Lemay, *The Life of Benjamin Franklin*, vol. 3, *Soldier, Scientist, and Politician, 1748–1757* (Philadelphia, 2009), 126.

4. Ebenezer Kinnersley to Franklin, Mar. 12, 1761, PBF, 9:293.

5. Franklin to Cadwallader Colden, Apr. 12, 1753, PBF, 4:463.

6. Frank Lambert, *"Pedlar in Divinity": George Whitefield and the Transatlantic Revivals* (Princeton, N.J., 1994), 128; Walter Isaacson, *Benjamin Franklin: An American Life* (New York, 2003), 111.

7. *Pennsylvania Gazette*, June 12, 1740; May 20, 1742, PBF, 2:287–288, 361.

8. Lambert, *"Pedlar in Divinity,"* 128.

9. Lambert, *"Pedlar in Divinity,"* 128; *Pennsylvania Gazette*, June 12, 1740.

10. *Pennsylvania Gazette*, Aug. 10, 1738; William Seward, *Journal of a Voyage from Savannah to Philadelphia* (London, 1740), 6; J. A. Leo Lemay, *The Life of Benjamin Franklin*, vol. 2, *Printer and Publisher, 1730–1747* (Philadelphia, 2006), 427.

11. *Pennsylvania Gazette*, May 1, 1740.

12. Seward, *Journal*, 22.

13. *Pennsylvania Gazette*, May 8, 1740, PBF, 2:257–259.

14. *Pennsylvania Gazette*, May 15, 1740; Lemay, *Life of Franklin*, 2:429.

15. *Pennsylvania Gazette*, May 15, 1740; Gordon S. Wood, *The Americanization of Benjamin Franklin* (New York, 2004), 47; William A. Pencack, "The Beginning of a Beautiful Friendship: Benjamin Franklin, George Whitefield, the Dancing School, and a Defense of the 'Meaner Sort,' " in William A. Pencack, ed., *Contested Commonwealths: Essays in American History* (Bethlehem, Penn., 2011), 204–205; Todd N. Thompson, "Representative Nobodies: The Politics of Benjamin Franklin's Satiric Personae, 1722–1757," *Early American Literature* 46, no. 3 (Nov. 2011): 470–471.

16. *Pennsylvania Gazette*, May 22, 1740.

17. *Pennsylvania Gazette*, May 22, 1740.

18. "Tom Trueman," *American Weekly Mercury*, May 22, 1740.

19. "Tom Trueman," *American Weekly Mercury*, May 22, 1740; [Franklin], "Obadiah Plainman," *Pennsylvania Gazette*, May 29, 1740.

20. Franklin, *Autobiography*, 175; Thomas S. Kidd, *George Whitefield: America's Spiritual Founding Father* (New Haven, Conn., 2014), 87; Ralph Lerner, "Franklin, Spectator," in *The Thinking Revolutionary: Principle and Practice in the New Republic* (Ithaca, N.Y., 1987), 57.

21. Franklin, *Autobiography*, 176; Douglas Anderson, *The Unfinished Life of Benjamin Franklin* (Baltimore, 2012), 144.

22. Franklin, *Autobiography*, 176; Thompson Westcott, *The Historic Mansions and Buildings of Philadelphia* (Philadelphia, 1895), 160; Lemay, *Life of Franklin*, 2:435–436.

23. "Memoirs of Mrs. Hannah Hodge," *General Assembly's Missionary Magazine*, Jan. 1806, 2:46; Lemay, *Life of Franklin*, 2:438.

24. *Pennsylvania Gazette*, July 24, 1740; Lemay, *Life of Franklin*, 2:438.

25. "Statement of Editorial Policy," *Pennsylvania Gazette*, July 24, 1740, PBF, 2:259–261; see 259n6 on Kinnersley's career; Lemay, *Life of Franklin*, 2:439.

26. *Pennsylvania Gazette*, Nov. 27, 1740, PBF, 2:291; Lemay, *Life of Franklin*, 2:427.

27. Franklin, *Autobiography*, 178.

28. Lemay, *Life of Franklin*, 2:300.

29. Theophilus, "To the Author," *General Magazine*, Mar. 1741, 201. On Franklin's authorship, see J. A. Leo Lemay, *The Canon of Benjamin Franklin, 1722–1776: New Attributions and Reconsiderations* (Cranbury, N.J., 1986), 103–104; and Elizabeth E. Dunn, "From a Bold Youth to a Reflective Sage: A Reevaluation of Benjamin Franklin's Religion," *Pennsylvania Magazine of History and Biography* 111, no. 4 (Oct. 1987): 509n19.

30. Hugh Bryan, "A Letter from Mr. Hugh Bryan," *General Magazine*, Mar. 1741, 202. On Bryan's and Whitefield's detention, see Kidd, *George Whitefield*, 141–142.

31. Lemay, *Life of Franklin*, 2:305–306, 509–511.

32. [Franklin], "The Religion of the Indian Natives of America," *American Magazine*, Mar. 1, 1741, 91; Lemay, *Life of Franklin*, 2:511. Gerald R. McDermott notes that many deists reacted against the "scandal of particularity," or the idea that God had specially revealed himself to only certain people at certain times. McDermott, *Jonathan Edwards Confronts the Gods: Christian Theology, Enlightenment Religion, and Non-Christian Faiths* (New York, 2000), 24–25.

33. [Franklin], "Religion of the Indian Natives of America," 91–92.

34. [Franklin], "Religion of the Indian Natives of America," 92.

35. [Franklin], "Religion of the Indian Natives of America," 92–93; Franklin, "To All Commanders of Armed Vessels Belonging to the United States," June 22, 1778, PBF, 26:667.

36. [Franklin], "Religion of the Indian Natives of America," 93.

37. [Franklin], "Religion of the Indian Natives of America," 93–94; Lemay, *Life of Franklin*, 2:306.

38. Franklin, *Remarks Concerning the Savages of North America* (Paris, [1784]), PBF, 41:418–420; A. Owen Aldridge, *The Dragon and the Eagle: The Presence of China in the American Enlightenment* (Detroit, 1993), 68–69.

39. Franklin to Jane Mecom, July 28, 1743, PBF, 2:384–385.

40. Franklin to Jane Mecom, July 28, 1743, PBF, 2:384–385; Jill Lepore, *Book of Ages: The Life and Opinions of Jane Franklin* (New York, 2013), 77–79.

41. Franklin to Jane Mecom, July 28, 1743, PBF, 2:384–385.

42. Franklin to Jane Mecom, July 28, 1743, PBF, 2:384–385; Norman Fiering, *Jonathan Edwards's Moral Thought and Its British Context* (Chapel Hill, N.C., 1981), 346–349.

43. Lemay, *Life of Franklin*, 2:311; Franklin, *Autobiography*, 240. On the date of Franklin's encounter with "Dr. Spence," as the *Autobiography* calls him, see I. Bernard Cohen, *Benjamin Franklin's Science* (Cambridge, Mass., 1990), 51.

44. James Delbourgo, *A Most Amazing Scene of Wonders: Electricity and Enlightenment in Early America* (Cambridge, Mass., 2006), 22–25; Richard Godbeer, *The Devil's Dominion: Magic and Religion in Early New England* (New York, 1992), 130–131; Lemay, *Life of Franklin*, 2:489.

45. *Pennsylvania Gazette*, Feb. 11, 1735; Lemay, *Life of Franklin*, 2:488–489.

46. Franklin, "Proposal for Promoting Useful Knowledge," May 14, 1743, PBF, 2:382.

47. Cadwallader Colden to Franklin, [Oct. 1743], PBF, 2:387; Colden to Peter Collinson, Nov. 13, 1744, in Asa Gray, ed., *Selections from the Scientific Correspondence of Cadwallader Colden* (New Haven, Conn., 1843), 40; John M. Dixon, *The Enlightenment of Cadwallader Colden: Empire, Science, and Intellectual Culture in British New York* (Ithaca, N.Y., 2016), 4–5, 89–92.

48. James N. Green, "English Books and Printing in the Age of Franklin," in Hugh Amory and David D. Hall, eds., *A History of the Book in America*,

vol. 1, *The Colonial Book in the Atlantic World* (New York, 2000), 260; *Pennsylvania Gazette*, Nov. 22, 1744, Sept. 12, 1745.

49. *Pennsylvania Gazette*, June 2, 1743, Apr. 3, 1746; George Whitefield to Franklin, [Apr. 16,] 1746, PBF, 3:73; Kidd, *George Whitefield*, 209.

50. George Whitefield to Franklin, June 23, 1747, PBF, 3:143–144; Kidd, *George Whitefield*, 199.

51. Franklin to [Thomas Hopkinson?], [Oct. 16, 1746], PBF, 3:85.

52. Franklin to [Thomas Hopkinson?], [Oct. 16, 1746], PBF, 3:88. Compare Andrew Baxter, *An Enquiry into the Nature of the Human Soul*, 2nd edn. (London, 1737), 8.

53. Franklin to [Thomas Hopkinson?], [Oct. 16, 1746], PBF, 3:88.

54. Franklin to [Thomas Hopkinson?], [Oct. 16, 1746], PBF, 3:88–89.

55. Edwin Wolf II, "The Romance of James Logan's Books," *William and Mary Quarterly*, 3rd ser., 13, no. 3 (July 1956): 342, 347.

56. James Logan to Franklin, Feb. 23, 1747, PBF, 3:110–111.

57. Franklin to Peter Collinson, Mar. 28, 1747, PBF, 3:118–119; James Logan to the Proprietary of Pennsylvania, Feb. [1749/1750], cited in Wolf, "James Logan's Books," 350.

Chapter 7. Tribune of the People

1. Franklin, "Notes on Assembly Debates," [Feb. 26–28, 1745], PBF, 3:17.

2. Franklin to John Franklin, [May] 1745, PBF, 3:26–27.

3. *Pennsylvania Gazette*, June 6, 1745.

4. Franklin, "Gazette Extracts, 1746," and *Poor Richard Improved, 1748* (Philadelphia, [1747]), PBF, 3:97–98, 255.

5. Jessica Choppin Roney, *Governed by a Spirit of Opposition: The Origins of American Political Practice in Colonial Philadelphia* (Baltimore, 2014), 86.

6. Franklin, *Autobiography*, 182; J. A. Leo Lemay, *The Life of Benjamin Franklin*, vol. 3, *Soldier, Scientist, and Politician, 1748–1757* (Philadelphia, 2009), 4.

7. Franklin, *Plain Truth* (Philadelphia, 1747), PBF, 3:192–193; Franklin, "A Dialogue between X, Y, and Z," Dec. 18, 1755, PBF, 6:304–305.

8. Franklin, *Plain Truth*, PBF, 3:198–199.

9. Franklin, *Plain Truth*, PBF, 3:201.

10. Franklin, *Plain Truth*, PBF, 3:204.

11. Roney, *Governed by a Spirit of Opposition*, 85–89.

12. Franklin, "Proclamation for a General Fast," [Dec. 9, 1747], PBF, 3:228; Franklin, *Autobiography*, 184–185; Lemay, *Life of Franklin*, 3:28.

13. [Franklin], "The Necessity of Self-Defence," 1747, in J. A. Leo Lemay, ed., *Benjamin Franklin: Writings* (New York, 1987), 314.

14. [Franklin], "The Necessity of Self-Defence," in Lemay, ed., *Writings*, 315–318.

15. "Devices and Mottoes of the Association," *Pennsylvania Gazette*, Jan. 12, Apr. 16, 1748, in Lemay, ed., *Franklin: Writings*, 318–319.

16. "Devices and Mottoes of the Association," *Pennsylvania Gazette*, Jan. 12, Apr. 16, 1748, in Lemay, ed., *Franklin: Writings*, 319.

17. Roney, *Governed by a Spirit of Opposition*, 88–91; Lemay, *Life of Franklin*, 3:49.

18. Franklin, *Autobiography*, 149–150.

19. Franklin, *Autobiography*, 153–156; James Thomson, *Winter*, 4th edn. (London, 1726), 40.

20. Franklin, *Autobiography*, 157; Henry F. May, *The Enlightenment in America* (New York, 1976), 128; Mitchell Robert Breitwieser, *Cotton Mather and Benjamin Franklin: The Price of Representative Personality* (New York, 1984), 8; Robert A. Ferguson, *The American Enlightenment, 1750–1820* (Cambridge, Mass., 1994), 75; Oscar Reiss, *The Jews in Colonial America* (Jefferson, N.C., 2004), 198; "Subscription List for Congregation Mikveh Israel," Apr. 20, 1788, franklinpapers.org.

21. D. H. Lawrence, "Benjamin Franklin," in J. A. Leo Lemay and P. M. Zall, eds., *Benjamin Franklin's Autobiography* (New York, 1986), 292–294, 297.

22. Norman S. Fiering, "Benjamin Franklin and the Way to Virtue," *American Quarterly* 30, no. 2 (Summer 1978): 206–207; Ralph Lerner, "The Gospel According to the Apostle Ben," *American Political Thought* 1, no. 1 (Spring 2012): 147.

23. Franklin, "Advice to a Young Tradesman," 1748, PBF, 3:308; *Poor Richard Improved, 1749* (Philadelphia, [1748]), PBF, 3:336–337, 340.

24. Franklin, *Poor Richard Improved, 1758* (Philadelphia, [1757]), PBF, 7:341, 342; Gordon S. Wood, *The Americanization of Benjamin Franklin* (New York, 2004), 83; Edmund S. Morgan, *Benjamin Franklin* (New Haven, Conn., 2002), 24–25; Franklin, *Autobiography*, 164n2.

25. Franklin, *Poor Richard Improved*, PBF, 7:347; Franklin, *Autobiography*, 164; Franklin to George Whitefield, July 6, 1749, PBF, 3:383.

26. Franklin, *Poor Richard Improved*, PBF, 7:349.

27. Franklin, *Poor Richard Improved*, PBF, 7:350.

28. Franklin, *Poor Richard Improved*, PBF, 7:350; Franklin to George Whitefield, July 6, 1749, PBF, 3:383. By "inventor of the longitude," Franklin likely meant John Harrison, an inventor of the marine chronometer.

29. Franklin, "On the Need for an Academy," *Pennsylvania Gazette*, Aug. 24, 1749, PBF, 3:385–387.

30. Franklin, *Proposals Relating to the Education of Youth in Pennsylvania* (Philadelphia, 1749), PBF, 3:405–407, 415.

31. Franklin, *Education of Youth*, PBF, 3:412–413.

32. Franklin, *Education of Youth*, PBF, 3:413; George Turnbull, *Observations upon Liberal Education, in All Its Branches*, ed. Terrence O. Moore, Jr. (1742; Indianapolis, 2003), http://oll.libertyfund.org/titles/892.

33. Franklin, *Education of Youth*, PBF, 3:419–421; John Milton, *Of Education*, in John Milton, *Paradise Regain'd. A Poem. In Four Books. To Which Is Added*

Samson Agonistes. And Poems upon Several Occasions. With a Tractate of Education, 5th edn. (London, 1713), 373.

34. George Whitefield to Franklin, Feb. 26, 1750, PBF, 3:467–469.

35. George D. Johnson, "The Reverend Samuel Johnson, D.D., of Connecticut," *New-England Historical and Genealogical Register* 27 (1873): 44; Melvin H. Buxbaum, *Benjamin Franklin and the Zealous Presbyterians* (University Park, Penn., 1975), 156–159.

36. Franklin to Samuel Johnson, Sept. 13, 1750; Aug. 23, 1750, PBF, 4:63, 41–42; Jeanne E. Abrams, *Revolutionary Medicine: The Founding Fathers and Mothers in Sickness and Death* (New York, 2013), 93.

37. Franklin, "Idea of the English School," in Richard Peters, *A Sermon on Education* (Philadelphia, 1751), PBF, 4:106–107.

38. Samuel Johnson to Franklin, [January? 1752], PBF, 4:260–261; Lemay, *Life of Franklin*, 3:202–203; Lorraine Smith Pangle and Thomas L. Pangle, *The Learning of Liberty: The Educational Ideals of the American Founders* (Lawrence, Kans., 1993), 77–78; Buxbaum, *Franklin and the Zealous Presbyterians*, 166–167.

39. Franklin, *Autobiography*, 199.

40. Franklin, "Appeal for the Hospital," *Pennsylvania Gazette*, Aug. 8, 15, 1751, PBF, 4:148–149; Franklin, *Poor Richard Improved*, 1757 (Philadelphia, [1756]), PBF, 7:89; Lemay, *Life of Franklin*, 3:587. Although some attribute the "archives of eternity" quote to Franklin, it appears to be taken from an edition of *Letters Writ by a Turkish Spy* (London, 1748), 5:64.

41. Franklin, "Appeal for the Hospital," PBF, 4:150–151; Stanley Finger, *Doctor Franklin's Medicine* (Philadelphia, 2006), 73–76.

42. Franklin, *Autobiography*, 201–202.

43. James Bowdoin to Franklin, Dec. 21, 1751, PBF, 4:216; Lemay, *Life of Franklin*, 3:82, 91; James Delbourgo, *A Most Amazing Scene of Wonders: Electricity and Enlightenment in Early America* (Cambridge, Mass., 2006), 72–73; *Pennsylvania Gazette*, Apr. 11, 1751.

44. Lemay, *Life of Franklin*, 3:104–108; *Pennsylvania Gazette*, Oct. 19, 1752.

45. Joseph Priestley, *The History and Present State of Electricity*, 3rd edn. (1767; London, 1775), 1:108.

46. Joyce E. Chaplin, *The First Scientific American: Benjamin Franklin and the Pursuit of Genius* (New York, 2006), 132–133.

47. Gilbert Tennent, *All Things Come Alike to All* (Philadelphia, 1745), 34–36; Delbourgo, *Scene of Wonders*, 66.

48. Thomas Prince, *Earthquakes the Works of God* (Boston, 1755), 20–23.

49. John Winthrop, *A Lecture on Earthquakes* (Boston, 1755), 33–35; Delbourgo, *Scene of Wonders*, 68.

50. Delbourgo, *Scene of Wonders*, 68–69.

51. Delbourgo, *Scene of Wonders*, 3, 285n2.

Chapter 8. Diplomat

1. Franklin to Cadwallader Colden, Apr. 23, 1752, PBF, 4:301; Thomas F. Mayer, *The Roman Inquisition: Trying Galileo* (Philadelphia, 2015), 3–4.
2. Franklin to Joseph Huey, June 6, 1753, PBF, 4:505–506; George Whitefield to Franklin, Aug. 17, 1752, PBF, 4:343.
3. George Whitefield to Franklin, Aug. 17, 1752, PBF, 4:343.
4. George Whitefield to Franklin, Jan. 17, 1755, PBF, 5:475–476; Franklin to Whitefield, June 19, 1764, PBF, 11:231–232; Franklin to William Strahan, June 25, 1764, PBF, 11:241; Kerry S. Walters, *Benjamin Franklin and His Gods* (Urbana, Ill., 1999), 111, 186–187n47; Claude-Anne Lopez and Eugenia W. Herbert, *The Private Franklin: The Man and His Family* (New York, 1975), 76.
5. Franklin, *Autobiography*, 197.
6. Judith Ridner, *A Town In-Between: Carlisle, Pennsylvania, and the Early Mid-Atlantic Interior* (Philadelphia, 2010), 78.
7. Franklin, *Autobiography*, 198–199.
8. David Hume, *Essays, Moral and Political* (1742), in Isaac Kramnick, ed., *The Portable Enlightenment Reader* (New York, 1995), 629.
9. Franklin, *Observations Concerning the Increase of Mankind* (Boston, 1755), PBF, 4:234; David Waldstreicher, *Runaway America: Benjamin Franklin, Slavery, and the American Revolution* (New York, 2004), 137; Carla J. Mulford, *Benjamin Franklin and the Ends of Empire* (New York, 2015), 154–155, 161–162.
10. Franklin, *Observations Concerning the Increase*, PBF, 4:234; Waldstreicher, *Runaway America*, 138–139.
11. *Pennsylvania Gazette*, May 9, 1754.
12. Franklin, "Reasons and Motives for the Albany Plan of Union," in Benjamin Vaughan, ed., *Political, Miscellaneous, and Philosophical Pieces* (London, 1779), PBF, 5:399.
13. Franklin, *Autobiography*, 224; H. W. Brands, *The First American: The Life and Times of Benjamin Franklin* (New York, 2000), 250.
14. James Read to Benjamin Franklin, July 25, 1755, in Alan Houston, ed., "Benjamin Franklin and the 'Wagon Affair' of 1755," *William and Mary Quarterly*, 3rd ser., 66, no. 2 (Apr. 2009): 281–282.
15. "Oath of Trustees and Officers of the College," June 10, 1755, PBF, 6:70–71; Francis Jennings, *Benjamin Franklin, Politician: The Mask and the Man* (New York, 1996), 70.
16. Franklin, "Parable against Persecution," [1755?], PBF, 6:114–121. A critical piece in a 1781 edition of the *Gentleman's Magazine* shows similarities between Franklin's parable and a section from a book by Jeremy Taylor, but Taylor had taken his story from earlier sources as well. "H.S." to "Mr. Urban," *Gentleman's Magazine*, Nov. 1781, 514–515.
17. Franklin, "Parable against Persecution," PBF, 6:122–124.

18. Franklin, "A Parable on Brotherly Love," [1755?], PBF, 6:124–128; Eran Shalev, " 'Written in the Style of Antiquity': Pseudo-Biblicism and the Early American Republic, 1770–1830," *Church History* 79, no. 4 (Dec. 2010): 820; David F. Holland, *Sacred Borders: Continuing Revelation and Canonical Restraint in Early America* (New York, 2011), 70–71.

19. Franklin to Catherine Ray, Mar. 4, 1755, PBF, 5:503.

20. Franklin to Catherine Ray, Sept. 11, 1755, PBF, 6:182, 184; Sheila Skemp, "Family Partnerships: The Working Wife, Honoring Deborah Franklin," in Larry E. Tise, ed., *Benjamin Franklin and Women* (University Park, Penn., 2000), 25.

21. Franklin to Catherine Ray, Oct. 16, 1755, PBF, 6:225; Franklin to Deborah Franklin, Feb. 19, 1758, PBF, 7:384; Franklin to Sally Franklin, Nov. 8, 1764, PBF, 11:449–450; Isabel Rivers, *Reason, Grace, and Sentiment: A Study of the Language of Religion and Ethics in England, 1660–1780* (New York, 1991), 1:22–23; Lopez and Herbert, *Private Franklin*, 75.

22. Franklin to Catherine Ray, Oct. 16, 1755, PBF, 6:225.

23. Walter Isaacson, *Benjamin Franklin: An American Life* (New York, 2003), 162–165; Lopez and Herbert, *Private Franklin*, 56; Jan Lewis, "Sex and the Married Man: Benjamin Franklin's Families," in Tise, ed., *Franklin and Women*, 67–68.

24. Franklin, *Autobiography*, 234–235; Franklin to Unknown, Jan. 20, 1756, PBF, 6:363.

25. Franklin to George Whitefield, July 2, 1756, PBF, 6:468–469.

26. Franklin to George Whitefield, July 2, 1756, PBF, 6:469.

27. Thomas S. Kidd, *George Whitefield: America's Spiritual Founding Father* (New Haven, Conn., 2014), 227.

28. Franklin to Deborah Franklin, June 27, 1760, PBF, 9:174–175; Franklin to John Waring, June 27, 1763, Dec. 17, 1763, PBF, 10:299, 395–296; Waldstreicher, *Runaway America*, 194–195; Joyce E. Chaplin, *The First Scientific American: Benjamin Franklin and the Pursuit of Genius* (New York, 2006), 180–181.

29. Franklin to Deborah Franklin, July 17, 1757, PBF, 7:243.

30. Gordon S. Wood, *The Americanization of Benjamin Franklin* (New York, 2004), 84–88, 92–94; John Fothergill to Israel Pemberton, June 12, 1758, PBF, 8:100–101n2; Franklin to Lord Kames, Jan. 3, 1760, PBF, 9:6, 8; Mulford, *Ends of Empire*, 235–236.

31. Franklin to Jane Mecom, Sept. 16, 1758, PBF, 8:153–154; Jill Lepore, *Book of Ages: The Life and Opinions of Jane Franklin* (New York, 2013), 116–117.

32. Franklin to Jane Mecom, Sept. 16, 1758, PBF, 8:154.

33. Franklin to Jane Mecom, Sept. 16, 1758, PBF, 8:154–155.

34. Franklin to Jane Mecom, Sept. 16, 1758, PBF, 8:155.

35. Franklin to Jane Mecom, July 14, 1759, PBF, 8:414.

36. Franklin to Jane Mecom, Jan. 9, 1760, PBF, 9:17–18.

37. Lord Kames, *Sketches of the History of Man* (Edinburgh, 1788), 4:354; Franklin to Lord Kames, May 3, 1760, PBF, 9:104n7; Franklin to Benjamin Vaughan, Nov. 2, 1789, in Benjamin Franklin, *The Works of Benjamin Franklin*, vol. 12, *Letters and Miscellaneous Writings, 1788–1790, Supplement, Indexes* (New York, 1904), http://oll.libertyfund.org/titles/franklin-the-works-of-benjamin-franklin-vol-xii-letters-and-misc-writings-1788-1790-supplement-indexes.

38. Franklin to Lord Kames, May 3, 1760, PBF, 9:104–105, 104n9; Franklin to Joseph Priestley, Feb. 8, 1780, PBF, 31:456; Ronald A. Bosco, " 'He That Best Understands the World, Least Likes It': The Dark Side of Benjamin Franklin," *Pennsylvania Magazine of History and Biography* 111, no. 4 (Oct. 1987): 532.

39. David Hume to Franklin, May 10, 1762, PBF, 10:81–82; Franklin to William Strahan, Oct. 27, 1771, Nov. 17, 1771, PBF, 18:236, 251; Paul Giles, *Transatlantic Insurrections: British Culture and the Formation of American Literature, 1730–1860* (Philadelphia, 2001), 88.

40. Franklin to David Hume, May 19, 1762, PBF, 10:83; Nancy Glazener, "Benjamin Franklin and the Limits of Secular Civil Society," *American Literature* 80, no. 2 (June 2008): 210–211, 215.

41. Franklin to Mary [Polly] Stevenson, June 11, 1760, PBF, 9:120–121; Franklin to Deborah Franklin, June 27, 1760, PBF, 9:174; Lopez and Herbert, *Private Franklin*, 84; George Goodwin, *Benjamin Franklin in London: The British Life of America's Founding Father* (New Haven, Conn., 2016), 118–121; Lewis, "Sex and the Married Man," 81.

42. Mary [Polly] Stevenson to Franklin, [1760–1762], PBF, 9:264–265; Franklin to Mary [Polly] Stevenson, Sept. 2, 1769, PBF, 16:193; Whitfield J. Bell, Jr., " 'All Clear Sunshine': New Letters of Franklin and Mary Stevenson Hewson," *Proceedings of the American Philosophical Society* 100, no. 6 (Dec. 1956): 526.

43. Mary [Polly] Stevenson to Franklin, [1760–1762], PBF, 9:265–266; J. C. D. Clark, *The Language of Liberty, 1660–1832: Political Discourse and Social Dynamics in the Anglo-American World* (New York, 1994), 329. Hugh Farmer's preface indicates a 1761 composition. Farmer, *Inquiry into the Nature and Design of Christ's Temptation in the Wilderness*, 2nd edn. (London, [1765]), iv.

44. Mary [Polly] Stevenson to Franklin, [1760–1762], PBF, 9:266.

45. Mary [Polly] Stevenson to Franklin, May 19, 1761, PBF, 9:319–320.

46. William Franklin to Sarah Franklin, Oct. 10, 1761, PBF, 9:365–366; Mary [Polly] Stevenson to Franklin, Aug. 29, 1761, PBF, 9:353.

47. Mary [Polly] Stevenson to Franklin, Aug. 29, 1761, PBF, 9:353.

48. Franklin to Jared Ingersoll, Dec. 11, 1762, PBF, 10:175–176; Franklin to Jonathan Williams, Sr., Apr. 13, 1785, franklinpapers.org.

49. Richard R. Beeman, *The Varieties of Political Experience in Eighteenth-Century America* (Philadelphia, 2004), 229.

50. Franklin, *A Narrative of the Late Massacres* (Philadelphia, 1764), PBF, 11:52, 55. The phrase "sins that cry to heaven for vengeance" was common in English, but it also referred to a particular category of sin in Catholic theology. Murder was one of those sins. See, for example, Robert Bellarmine, *Christian Doctrine* (N.p., 1676), 36.

51. Franklin, *A Narrative of the Late Massacres*, PBF, 11:56, 66.

52. [Franklin], *Remarks on a Late Protest* ([Philadelphia, 1764]), PBF, 11:434; Isaacson, *An American Life*, 213; Melvin H. Buxbaum, *Benjamin Franklin and the Zealous Presbyterians* (University Park, Penn., 1975), 204–205.

53. [William Smith], *Answer to Mr. Franklin's Remarks* (Philadelphia, 1764), PBF, 11:505; Benjamin Franklin, *Cool Thoughts on the Present Situation of Our Public Affairs* (Philadelphia, 1764), 9–10; Wood, *Americanization*, 97–101; Nathan R. Kozuskanich, *Benjamin Franklin: American Founder, Atlantic Citizen* (New York, 2015), 85.

54. Franklin to Jane Mecom, Mar. 1, 1766, PBF, 13:188; Wood, *Americanization*, 106–108.

55. Franklin to Jane Mecom, Mar. 2, 1767, PBF, 14:72–73.

56. A week after Franklin's testimony, Whitefield visited Franklin in London and shared news that one of Franklin's relatives had received Anglican ordination. Franklin to Deborah Franklin, Feb. 27, 1766, PBF, 13:176.

57. Wood, *Americanization*, 119–120; Kidd, *George Whitefield*, 242. William Franklin seemed to attribute the clergyman's letter to Whitefield; see William Franklin to Franklin, Apr. 30, 1766, PBF, 13:254–255. Whitefield quoted in Ralph Frasca, *Benjamin Franklin's Printing Network: Disseminating Virtue in Early America* (Columbia, Mo., 2006), 152.

58. Franklin, "A New Version of the Lord's Prayer," [1768?], PBF, 15:301–303; Franklin to Samuel Mather, July 7, 1773, PBF, 20:289; Walters, *Franklin and His Gods*, 146; Alfred Owen Aldridge, *Benjamin Franklin and Nature's God* (Durham, N.C., 1967), 175–179.

59. Franklin, "Proposed New Version of the Bible," Apr. 1, 1782, franklinpapers.org.

60. Aldridge, *Franklin and Nature's God*, 166–171; Goodwin, *Franklin in London*, 234–235.

61. "Franklin's Contributions to an Abridgment of the Book of Common Prayer," [before Aug. 5, 1773], PBF, 20:345–346, 348, 350; Franklin to Granville Sharp, July 5, 1785, franklinpapers.org; Aldridge, *Franklin and Nature's God*, 170–173. English Unitarians also produced a "reformed" version of the Book of Common Prayer in 1774. Thomas Coombe, Jr., to Franklin, Sept. 24, 1774, PBF, 21:313n1.

62. Franklin to Ezra Stiles, Jan. 13, 1772, PBF, 19:31; Richard H. Popkin, *Spinoza* (London, 2004), 122.

63. Franklin to Unknown, [Dec. 13, 1757], PBF, 7:294–295; Howard L. Lubert, "Benjamin Franklin and the Role of Religion in Governing Democracy," in Daniel L. Dreisbach, Mark D. Hall, and Jeffry H.

Morrison, eds., *The Founders on God and Government* (Lanham, Md., 2004), 156–157.

64. Deborah Franklin to Franklin, Oct. 14, 1770, PBF, 17:251; Franklin to Jane Mecom, Nov. 7[–9], 1770, PBF, 17:284.

65. Franklin to George Whitefield, [before Sept. 2, 1769], PBF, 16:192.

66. George Whitefield to Franklin, Jan. 21, 1768, PBF, 15:29; Franklin, *Autobiography*, 178; Franklin to Noble Wimberly Jones, Mar. 5, 1771, PBF, 18:53.

Chapter 9. The Pillar of Fire

1. Walter Isaacson, *Benjamin Franklin: An American Life* (New York, 2003), 311–312.

2. Franklin, "Proposal for the Great Seal of the United States," [before Aug. 14, 1776], PBF, 22:562–563. On the origin of the motto, see Carla J. Mulford, *Benjamin Franklin and the Ends of Empire* (New York, 2015), 278–281.

3. Franklin to Mary [Polly] Stevenson, Sept. 14, 1767, PBF, 14:253; Gordon S. Wood, *The Americanization of Benjamin Franklin* (New York, 2004), 124, 130.

4. Claude-Anne Lopez and Eugenia W. Herbert, *The Private Franklin: The Man and His Family* (New York, 1975), 170, 174; Wood, *Americanization*, 136–137.

5. Wood, *Americanization*, 141–146; Franklin, "Tract Relative to the Affair of Hutchinson's Letters" (1774), PBF, 21:430.

6. Wood, *Americanization*, 146–147; Isaacson, *An American Life*, 278; Jane Mecom to Franklin, Nov. 3, 1774, PBF, 21:346–349.

7. Franklin to Thomas Viny, Feb. 12, 1775, PBF, 21:487; Jane Mecom to Franklin, Dec. 5[–15], 1774, PBF, 21:371; Joseph Priestley, *Memoirs of Joseph Priestley* (Northumberland, Eng., 1806), 1:90; Richard Price to Franklin, [May 30, 1790], in Franklin, *Autobiography*, 242; Mulford, *Ends of Empire*, 264–265; George Goodwin, *Benjamin Franklin in London: The British Life of America's Founding Father* (New Haven, Conn., 2016), 244–245.

8. Franklin to Benjamin Vaughan, Oct. 24, 1788, franklinpapers.org; J. D. Bowers, *Joseph Priestley and English Unitarianism in America* (University Park, Penn. 2007), 138.

9. Priestley, *Memoirs of Joseph Priestley*, 1:90; Richard Allen, "David Hartley," in Edward N. Zalta, ed., *The Stanford Encyclopedia of Philosophy* (summer 2015 edn.), http://plato.stanford.edu/archives/sum2015/entries/hartley/; Gerald R. Cragg, *Reason and Authority in the Eighteenth Century* (Cambridge, Eng., 1964), 229–230.

10. Priestley, *Memoirs of Joseph Priestley*, 1:90; Franklin to David Hartley, Oct. 3, 1775, PBF, 22:217; Wood, *Americanization*, 154–155, 159.

11. Franklin to Richard Bache, Sept. 30, 1774, PBF, 21:325; Carl Van Doren, *Benjamin Franklin* (New York, 1938), 551.

12. Franklin to John Calder, Aug. 21, 1784, franklinpapers.org. The Franklin Papers identify Calder as the recipient of this letter, while J. A. Leo Lemay and Alfred Owen Aldridge identified the recipient as Joseph Priestley. J. A. Leo Lemay, *The Life of Benjamin Franklin*, vol. 2, *Printer and Publisher, 1730–1747* (Philadelphia, 2006), 592n28; Alfred Owen Aldridge, *Benjamin Franklin and Nature's God* (Durham, N.C., 1967), 191; "Pennsylvania Constitution of 1776," in Daniel L. Dreisbach and Mark David Hall, eds., *The Sacred Rights of Conscience: Selected Readings on Religious Liberty and Church-State Relations in the American Founding* (Indianapolis, 2009), 242.

13. Franklin to Richard Price, Oct. 9, 1780, PBF, 33:390; Thomas S. Kidd, *God of Liberty: A Religious History of the American Revolution* (New York, 2010), 169–170.

14. Franklin, *Information to Those Who Would Remove to America* (Paris, [1784]), PBF, 41:608; Melvin H. Buxbaum, *Benjamin Franklin and the Zealous Presbyterians* (University Park, Penn., 1975), 45.

15. Franklin to [Samuel Cooper], Oct. 25, 1776, PBF, 22:670; [Cooper] to Franklin, Feb. 27, 1777, PBF, 23:400; Franklin to Cooper, May 1, 1777, PBF, 24:7; Franklin to Thomas Viny, May 4, 1779, PBF, 29:431; Kidd, *God of Liberty*, 74.

16. Lopez and Herbert, *Private Franklin*, 236; Franklin to Mary [Polly] Hewson, Jan. 12, 1777, PBF, 23:155; Franklin to Jane Mecom, Oct. 25, 1779, PBF, 30:583; Edward E. Hale, *Franklin in France* (Boston, 1888), 90; John Adams, diary, June 23, 1779, in C. James Taylor et al., eds., *The Adams Papers Digital Edition* (Charlottesville, Va., 2008–2016), http://rotunda.upress.virginia.edu/founders/default.xqy?keys=ADMS-search-1-3&expandNote=on#match1; Wood, *Americanization*, 177, 179.

17. Stacy Schiff, *A Great Improvisation: Franklin, France, and the Birth of America* (New York, 2005), 36; Joyce E. Chaplin, *The First Scientific American: Benjamin Franklin and the Pursuit of Genius* (New York, 2006), 262–263.

18. *New-York Gazette*, Feb. 2, 1778. The report was drawn from London newspaper accounts of November 1777. Jane Mecom to Franklin, May 5, 1778, PBF, 26:402.

19. Franklin to [David Hartley], Feb. 3, 1779, PBF, 28:462.

20. Sarah Bache to Franklin, Jan. 17, 1779, PBF, 28:391; Franklin to John Quincy Adams, Apr. 21, 1779, PBF, 29:351; Franklin to Bache, June 3, 1779, PBF, 29:614; Lopez and Herbert, *Private Franklin*, 223, 229.

21. Franklin to Samuel Cooper Johonnot, Jan. 7, 1783, PBF, 38:558.

22. Franklin to John Thornton, May 8, 1782, PBF, 37:284; William Cowper, *Poems*, 2nd edn. (London, 1786), 1:208; "Charity, Cupidity," in David L. Jeffrey, ed., *A Dictionary of Biblical Tradition in English Literature* (Grand

Rapids, Mich., 1992), 135; Edwin Wolf and Kevin J. Hayes, eds., *The Library of Benjamin Franklin* (Philadelphia, 2006), 223. Thanks to Justin Taylor for pointing out the Cowper commendation to me.

23. Claude-Anne Lopez, *Mon Cher Papa: Franklin and the Ladies of Paris* (New Haven, Conn., 1966), 29, 32; Isaacson, *An American Life*, 357.

24. Lopez, *Mon Cher Papa*, 38–39.

25. Franklin to Anne-Louise Brillon, Mar. 10, 1778, PBF, 26:85–86.

26. Lopez, *Mon Cher Papa*, 40–41, 56, 58; Jan Lewis, "Sex and the Married Man: Benjamin Franklin's Families," in Larry E. Tise, ed., *Benjamin Franklin and Women* (University Park, Penn., 2000), 69.

27. Franklin to Anne-Louise Brillon, Nov. 10, 1779, PBF, 31:73; Lopez, *Mon Cher Papa*, 68–69, 72.

28. Franklin to Jonathan Shipley, Feb. 24, 1786; Franklin to George Whatley, May 23, 1785, both franklinpapers.org; Kerry S. Walters, *Benjamin Franklin and His Gods* (Urbana, Ill., 1999), 111. In 1785, he asserted that "consciousness and memory remain in a future state." Franklin to Jan Ingenhousz, Aug. 28, 1785, franklinpapers.org.

29. Lopez, *Mon Cher Papa*, 89–90.

30. Lopez, *Mon Cher Papa*, 92–96.

31. Lopez, *Mon Cher Papa*, 254–255; Woody Holton, *Abigail Adams: A Life* (New York, 2009), 206; Wood, *Americanization*, 208–209.

32. Franklin to John Adams, Feb. 22, 1781; Feb. 12, 1782, PBF, 34:390, 36:561.

33. John Adams to Thomas McKean, Sept. 20, 1779, in C. James Taylor et al., eds., *The Adams Papers Digital Edition* (Charlottesville, Va., 2008–2016), http://rotunda.upress.virginia.edu/founders/ADMS-06-08-02-0112; Franklin to Robert Morris, Mar. 7, 1783, PBF, 39:301–302; Franklin to Adams, Oct. 12[–16], 1781, PBF, 35:582; Wood, *Americanization*, 192, 195.

34. Franklin to William Hodgson, Apr. 1, 1781, July 8, 1781, PBF, 34:507, 35:234; Sheldon S. Cohen, *British Supporters of the American Revolution, 1775–1783* (Rochester, N.Y., 2004), 39.

35. Franklin to Samuel Mather, July 7, 1773, PBF, 20:289; Jack P. Greene, "Pride, Prejudice, and Jealousy: Benjamin Franklin's Explanation for the American Revolution," in J. A. Leo Lemay, ed., *Reappraising Benjamin Franklin: A Bicentennial Perspective* (Cranbury, N.J., 1993), 134–135; Franklin to Joseph Priestley, Jan. 27, 1777, PBF, 23:238; Edmund S. Morgan, *Benjamin Franklin* (New Haven, Conn., 2002), 273.

36. Franklin to Joseph Priestley, June 7, 1782, PBF, 37:444; Daniel Walker Howe, "Franklin, Edwards, and the Problem of Human Nature," in Barbara B. Oberg and Harry S. Stout, eds., *Benjamin Franklin, Jonathan Edwards, and the Representation of American Culture* (New York, 1993), 76–77.

37. Franklin to Joseph Priestley, June 7, 1782, PBF, 37:445.

38. Franklin to Joseph Priestley, June 7, 1782, PBF, 37:445; Franklin to John Jay, Jan. 6, 1784, PBF, 41:411; Ronald A. Bosco, " 'He That Best Understands the World, Least Likes It': The Dark Side of Benjamin Franklin," *Pennsylvania Magazine of History and Biography* 111, no. 4 (Oct. 1987): 527–528, 534.

39. Franklin to James Hutton, July 7, 1782, PBF, 37:586–587.

40. Franklin to James Hutton, July 7, 1782, PBF, 37:587–588; [Franklin], "Supplement to the Boston *Independent Chronicle*," 2nd edn. (Paris, 1782), PBF, 37:184–197; Gregory E. Dowd, *Groundless: Rumors, Legends, and Hoaxes on the Early American Frontier* (Baltimore, 2015), 190–193.

41. Peter Labilliere to Franklin, Dec. 8, 1781, PBF, 36:223; Jane Mecom to Franklin, Oct. 29, 1781, PBF, 35:666; Mecom to Franklin, July 4, 1784, franklinpapers.org; Lopez, *Mon Cher Papa*, 110.

42. Thomas Pownall to Franklin, Feb. 28, 1783, PBF, 39:227; H. W. Brands, *The First American: The Life and Times of Benjamin Franklin* (New York, 2000), 616–620.

43. Franklin to William Strahan, Aug. 19, 1784, franklinpapers.org; Franklin to Jonathan Shipley, June 10, 1782, PBF, 37:457; Franklin to Jane Mecom, July 4, 1786, franklinpapers.org. Strahan replied that he was "much disposed to attribute to the Interposition of Providence whatever seems to promote the Liberty and Happiness of any of his Creatures: but we are but short sighted Mortals." Strahan to Franklin, Nov. 21, 1784, franklinpapers.org; Buxbaum, *Franklin and the Zealous Presbyterians*, 42–43.

44. Franklin to John Calder, Aug. 21, 1784, franklinpapers.org.

45. Pennsylvania General Assembly to Franklin, Sept. 15, 1785, franklinpapers.org; Benjamin Rush to Richard Price, Oct. 15, 1785, Apr. 22, 1786, *The Founders' Constitution*, http://press-pubs.uchicago.edu/founders/documents/a6_3s8.html; Steven K. Green, *The Second Disestablishment: Church and State in Nineteenth-Century America* (New York, 2010), 82.

46. Wood, *Americanization*, 216.

Conclusion

1. Gordon S. Wood, *The Americanization of Benjamin Franklin* (New York, 2004), 216; H. W. Brands, *The First American: The Life and Times of Benjamin Franklin* (New York, 2000), 674–675.

2. Franklin to Jane Mecom, May 30, 1787, franklinpapers.org.

3. Franklin, "Convention Speech on Salaries," June 2, 1787, franklinpapers.org; Jeffery A. Smith, *Franklin and Bache: Envisioning the Enlightened Republic* (New York, 1990), 18.

4. Franklin, "Convention Speech on Salaries," franklinpapers.org; [James Madison or Alexander Hamilton], *Federalist*, no. 51, Feb. 8, 1788, at https://www.congress.gov/resources/display/content/The+Federalist+Papers#

TheFederalistPapers-51; Howard L. Lubert, "Benjamin Franklin and the Role of Religion in Governing Democracy," in Daniel L. Dreisbach, Mark David Hall, and Jeffry H. Morrison, eds., *The Founders on God and Government* (Lanham, Md., 2004), 164; Wood, *Americanization*, 216–218.

5. Franklin, "Convention Speech Proposing Prayers," June 28, 1787, franklinpapers.org.

6. Franklin, "Convention Speech Proposing Prayers," June 28, 1787, franklinpapers.org; Brands, *First American*, 678.

7. Joseph C. Morton, *Shapers of the Great Debate at the Constitutional Convention of 1787* (Westport, Conn., 2006), 103.

8. Franklin, "Speech in the Convention on the Constitution," [Sept. 17, 1787], franklinpapers.org; John R. Vile, *The Constitutional Convention of 1787: A Comprehensive Encyclopedia of America's Founding* (Santa Barbara, Calif., 2005), 1:296.

9. Jane Mecom to Franklin, Nov. 9, 1787; Franklin to the Editor of the *Federal Gazette*, Apr. 8, 1788, both franklinpapers.org.

10. Franklin, "Speech in the Convention on the Constitution," [Sept. 17, 1787], Granville Sharp to Franklin, Jan. 10, 1788, both franklinpapers. org; David Waldstreicher, *Runaway America: Benjamin Franklin, Slavery, and the American Revolution* (New York, 2004), 234–235.

11. Waldstreicher, *Runaway America*, 225; Franklin to Benjamin Rush, July 14, 1773, franklinpapers.org; Pennsylvania Society for Promoting the Abolition of Slavery, "An Address to the Public," Nov. 9, 1789, in William Temple Franklin, *Memoirs of the Life and Writings of Benjamin Franklin* (London, 1818), 403.

12. "Petition from the Pennsylvania Abolition Society to Congress, 1790," in Kenneth Morgan, ed., *Slavery in America: A Reader and Guide* (Athens, Ga., 2005), 130; William Maclay, *Sketches of Debate in the First Senate* (Harrisburg, Penn., 1880), 169; "Proceedings of Congress," Mar. 16, 1790, in *Federal Gazette and Philadelphia Evening Post*, Mar. 22, 1790, 2.

13. [Franklin], "To the Editor of the *Federal Gazette*," Mar. 23, 1790, franklin papers.org.

14. Franklin to Benjamin Vaughan, Nov. 2, 1789, in Benjamin Franklin, *The Works of Benjamin Franklin*, vol. 12, *Letters and Miscellaneous Writings, 1788–1790, Supplement, Indexes* (New York, 1904), http://oll.libertyfund. org/titles/franklin-the-works-of-benjamin-franklin-vol-xii-letters-and-misc-writings-1788-1790-supplement-indexes; Jane Mecom to Franklin, Nov. 21, 1788, franklinpapers.org; Franklin to Robert Livingston, Dec. 5[–14], 1782, PBF, 38:416–417.

15. John T. Hassam, "Registers of Probate for the County of Suffolk, Massachusetts, 1639–1799," *Proceedings of the Massachusetts Historical Society* 16 (Mar. 1902): 116n3; Clifford K. Shipton, *New England Life in the Eighteenth Century* (Cambridge, Mass., 1963), 257; Franklin to Elizabeth Partridge, Nov. 25, 1788, franklinpapers.org.

16. Jane Mecom to Franklin, Jan. 17, 1790, franklinpapers.org.

17. Ezra Stiles to Franklin, Jan. 28, 1790, franklinpapers.org; Edmund S. Morgan, *The Gentle Puritan: A Life of Ezra Stiles, 1727–1795* (Chapel Hill, N.C., 1962), 96; Richard Price to Franklin, [May 30, 1790], in J. A. Leo Lemay and P. M. Zall, eds., *Benjamin Franklin's Autobiography* (New York, 1986), 242.

18. Ezra Stiles to Franklin, Jan. 28, 1790; Franklin to Stiles, Mar. 9, 1790, both franklinpapers.org.

19. Nicholas Collin to William Temple Franklin, Oct. 30, 1790, franklin papers.org.

20. Franklin to Ezra Stiles, Mar. 9, 1790, franklinpapers.org.

21. Franklin to Ezra Stiles, Mar. 9, 1790; Franklin, "Will and Codicil," July 17, 1788, both franklinpapers.org.

22. "Anecdotes of Mary H—," *Pennsylvania Magazine of History and Biography* 19, no. 3 (1895): 408–409.

23. M. L. Weems, *The Life of Benjamin Franklin* (Philadelphia, 1873), 237.

Acknowledgments

I am grateful for the many people who helped me to complete this book. At Baylor University, these include my research assistants Kristina Benham, Tim Grundmeier, Paul Gutacker, and Elise Leal, and wonderful colleagues including Beth Allison Barr, Barry Hankins, Philip Jenkins, Byron Johnson, Kim Kellison, Joe Stubenrauch, and Andrea Turpin. We were also blessed to have George Marsden, my doctoral advisor, at Baylor during spring 2016, and he and I had a number of helpful discussions about Ben Franklin. At Yale University Press, it has been a delight to work with my editors Jennifer Banks and Chris Rogers, as well as Heather Gold, Erica Hanson, Margaret Otzel, and the rest of the Yale team. Thanks to Margaret Hogan for a splendid job on copyediting the manuscript. I remain ever appreciative of the work of my friend and literary agent Giles Anderson. As always, I am most thankful for my wife, Ruby, and my boys, Jonathan and Josh.

Index